FERMENT

FERMENT

A MEMOIR OF MENTAL ILLNESS, REDEMPTION, AND WINEMAKING IN THE MOSEL

PATRICK DOBSON

Skyhorse Publishing

Skyhorse Publishing books may be purchased in bulk at special discounts for sales promotion, corporate gifts, fund-raising, or educational purposes. Special editions can also be created to specifications. For details, contact the Special Sales Department, Skyhorse Publishing, 307 West 36th Street, 11th Floor, New York, NY 10018 or info@skyhorsepublishing.com.

The chapter "Prelude: Diagnoses" appeared May 18, 2018 in *The Furious Gazelle* (www.thefuriousgazelle.com) under the title, "Why I Hate Spring, or How I Almost Hung Myself but Went to the Nervous Hospital Instead."

Visit our website at www.skyhorsepublishing.com.

10 9 8 7 6 5 4 3 2 1

Library of Congress Cataloging-in-Publication Data is available on file.

Cover design by Brian Peterson
Cover photo credit: Getty Images

ISBN: 978-1-5107-5731-8
Ebook ISBN: 978-1-5107-5732-5

Printed in the United States of America

This book is for Josef and Marlies Frick and the men of the Gemeinschaft Glas und Glaube.

CONTENTS

Prelude: Diagnoses ix

Chapter One: Taking Flight 1

Chapter Two: My Escape 7

Chapter Three: The Old Country 22

Chapter Four: Ivo and Martin 38

Chapter Five: Coming Home 59

Chapter Six: A Lost Friend 76

Chapter Seven: The Fricks 94

Chapter Eight: Saarburg and Trier 107

Chapter Nine: The Last Resort 122

Chapter Ten: Into France 137

Chapter Eleven: Guedelon 155

Chapter Twelve: Hotel du Commerce 170

Chapter Thirteen: The Waffle 188

Chapter Fourteen: Andrea 205

Chapter Fifteen: Days of Rest 224

Chapter Sixteen: Love and Loss 236

Chapter Seventeen: Leaving Home 253

Epilogue 260

PRELUDE
DIAGNOSES

In January 2011, my good friend and soul mate Joachim Frick was dying. He had been diagnosed with glioblastoma the previous October, and I arranged to visit him in Berlin during my semester break. His diminished state stunned me. He was closer to me than my own brother, and I took his illness personally. After I returned to Kansas City, I plunged into the depths of despair. My usual spring downturn, combined with increasing grief over Joachim's condition, turned into unchecked agitation and deep depression at the same time. At home, I barely talked to my family. I hid in books and read with hungry ferocity. Activities with my eight-year-old, Nick, felt obligatory and difficult. I could hardly function, much less be a father to a boy rife with all the energy and curiosity kids his age possess.

Soon, I wanted nothing to do with the outside world. I couldn't sleep. It felt as if fierce wind and booming thunder washed over my consciousness in wave after wave. I hoisted myself out of bed solely because the alarm clock told me to. My impulse was to burrow in, turn off the world around me, and try to sleep. I went through my community college teaching responsibilities as if under robotic control. Everything moved in slow motion. Even walking to my car was like slogging through warm mud. I dodged my students and didn't talk to my colleagues.

Around the end of February, I found myself devising how I'd string myself up in the basement so Nick wouldn't be the first to find me. These suicidal thoughts seemed rational. Of course, I reasoned, there was one way out of my despair. The weight of life pressed on me, as it should, since I have always done penance for being me. The end of a rope was a reasonable way to deal with the darkness and fear.

I hove out of bed at 11 a.m. Sunday morning, March 13, 2011. My T-shirt and jeans hung on me as if made of lead. I could feel my face, heavy and sagging. I obsessed over which rope I would use to attach my neck to the beam in the basement. I went down, found a piece of nylon cord I use when canoeing, and started tying the knot in the receiving end. As I worked, hands shaking, Nick called me from the living room. I ignored him. He called again and again. Rage welled up inside me. I raced upstairs and encountered a smiling child who took all the wind out of me. He asked what we were doing that day. I stood there, empty. I didn't have an answer.

I sat with him, brooding and calculating for about an hour. He was watching cartoons, jumping around like he does when he's in front of the television for too long. Suddenly, something inside me broke like a watch spring wound too tightly. Even in my addled state, I knew something was seriously wrong. I dragged myself into the bathroom, knees weak and body trembling. I stuffed my medications into a sandwich bag. My voice cracking, I called friends and made arrangements for Nick for that evening and night. I woke Virginia, who was sleeping before another night shift at the hospital, where she worked as an oncology nurse. She lifted her head and opened a sleepy eye. I told her, "I'm going to the mental hospital." I told her not to worry, Nick was taken care of. She looked up and told me whatever I needed to do, I should.

With Virginia's blessing, I took that bag of pill bottles and drove, as well as I could—even stoplights overwhelmed me—to the psychiatric facility attached to the hospital where Virginia worked. I remembered that Karl Childers, the main character in the movie *Sling Blade,* called the mental hospital the "nervous hospital." I liked that. My chest buzzed as if filled with electricity. My head spun. I was anxious, nervous, and upset, using all my energy to walk across the parking lot.

I walked up to the counter and shoved my medications at the clerk. "I'm here to check in," I insisted, not looking at him. When these episodes occur, I don't make eye contact. I look at the floor.

"Yes, well . . . uh . . . people usually call before they come in," he said. He looked confused and held the bag of medications as if he didn't really know what to do with them.

"Yeah, well," I said. "I'm not leaving."

"Well, uh . . . yeah, fill this out and take a seat." The kid looked scared. "Someone'll be right with you."

I filled in the blanks in the admitting form. My script looked forced and arthritic. I returned, gave the form to the clerk, and hid in the corner as best I could from the other people, probably families waiting to visit inmates. A security guard took up a position opposite me in the room, watching me, immobile, hands crossed.

After an excruciating hour, a woman came out from behind the counter and asked me if I was Patrick Dobson. She ushered me to her office. During the admitting interview, she asked about my medications, what doctor I was seeing, and if I had any medical conditions the doctors should be aware of. She asked if I struggled with depression. I said yes. Then she asked a series of standard questions about mental illness, probing to see if I really needed to be there.

"Have you had any thoughts of suicide or hurting yourself?" she said finally.

"Of course," I said. "What's a good depression without them?"

She stood up quickly, waved me over with a weapons wand, and led me into the nervous part of the nervous hospital.

A doctor showed me to my bed first and then around the facility. I shuffled behind him with my eyes to the floor. When he left, the other patients gathered around.

"Doctor," a woman in a gray, faded gabardine jacket said. "When's my appointment tomorrow?" I glanced up for a half-second. Her face twitched all over.

"Doctor?" I said.

"You mean you're staying?" the woman asked. A group of people had gathered around me.

"Sure. I'm staying," I said. I shoved through the crowd and made for my room.

"But, wait," a man in T-shirt and jeans and slippers said. I stopped and faced him. "You're not a doctor?"

I don't know what would have given them the idea that I was a psychiatrist. I was dressed in jeans and a black, long-sleeved pullover shirt. Maybe it was my demeanor, aloof and distant, I thought.

"No," I said. "I just checked in." I stood there a minute, looking at the floor. Then, I went off with the crowd shambling behind me to my room. I squinted at the hopeful faces as I closed the door and thought, wow, I'm really in it now.

That evening was a long one. I didn't turn on the light or leave the room. Though there was another bed next to mine, I had no roommate. When I peeked outside, the halls of the institution were white and fluorescent. Even tiny noises echoed through the place. Plastic covered the mattress underneath the sheet. Bedwetters, I thought. The bottom of the bathroom door stood a foot and a half above the floor. The top of the door was cut at a steep angle, I supposed, to keep people from hanging themselves, which I found ironic. They told me at check-in that I'd only be allowed to shave under supervision. They took my shoestrings.

I spent eight days in the nervous hospital. I met with a doctor every mid-morning for about two hours. After a couple of these chats, he thought the treatment I'd been receiving for depression was flawed. I had been on selective serotonin reuptake inhibitors for about ten years. He determined that I was bipolar depressive with chronic monopolar characteristics. This meant, in effect, that I was always depressed, sometimes worse than others—when I wasn't in exaggeratedly high spirits. Bipolar disorder is often hard to diagnose, he said. Manic-depressives often talk about depression with their doctors, but rarely report elevated moods or hyperactivity. This made sense. I experienced days and weeks—and even months—when I felt fantastic and that I could do anything, and, in fact, took on and managed more than most people. As I spun out of control, I alienated friends and family. They just couldn't keep up and too bad for them. But I'd always crashed into chin-jarring depressions. The doctor said I likely entered the hospital in a dysphoric state, suffering from a combination of depression and intense mania, exacerbated by seasonal affective disorder. Most people who suffer seasonal depression have it in the dark of winter. I belonged to a significant minority who experience the depression in the spring.

The answer, he believed, lay in a drug from the 1960s called oxcarbazepine, an anticonvulsant first developed for epileptics. The drug's side effects eased problems of anxiety and mood disorders. This combined with lamotrigine, another anticonvulsant implemented as a mood stabilizer for bipolar disorder, might solve my chronic depressions and even out my mood swings. On any medication, he said, I might do very well but still suffer "breakout" episodes of mania or depression. It would depend on many factors, not all of which he could predict. A psychologist, he added, "might help you with your feelings of inadequacy and this strange feeling you have of being a fraud."

While I was in the hospital, I began eating again. I'd lost a lot of weight in the weeks leading up to my almost-suicide. The psych ward food was surprisingly good and plentiful. Three times a day, inmates lined up at the cafeteria door. The staff laid out all kinds of wonderful things in hotel pans. Since we—there were about twenty of us in the facility at the time—were the only customers, the food was always fresh, with piles of fruit and vegetables, beautiful desserts, and, I supposed, since I don't eat meat, plenty of tasty animals.

In addition, two refrigerators stood in the nervous hospital dayroom, where people milled about or watched television between smoking cigarettes. The fridges harbored healthy juices, yogurts, and fruit. Cabinets between the refrigerators were stocked with granola bars and cereals. Between meals, talking to doctors, and attending group therapy, I grazed in the dayroom, eating just because I could.

Nearly everyone in the place smoked but me. Here's how I found out: The first time I went out to the tiny, sad, worn courtyard surrounded by a tall privacy fence, the other patients shuffled in the door quietly like I had a disease. Then, they stood with their faces at the windows until I went inside, at which time they filed out and lit their cigarettes. This was disconcerting. I finally asked one of the smokers what I was doing wrong.

"N-n-nothing," he said. "They d-d-d-don't let us smokers outside with the n-n-non-smokers."

One woman in the nervous hospital with me wore bandages around her arms above the wrists. She was very beautiful and seemed sweet. She asked me how I came to be there.

"I checked myself in," I said. "I was going to hang myself."

She laughed and held up her arms. "Yeah," she said. "They found me on the bathroom floor."

A tall, lanky, and jovial guy was in for alcohol treatment. We developed a kind of comradery over a couple of days. When he found out that I had not had a drink in two decades, he said, "Twenty years and you're in the psych ward? What's in sobriety for me?"

"At least," I said, "I don't have to go through this thing drunk. I can't imagine the horror."

"Well, I suppose that's something," he said thoughtfully. "I gotta sober up, but you're not going to be my role model."

About the third day, the mental fog and psychic pain began to lift. I struck up a rapport with the hospital staff and my fellow inmates. Still manic, I led art therapy sessions where we worked with plaster, paints, and colored markers. In group therapy sessions, I wound up leading discussions. Every evening, I'd hide in my room and do push-ups. I shoved against the walls and beds—which were firmly anchored to the floor—to get some physical exercise that eased my depressed emotions. A man came in late one night. He snored, moaned, and talked in his sleep. After he left in the morning, I never saw him again.

Virginia and Nick came to see me twice that week. It reminded me of visits I'd made to my friends in prison. We sat at a round table and talked about little things—how Nick was doing in school, how did walking the dogs go, and so on.

"Is this place all right?" Virginia asked. "Are they taking good care of you? Are you eating?"

I asked Nick what he thought of all this. "You're here because you're sick," he said. "I want you to get better and come home."

It was nice to have them there. When the visits ended, Virginia said I should continue calling home every night.

One evening, I couldn't stand any more of *The Real Housewives of Orange County*. I commandeered the television and turned to the classic movie channel. We watched *Joan of Arc* with Ingrid Bergman. At first, my fellow inmates groused about missing their reality shows. But I took control of the room and gave them a brief bio of Bergman and explained that critics considered this role one of her greatest. The other patients took an interest in the movie. Soon, people filled the dayroom. When someone came in and started talking, my mates shushed them. It was a night at the movies with popcorn and apple juice.

After a week, the doctor told me I was good to go. I'd started the new drug regimen and was feeling relief at having taken a break from my own brain. I drove home. The stoplights didn't throw me into anxious fits. The sun was shining, which irritated me, but I didn't feel the need to hide.

* * *

I thought I'd told Virginia about my suicide wish when she visited me in the nervous hospital. In spring 2014, I explained I felt a breakout depressive episode on the way and things might be difficult for me for the next couple of weeks. Although I'm not always good at it, I try to tell her when I'm feeling significant changes in my moods.

This time, I happened to say, "At least I'm not hanging myself in the basement like I did before I went to the nervous hospital."

She immediately began to cry. Why? What's wrong? I asked anxiously.

"You never told me you were going to kill yourself that day," she said, raising her hands to her face. "This is the first I've heard of it."

CHAPTER ONE

TAKING FLIGHT

In July 2014, I celebrated my twenty-fourth sobriety anniversary. In the three years since I'd been to the nervous hospital, I'd plumbed my insides but had barely begun to understand my mental illness' effects on my drinking and sober lives. I made up with friends I'd alienated when euphoric and informed my closest friends of my difficulties with depression. Most of them just nodded and said something akin to, "That explains a lot."

The suicide attempt and new awareness of mental illness brought my relationship with Joachim and many aspects of my confused and eventful past into question. Over the years, I'd ditched jobs, apartments, and personal belongings to set out on journeys that changed the course of my existence irrevocably. The first and perhaps most formative of all was my attempt to start a new life in Germany when I was twenty-two. In 1985, I sold all my worldly possessions and left for the Vaterland on a whim and in the middle of a deep depression. The friends I made there would essentially usher me into a new existence. Every occasion I'd seen them either in the States or in Germany in the thirty years since my first jaunt in the country, we learned more about my selves—the person I used to be, the one I am, and the one I was becoming. Each new revelation transformed me a little. I grew more mature, became more patient with myself and others, and gained self-awareness.

It was fortunate that this impulse to set mental illness into context came to me when it did. Virginia and I had been planning a trip to Germany for more than two years. Something always came up in the weeks before we bought our tickets—a death in the family, a wedding, schooling needs for Nick. We were determined this time. Leading up to our departure, no close relatives or friends died or decided to get married. We buttoned up all of Nick's outstanding and future school projects.

A journey to visit my German friends would mean far more to Virginia, Nick, now twelve years old, and me than a tourist romp through Europe. Our contact with the Germans through phone calls and emails sufficed no longer. We needed to see our friends in the flesh. They had become elderly or, like me, were on the edge of senior citizenship. Who knew how many years we had left, how many trips between continents, how long before we'd visit gravestones?

With this journey, I'd also embark on a quest to understand the young man who made the impulsive decision to hop a plane for Europe. I'd contemplate relationships he established and their endurance. Through him, I'd discover more of my old self, which I knew would lead to further self-awareness in the present.

It was also time for me to survey the course of the years and see what had become of them. I'd often contemplated my stay in Germany. I had never written on paper what was most important of that time. Memory isn't fixed. It's malleable and it fades. I felt a sense of loss beyond the people whose lives were slipping away. I felt I might be losing sight of my old self. The trip, then, would serve several purposes. I'd write the journey through Germany and through self-discovery, pin down their lessons so they would never escape me.

* * *

As the summer heat mounted and the grass browned in 2014, I bided my time, living a paradox. I treated each day as if it were my last but looked forward—counted the days—to another journey to Germany. Shimmering vineyards and lush, green valleys haunted my dreams, woke me in the night, and made my heart skip. I reveled in memories of evenings with friends in *Biergarten* and strolling cobbled medieval streets.

As our departure approached, mania's prickly edges crawled up my neck and clawed at my forehead. The end of another semester drew near. I taught my online and face-to-face classes, wrote, and went with Nick to the neighborhood park pool in the late afternoons. Evenings began more rounds of student e-mails and grading. I grew more excited and started to feel jumpy and wired. Mania threatened to "break through" despite the medication I took to control it. It huddled beneath, ready to spring. So, without thinking much about it, I sunk deeper into the tasks before me. Intellectual work felt sometimes as challenging and exhilarating as physical labor, like carrying several tons of rebar in a day, as I had done in my years as an ironworker.

Some days, I ached to ditch teaching and re-up my union card.

When I began to understand what was happening, I calmed myself using techniques I'd learned from my short years of awareness of manic-depressive illness and what it does to me. (Despite the professionals' judgment, I use the terms "manic-depressive" and "manic depression" here on purpose. For me, "bipolar disorder" doesn't take on or describe the condition well. I suffer manias and depressions, each distinct states, and sometimes I experience both simultaneously.) As I sat down to my teaching responsibilities, I took deep breaths, paused frequently to contemplate my actions, and walked the dogs farther and faster. Heavy yardwork between grading essays and caring for Nick mortified my body and distracted my mind. Sleepy or not, I made sure to go bed and rise at regular hours.

I kept a lid on it. The mania crept away, and my head cleared. My thoughts slowed. Physically, I remained steady. I conscientiously calculated student grades and completed administrative work.

* * *

We'd blocked out three weeks for our expedition. During that time, we planned to visit Josef and Marlies Frick, a couple now in their 80s who are closer to me than my own parents. I met them the day I first stepped foot in Germany on September 23, 1985, and they've influenced my life ever since. When I met their son Joachim, he quickly felt like my brother. Until his death in December 2011, when we were both forty-nine. I shared a closeness with him I never had with my siblings.

The other people we planned to visit had befriended me during my year and a half in Trier, an ancient city in the west of Germany. My friends taught me the language. They fed me when I was hungry. They nursed me when I fell ill. When I faced weekends alone in my room, they opened their homes to me. As the weather changed, they dressed me—clothes, boots, shoes, coats, and gloves. They ushered me through the heights and depths of undiagnosed manic-depressive illness. They shaped the person I am today.

Ivo Rauch lives above the Rhein in Koblenz. I met him in early 1986 by chance when he worked as an apprentice at a stained-glass window-restoration firm in Trier. Finding social outlets, let alone steady companionship, escaped me during my first months in the city.

Loneliness haunted me as I plunged headlong into manic and depressive episodes and periods of calm between. In one of those lonely depressions, I despaired. I contemplated giving up my Germany experiment and heading back to Kansas City. Suicide seemed a fitting escape.

Meeting Ivo changed my plans and my life. He opened avenues of friendship and acquaintance that kept me afloat. He taught me more about Trier, its Roman origins, and its medieval history than I could have learned on my own. He took me to cafés and coffeehouses. Walking the city's ancient ruins and parks, we shared long, deep conversations. In subsequent years, he went on to earn a doctorate in art history. He now runs his own stained-glass conservatory business.

When I first met Ivo, he presented me to his roommates, who all lived in a house on Trier's Saarstrasse on the south side of the city. Udo Bethke worked as an apprentice at the same company as Ivo. Udo was a giant man with huge hands. Whatever he handled, he did gently and with firm intention. He thought through everything thoroughly, sometimes to his detriment. But he taught me to slow down and live more thoughtfully. His considered movements and actions showed me I needn't rush through life looking for the next adventure. It would find me if I opened myself to it. He'd go on to become a master stained-glass artist with his own workshop.

For our visit, Udo planned a weeklong camping trip for us through central France from where he lived in Reutlingen, near Stuttgart. We'd then circle back through Belgium and Luxembourg to Koblenz, where we'd meet up with Ivo and Martin Streit, who had once worked with Ivo and Udo in the stained-glass-restoration firm.

When Martin lived in the Saarstrasse, he drew and painted in his evenings after work, gaining skill as time passed. Since his apprenticeship, he'd labored to establish himself as an artist. After Trier, he attended the famous Kunstakademie Düsseldorf, where he studied under renowned German painter Gotthard Graubner. He has since achieved more success as an independent painter and photographer than any of us ever dreamed possible for him when we lived in Trier. Like Udo, he was introverted and contemplative. I learned the vagaries and joys of creative endeavor from Martin, and that the creative mind needs space. Distractions I indulged in from habit, I discovered, provided excuses not to know myself.

On this trip, Virginia, who had been with me to Germany before, would see some things for the first time, and Nick would experience things wholly new. Except for the sojourn to France, I'd revisit familiar territories and see myself in those places again. I didn't look forward to the task. There were ugly truths yet to discover, things I might not want to know about myself. But now we'd checked our bags at the airport counter, taken off our shoes, and made our way past security.

CHAPTER TWO

MY ESCAPE

IT BEGINS LIKE this:

I got drunk the day of my first communion.

Our little seven-year-old voices echoed in the church as each of us answered "Amen" before receiving the host. The ritual awed us, and we stood quietly in the vestibule after the ceremony while proud parents shook hands and congratulated one another. The sun was drawing low in the oak trees, casting the houses across the street from the church in orange and red, the sky purple above.

We arrived home at dusk, the house dark but for a lamp by the front door. My grandparents and a few uncles filed into the tight spaces between the dining room table and china hutch. My mother lit candles that made our faces glow. A hush fell when everyone found a place. My dad poured everybody a glass of wine, including me, and said a prayer. He had me put the gallon bottle in the refrigerator.

The wine tasted heavenly, sweet and lush. After toasts and prayers, Dad sent me to fetch the jug from the darkened kitchen. The rosé glowed in the lighted refrigerator. The rest of the evening, I ferried the jug from the fridge in the dark to the dining room as my parents and relatives grew increasingly cheerful. During transit, I unscrewed the cap and humped the bottle up on my chest and gulped. The nectar burned in my stomach. Warmth flowed out along my limbs. My face tingled. About 7 p.m., I felt buoyant and unsteady. Fearing detection and not really knowing what was happening, I told my parents I needed to go to bed. They excused me, figuring I'd had a long day. Hugs and pats on the back sent me off for the evening.

I felt glorious. I bobbled around my room, doffing my clothes and dropping them to the floor. The bed felt like a slowly rotating barrel. My eyes pulled shut and I shook my head to stay awake. I slipped into the warmth and comfort of inebriated sleep.

After that communion celebration, I chased the euphoria I felt that night. I begged my dad for sips from his nightly beers. Remnants of wine, beer, and mixed drinks littered tables at family gatherings. I became the helpful child and snuck what remained in the glasses. One drink sparked an anxiousness that, I learned, would only be satisfied with more drink. I thought this was normal, something everyone felt.

In 1973 at age eleven, I joined the Boy Scouts and filched communion wine from the church basement during our weekly meetings. We tiptoed in the dark storage room illuminated only by a crack in the door. We took turns watching out for scout leaders, knowing they'd take up our transgression with the monsignor, who would report us to our parents and have our hides if we ever got caught. Betting that volunteers kept the wine inventory and would mark losses up to their mistake, we usually absconded with a full jug at a time. Sometimes the storage room was locked, resulting in me and my mates earning more merit badges by not skipping out on meetings.

These clandestine runs at the sacramental wine weren't enough for me. I graduated to furtive and exhilarating draws from my parents' liquor bottles. As a high school freshman, I befriended older boys who owned cars and had affinities for beer. We traveled from our Kansas City, Missouri, houses into the Kansas suburbs where eighteen-year-olds could legally buy beer at the time. Pooling our meager resources, we bought as much as we could whenever we could. We found willing retailers who'd sell us the goods if one of us "looked" old enough. I drank deeply and regularly after I bought my own car at sixteen. I ceased to draw a sober breath by the time I graduated high school in 1981.

Meanwhile, the ups and downs of being a kid masked the symptoms of incipient manic depression until I entered high school. During my years at Archbishop O'Hara High, I felt like an eccentric outsider. Hormones, teen angst, and rebelliousness made me miserable. Bursts of extraordinary energy preceded unbelievable lows, sometimes within the same hour.

Incredible flights of mind convinced me I could do anything. I tackled difficult projects and took on extracurricular activities. In high school, I enrolled in weightlifting classes and contemplated joining the wrestling team. (Even in my most agitated state, I realized this was foolish—I weighed 250 unmuscular pounds in high school.) As a sophomore, in one week, I joined the backpacking and the skeet-shooting clubs, the yearbook, and the student newspaper—all of which I would continue until graduation. When I was on top of things, I took charge and directed these operations. When I swung into depression, I made excuses for absences and poor performance. But I stuck with the extracurriculars out of duty and loyalty to my mates.

In college, I continued the same pattern. I introduced myself to strangers and made friends and then, the next day, retreated to a lonely corner in the library. During a heady burst one Wednesday afternoon while sitting in the university's commons, I impulsively decided to run for student government and campaigned fanatically. Campaign platforms came to me as if by magic. I bought poster paper and colored markers from the bookstore and plastered my name all over the Student Center. Stopping people on their way in for lunch or coffee, I shook hands by the score. By Friday afternoon, I'd won a seat on the All Student Association and came crashing down. I slunk home to hide in my bedroom.

When in manic mode, I received enough positive feedback from my endeavors to convince me of my abilities. I wrote well, and teachers admired my enthusiasm and productivity. I took front-row seats in classes and drove teachers to distraction. Other students sought my company at the local pub, where I drank underage and gave everyone a good time until I passed out in a back booth.

Many times, some event set off a depressive or manic episode. But usually my mental difficulties arose randomly and without cause. I isolated myself when depressed. Mania made me expansive and grandiose, sometimes delusional. During periods of manic euphoria, little things—a momentary setback or failure, the slightest resistance from people around me—even something as simple as lost keys—triggered wild bouts of irritability and outright fury. I spun into rages that ended with exhaustion or impact with impenetrable circumstance. I became convinced everyone was plotting against me. One fall afternoon my sister wouldn't let me use her car for a trip to a local vineyard.

"No, you can't use my car," she said. "Fix your own."

"Come on," I said. "I'm meeting friends. I've already said I'd go."

"You're just going to get drunk. No."

"Goddammit, give me the fucking keys!" I yelled. "I'm not getting drunk. I have to drive home." I was looking forward to lapping up tasty vintages. "You always fucking do this to me."

I bellowed and browbeat her until she moved to call the police. Faced with impending arrest, I apologized.

"Ah, come on," I said. "I'm sorry. I was looking forward to this all week. People expect me to show up. I promise I won't drink that much."

She put the phone down. I begged, promised, groveled, and scraped until she gave me the keys. I came to the next morning on her couch with her screaming at me. I remembered arriving at the vineyard, but nothing after that, including the forty-mile drive back to her house.

Euphoria and irritability never lasted. Seemingly within minutes, I would fall from great heights into bone-crushing depression. Feelings of worthlessness, remorse, and guilt plagued me. I often contemplated suicide—a crash against a highway abutment, a leap from a window, a rope from a rafter. I lost motivation. I ate too much and drank more. I played sick to stay in bed, curtains drawn. I suffered persistent insomnia but would fall asleep during the day or pass out drunk for fifteen or sixteen hours in a row only to suffer more nights of sleeplessness. Interest in school suffered, and I did the barest minimum to maintain B-average grades, keeping parents and teachers off my back.

I moved into my own apartment at age twenty in 1983. My drinking increased outside the confines of home. Generally, days started with a trip to the corner store for a couple of quarts of beer or a pint of whiskey, often both. The owner scoffed but didn't question my age or intent. I soon discovered that when I drank in the morning, I passed out by 2 p.m. I'd come to around 5 p.m., go to work making and delivering pizzas, and binge again after I clocked out at 11 p.m. or midnight. On days off, morning trips to the market started daytime sprees in which I passed out and recovered consciousness several times until the alcohol sent me under for good at 9 or 10 p.m.

I slept off drunks in front yards of friends' houses and apartments in the middle of the day. I'd regain consciousness in strange quarters of the city at odd hours with no way home. Many times, after I'd been out with friends or on my own, I emerged from a blackout in my apartment or somewhere strange to me, wondering how I got there.

Often, there was drama. Typical of my behavior, I popped out of a blackout one time in a crowd of people my workmates had introduced me to. I was opening beer bottles with my teeth. In a moment of stark clarity, I looked up into the tree canopy lit by streetlights underneath. I had a vague notion I'd done something wrong. The summer night was still but for the people gathered around me in the street. When I asked my friend Brian how I came to be with these people, he informed me that I'd just run his car into five parked vehicles on the next street over. We'd stashed the car behind the house of our pal who was having the party, hoping to escape detection.

The next day, Brian and I went to survey the damage to his car and found it gone. The heat was oppressive and my hangover severe. Sunlight through the leaves dappled tire marks in the bare dirt backyard. I felt my insides melt.

"Who would steal a wrecked car?" I asked Brian, who was just under five feet tall.

"You boob," he said, gesticulating with his hands as he often did to get people's attention. "You know the cops got it."

"Maybe not," I said hopefully. "Let's report it stolen."

We called the police and went down to the nearest station to fill out a report. A skinny, tired cop behind the window looked dubious and flipped through his files. He checked his computer. "This car's impounded pending criminal prosecution. We can't give it back until someone comes forward and takes responsibility."

We left. I told my parents what happened, and they decided to hire a lawyer they couldn't afford. Two days later, with counsel at my side, I surrendered myself at the station and was booked on destruction of property, leaving the scene of an accident, and hit-and-run. Stricken with impenetrable humiliation and remorse, I signed a signature bond and left the station. The lawyer told me that I was lucky. "You totaled five cars," he said. "By driving away from the wrecks, you avoided a more serious charge of driving while intoxicated. That would have put you in jail and made the other charges stick. As it is, you're a first-time offender and seem pretty sorry about what you've done. The prosecutor and judge might go easy on you."

When we appeared before a judge, two men whose cars I'd ruined were waiting to testify. I was so frightened I could hardly talk. The lawyer and the prosecutor met before the judge adjudicated my case. My attorney pled me down to the lesser charge of careless and imprudent driving, to which the prosecutor agreed. My fine was $35. The two men left in a huff and gave me a look that said if they ever saw me again, I'd lose my teeth and possibly a couple of limbs.

Barely escaping the clutches of the law didn't stop me. Drinkers often gather with or attract other drinkers. But my drinking wasn't a social disease. No one I knew drank like I did. My drinking pals and strangers I met drank too slowly for me. They didn't drink as much. Self-consciousness prevented me from making extra trips to the bar or drinking too frequently from the table's pitcher of beer. So, I'd excuse myself from a social situation and repair to another tavern or home where I could drink alone at my own pace. When I was with others, I'd develop grandiose schemes and outright lies. I grew loud and sloppy as the evening wore on. To sidestep the embarrassment I felt after such nights, I quit frequenting bars altogether and took to drinking alone in my apartment or while driving Kansas City streets.

Eventually, due to bad conscience and the need to keep a job, I only imbibed evenings and nights after work. It didn't matter how late I clocked out, I always drank the same way. I'd settle in front of the television or get behind the wheel and demolish a twelve-pack and a pint or two of liquor, or a couple jugs of wine in an hour and a half, often less. I couldn't get enough fast enough and resorted to pouring beer, wine, and liquor into quart jars, so I could slug without bottlenecks getting in my way. I passed out every night. I woke drunk in the morning and stayed that way well into the afternoon. About the time the shakes set in, it was time to start drinking again. When I wasn't drinking, I was thinking of drinking.

I denied I had a drinking problem and thought mania and depression were just parts of life. I contorted logic to justify my lifestyle. I kept a job, paid rent, and earned a 3.0 GPA at the university. It never occurred to me that alcoholism and manic impulsiveness kept me bouncing from job to job. I gained a certain moral flexibility. No one ever noticed or confronted me about stealing from employers. Legally, I lucked out. I drove drunk hundreds—thousands—of times but earned only that single citation for careless and imprudent driving. I never went to jail. Car wrecks—mine and others when I was a passenger with a drinking chum—landed me in hospital emergency departments and gave me facial scars and head trauma, but I bounced back quickly.

I'd take a job in a liquor and wine store to reduce my drinking bill and afford me access to better wines, mostly filched. After a while, I devoted myself to wine and experienced the illusion of climbing the enophile ladder. Later, a liquor and wine distributor hired me. I formulated designs on becoming a wine salesman, though my training for that position had me lugging cases and loading trucks in the warehouse. When feeling up, I hefted cases and loaded trucks faster than anyone else. In good cheer, I saw myself variously as a master sommelier, a vineyard owner, and a "somebody" in the wine trade. When depression hit, I dragged around the warehouse, doing enough to get by. I doubted the worth of this effort and often contemplated suicide.

I built the façade of the "wine professional." I became practiced at the wine game and possessed an acute taste memory. The Kansas City wine crowd fancied themselves sophisticated and urbane. I mimicked their language and mannerisms. I waxed poetically with them about the grape, reciting information I'd memorized from books on grape varieties, regions, vintages, and winemaking methods. They found me charming, and I found acceptance.

Recalling that time now, I see I was deluded. In truth, after the first drink, I couldn't stop. I might begin a night with other enophiles. Two or three glasses later, I left the proceedings and ensconced myself alone in my apartment with cheap beer and a plastic jug. I enrolled in a college class called Wine and Civilization. On the way home from an off-campus "tasting" one night in March 1984, the friend I'd brought—and talked into driving—ran a stoplight in front of my apartment as he drove me home. I don't recall the crash that totaled his car and sent the other driver to the hospital. I remember looking down from my window that night at the police lights knowing something awful had occurred. My friend went to jail. The professor nearly lost his position when the local paper caught wind of the incident. I suffered only crippling guilt that more alcohol easily wiped away.

* * *

About a year and a half after that accident in front of my apartment, escalating drinking, out-of-control mania and depression, and a dead-end job led me to believe Kansas City was going to be the death of me. The idea to leave the country and life as I knew it started with a phone call after a rough day at the liquor warehouse. My friend Larry, who'd been vagabonding in Germany, had found a broken pay phone on a street corner in Hamburg. He called everyone he knew stateside, but the phone charged him not one *pfennig*. When he hailed me, my evening bender was under way. Vodka and beer chasers relieved debilitating depression. I was watching reruns on my 12-inch black-and-white portable and was settling in to drink until I passed out.

I lived in the basement of a bare-bulb Midtown Kansas City apartment building. The front room had a kitchenette. A small bedroom stood to one side. During the day, light dribbled through a narrow, filmy, cobwebbed window at the very top of the wall. A sewer pipe hung about a foot and a half below the low ceiling. When I moved from room to room, I bent at the waist to avoid banging my head. I'd suspended a goldfish bowl in a cheap macramé plant hanger from a bend in the pipe. A discarded toilet stood by the door as an umbrella stand, though I had no umbrellas. The place lacked air-conditioning during the pounding-hot summer.

Larry's voice mercifully intruded on that solitary night. "Why don't you come to Germany and travel for a while?" he asked. "You talk about wanting to learn the wine business. Why not come to where the vineyards are?" In my depressive state, my nerves were dulled, and I was good and drunk. As he spoke, something clicked in my head and said "jump."

He'd caught me at the right moment. Empty and lonely, I was drinking harder as time unfolded. Fear of homelessness kept me at a job. But the grind had grown too burdensome, the work increasingly dreary and loaded with drudgery. The job's intense physical labor absorbed the heights of mania and depths of depression but did nothing to stop their onset. I packed box upon box with pints and half pints. I carted and heaved cases of wine and hard liquor. I loaded trucks and unloaded shipping containers, often shoving aside my workmates. Summer descended on the vast open space beneath the warehouse roof with a vengeance. The wastewater treatment plant next door filled the superheated building with sewer stench soon after we opened the loading dock doors in the morning. I always smelled of sweat, stale booze, and the excrement of an entire city. No amount of laundering removed the fug. Dust and shit lingered in my sinuses all the time, at work or not. Everything carried the odor of sewage—food, wine, beer. I mostly gave up food. I came home every night dehydrated and on the edge of heat prostration. I couldn't imagine a future for myself. Thoughts of suicide plagued me.

Larry made the notion of selling my meager possessions, packing a backpack, and bugging out of Kansas City seem like the best idea I ever had. Germany promised a way out of my miserable state. My depression would be healed forever, and I'd find myself prancing around vineyards in high moods. I put no thought into what a job in a foreign land would entail. I gave not one moment of contemplation to securing work visas or paying tax authorities. Picturing myself laboring in scenic vineyards, I imagined standing in candlelit cellars next to ancient barrels, tasting wines with rotund *Kellermeisters.*

By the end of the conversation, I'd decided. My trip to become a winemaker wouldn't resemble the youthful European frolic I'd read about in books or heard about from my acquaintances. No. This would be more important. I'd find a job in a winery and start my splendid career as a respected winemaker. Germany would solve my problems, plain and simple. It would save me without any effort on my part.

* * *

Getting busy eased depression. I quit my job and sold my possessions in a Saturday sale on my street corner. At the end of the day, I tossed what remained into a dumpster behind the building. I bought a one-way ticket to Luxembourg. The sale of my car yielded $400 in cash. My last check, the proceeds from my yard sale, and what I'd saved bought $400 in travelers' checks. I folded them into the back of a large wallet behind my passport in case the Germany experiment failed and I needed a way back to Kansas City.

Three weeks after my friend suggested I go to Germany, I boarded a plane with backpack and sleeping bag. I was a twenty-two-year-old drunken and mentally unbalanced kid with little self-awareness who had landed on a great, uncertain dream. Fear almost paralyzed me, but anxiety of not undertaking the journey overpowered the fear of doing it. After a month and a half of traveling Germany on trains—and before I went broke or committed suicide—I landed a job at a renowned winery in Trier, a German city west of the Luxembourg border that was ten times older than my country. The winery's director guided me to a sleeping room in the attic of the vineyard apprentices' school, where a small breakfast and coffee with some of the students came with the price of rent. I spent the next year learning the language and laboring in one of the most sublime places I've ever been.

I loved the country and the work and the people I met. I came back after a year and a half in pursuit of a Kansas City opera singer with whom I'd carried on a fiery affair in Germany. The relationship failed almost immediately on my return due to my severe neediness, mood swings, and dissolution. Again, on impulse, I went back to Germany again to attend the wine school in Geisenheim on the Rhein about eight months after I left the first time. But without means, having not planned at all, and deep into what I found later were the last days of my drinking career, I gave up after a semester and returned to a debauched life in my hometown. I was twenty-six years old.

* * *

By the time I was twenty-seven, drinking had done me in. I was sick, broke, and unemployable. Depression and despair brought me to the very bottom. Bereft of friends and isolated from family, I was alone in my universe. When I stopped drinking in July 1990, I made a new start—a sudden and complete break with the past. I thought, at the time, I'd leave all of the wreckage of my life behind and never look back.

Everything changed instantly and not all for the best. Unbuffered from the effects of manic depression, I cycled through suicidal pain and even greater heights of euphoria. I was immature, having dodged the emotional and life lessons one learns in their teens and twenties. I made poor decisions now not due to alcohol but to ineptitude, inexperience, and mental illness. Running four-square into myself, I didn't understand me one bit.

In other ways, life vastly improved. The drinker's physical ailments abated within a matter of weeks and months. My blood pressure dropped from 220/110 to normal. My kidneys stopped hurting, and my swollen liver returned to the size it was supposed to be. Mentally, but for frequent ups and downs, my head cleared. Reenrolling at the university, I earned A grades, and formulated designs on graduate school. I graduated with two degrees in May 1991, ten years after I started college. With manic confidence and determination, I resolved that nothing would hold me back. Even when my girlfriend got pregnant, I was resolute in making something of myself. I sought to become legitimate.

In that process and through dizzying bouts of mania and withering depressions, I denigrated and dismissed much of my old behavior and the person I once was. I made peace with the past and amends for the damage my drinking caused in other people's lives. For many years, I didn't worry too much about my former self. I negotiated single-fatherhood ineptly and mostly on intuition. I finished grad school at the University of Wyoming in 1993 and found a solid job. When I was four years sober, in a dysphoric state, I planned a long trip. A year later, in May 1995, I walked to Montana and then canoed home on the Missouri River, starting life all over again on my return. I landed my first writing gig, which turned into a full-time job and then into a career.

As I matured, I looked back into my drinking days and saw a "me" who also possessed positive qualities. I gave myself credit for good intention, thirst for experience, and eyes wide in wonder. My intentions were almost always good, and when not too looped, people considered me a nice guy. I made friends easily. I'd felt bad about stealing, lying, cheating, destroying private and public property, and wrecking my cars and those of others. My drunken "self" engaged freely in conversations and arguments with friends and strangers alike. I stood up for the underdog. I'd give what change and bills I had to anyone who asked. While an irritable workmate and mercurial friend, I tolerated other's beliefs and ideas and learned from them. My friends, uneducated and young, included strippers and hookers, alcoholics and drug addicts, and many jobless. I questioned everything I'd been told in school, church, and about every book I read. I cast off the religion of my youth and doubted the existence of a loving God. My intellectual universe broadened. Despite the drinking and perhaps because of manic depression, I did well in school and read books, hundreds of books—history, philosophy, classic works of fiction and nonfiction—anything that quenched the thirst for inquiry.

Slowly, I began to reexamine my relationships, and among these were the ones I developed with the friends I made in Germany who survived my entire fiasco of my hitting bottom and sobering up. They'd stuck with me through times of depression and mania, in part, because our friendships spanned continents. They weren't around for me to alienate or cling to in ways that alienated others. They escaped the worst of my drunken behavior. Their loyalty and kindness were unparalleled. Through phone calls, visits, letters, and then e-mails, I revealed the challenges and behaviors I'd hidden from them. They understood and empathized when I laid bare the nature of my worst offenses. I came to the realization that I was the luckiest person in the world.

CHAPTER THREE

THE OLD COUNTRY

FOR THE INTERNATIONAL flight out of Philadelphia, I was assigned a seat widely separated from Nick and Virginia, next to a window on an empty row. I needed the space. My old journals sat in my shoulder bag and I had pens and a new notebook. Since I cannot sleep on a plane, I'd stretch out with my notebook and journals for the duration of the flight and begin my journey into the past.

Soon, night fell and the blackness of the Atlantic absorbed me. Staring into it, I tried to focus on the fall of 1985 when I first decided to leave for Germany. But memory presented jumbled scenarios. For so many years I'd given myself and others differing accounts of my time in Germany, why I went, and what I did there. I understood my drinking history well. I had yet to discover all the ways manias and depressions affected my thinking and behavior. I sat back with my notebook not knowing what I'd find or if I'd even have the wherewithal for the task at hand.

So, I dove in knowing that when I do what's in front of me, I get something accomplished, even if it's not very much. After some initial notes, I checked on Virginia and Nick. Both slept soundly. They sprawled across their seats at odd angles, wrapped to their necks with blankets. I envied them. People who couldn't sit still any longer walked the length of the plane from first class to the tail and back—wraiths shuffling through the dark. The low roar of engines and the rushing of the air outside muffled all but a few coughs and sneezes.

I placed the notebook in the circle of light from the lamp above and began to write about the first time I was in Germany, pinning down memories that had rattled in my head for thirty years. First a series of bullet points arranged, scratched out, and rearranged splayed across the page. As I began to put them in order, the lines grew into blocks of text.

When I was twenty-two, nothing could have prepared me for a moment like this. I never thought I'd have a wife, much less a family. One of my children had already been to Germany three times. My then seven-year-old daughter Sydney went with me to visit our friends in 1998, before Virginia and I were married. She accompanied Virginia and me on Virginia's first trip to Germany in 2000. Sydney had also spent most of a summer vacation when she turned eighteen working with Udo in his shop and then traveling.

Now, it was Nick's turn. He came out of an impossible situation. His mother—my sister—shot and smoked meth for decades before she gave birth to Nick in 2002. By 2004, she'd developed severe schizophrenia and fallen into increasingly heavy meth use. One night in a psychotic and screaming fit, she tore up her apartment (again). The police found her scrubbing Nick in the bathtub with a hard-plastic cleaning brush and hydrogen peroxide. She was determined to scour microscopic cameras from beneath her two-year-old's skin. They took her to treatment. The Nevada Department of Child and Family Services settled Nick with my parents, and my sister signed formal documents giving up her parental rights. Meanwhile, Virginia and I started the lengthy adoption process. After a year of training and a gauntlet of social workers and psychologists, we picked Nick up in Reno in January 2007 and he became our son. He was four and a half years old.

We'd obviously done something right. Nick adapted well to school and felt comfortable at home. Over seven and a half years, he'd grown into his own person. He possessed a self-confidence and self-awareness I didn't at his age. He anticipated this trip after having met Ivo and Udo on their visit to us in Kansas City in 2012. With all the wide-eyed interest of a kid, he wanted to see where they came from and the many sights I'd told him about over the years.

Thinking these things through, I shifted from recording the moment to remembering that earlier journey. I'd spoken with Josef and Marlies and about their impressions of the man I once was, what I did, and how they perceived how I felt. She remembers me as a seeker who didn't know exactly what he was looking for. He was thrilled, sometimes like a child, at the cultural and material differences between Germany and his native land. He experienced great hope and expressed high expectations of himself. He was unsure but hopeful. Josef tells me he'd met a young man coming into his own, filled with curiosity and wonder. I scribbled, "Like Nick," in the margins as the thought came and went.

Shaking the fatigue from my writing hand, I breathed deeply the funk that can only emanate from an international flight.

I contemplated my scribblings and paged through the old journals. It was difficult to stay in the first person when reflecting on those thirty-year-old notes. I felt I was looking into the private meanderings of another person. The written hand was familiar. The language resembled that I use today. In some cases, I remembered the exact times when and places where he wrote those journal entries. Even the weather or the feeling of a breeze came back to me. As I read, I noticed how memories had changed in my mind over time. I could see through the emotional entries in my old journals and remember that's not really what happened. In some instances, he didn't write what occurred at the time but what he wanted me to remember. I could see him trying to shape what I'd think of myself.

* * *

On September 21, 1985, I stuffed everything I owned into a cheap backpack bought years before for a Boy Scout backpacking trip—a few clothes, a sweater, a copy of Maugham's *The Razor's Edge*, and a notebook with a couple of pens. My sleeping bag hung off the bottom of the pack. Tucked into my waistband, a large folding wallet held my passport and all my money. Though I was set to go to Europe for life, I had a plan B. If I didn't have a job by the time I'd spent my cash, I'd go to the airport with my travelers' checks and wait for a return flight at the price I could pay.

A friend dropped me at Kansas City's airport the next day. The sun shone through the puffy clouds and fall was in the air, though it was still warm and humid. Inside the terminal, electricity ran down my spine. I'd only been on an airplane once before, to Reno, Nevada, to visit my parents who had moved there from Kansas City. I checked my bags and waited anxiously at the gate. Gazing out over the airfield, I imagined the planes' passengers coming and going from exotic destinations. When, finally, I walked down the jetway with my notebook and pens in hand, I felt as on the first steps toward a new life, and it frightened me. Feelings of euphoria and despair ran through me as the plane lofted above the trees and farms.

A cacophony of taxi drivers hawking their cabs filled the halls of Chicago's O'Hare airport. More people than I'd ever seen in one place before thronged between gates. During the long walk from my arrival gate to the Icelandair flight to Luxembourg, I stopped for a drink at every bar along the way. Once in the air, the flight attendants kept bringing me little bottles of bourbon, which I paid for from the meager holdings of my pocket. By the time the plane eased into Luxembourg, my nerves jangled from in-flight drinks and lack of sleep.

From outside, the Luxembourg air terminal seemed comically small, a single building, like something from an old movie. The airplanes parked on the apron away from the building and had the stairs pulled up to them. I stumbled down the steps and toward the terminal with a young woman I'd met on the plane. She was a pretty Luxembourger with big gentle eyes. For hours on our flight, we'd talked about our hopes and dreams. She spoke flawless English, as well as French, German, Portuguese, and her native Luxembourgish. We parted on the apron, her telephone number in my pocket.

I spoke spits of German from a college course I drank through three years before. Fortunately, the Luxembourgers at passport control spoke English. After the claustrophobic officialdom of the customs counter, I lurched wide-eyed into the glass-and-metal terminal. People from around the world in all kinds of dress thronged through the hall. Everything seemed new and different. Advertising for cars, fashion, and cigarettes seemed larger, more fantastic than any I'd seen before. I stood in front of the screens announcing arrivals and departures. International capitals and strange and exotic destinations showed me I stood in a world much larger and deeper than Kansas City: Oslo, Helsinki, Copenhagen, Milan, Barcelona, Istanbul, and others—all places I'd only ever heard about. The lights were bright and the spaces echoed with indecipherable calls over the loudspeakers in three or four languages. My head spun from these new experiences; I had to stop and listen awhile.

Larry met me at the front doors of the terminal. His was a friendly and familiar face in the vast strangeness. He looked like the typical American student backpacking through Europe. He had a sturdy pack and tied his jacket around his waist. His moderate and solid build dropped from a mop of self-shorn hair into well-worn hiking boots.

We took a bus to the center of the city. As soon as we stepped off and watched it drive away, I realized I'd left my sleeping bag on board. It meant little to me in that moment. I couldn't muster the energy to be disturbed about it. Bone-tired, nerves dulled by depression, and still drunk, I told Larry it was gone. I'd figure things out as I went along. But he insisted and left on foot to retrieve my bag. I stayed at the bus stop nonplussed. I remember sitting on the bench with my backpack, my eyes as wide as I could open them, taking in the sights and smells of this new city. I began to feel hungover.

After a while, I regained my bearings some and worried Larry wouldn't get the sleeping bag back. Panic welled up. I fidgeted in my seat and stood up and sat down. When he returned sometime later with my sleeping bag, he'd performed a great feat. With it secured to my backpack, my heart still pounding, we lit out down a busy street. Unimaginably old buildings stood side by side with new, glass-and-steel structures. I wandered the narrow sidewalks hardly looking where I was going.

We walked down the Rue de Strasbourg to a row of shops and restaurants. I wanted nothing more than a big drink of water. We settled in at the Brasserie Journal, whose large windows swung open to the street. People sat at tables on the sidewalk. Inside, customers read newspapers and sipped drinks in the brass and wood interior. The smells of coffee blended with fresh bread and searing sausages. For an American who had only traveled on the Great Plains and into the Southwest, this Old World was new.

An older couple sat silently at the next table over, staring out the window. The sounds of traffic and people outside the shop settled in around them. Small glasses of wine sat on their narrow table. He wore a beret and a dark suit with no tie, his shirt unbuttoned at the collar. He held a cane at his side. She was plainly but elegantly dressed in a long, dark skirt, a silk blouse, and a matching waistcoat. She crossed her hands over a bag in her lap. As they turned their gaze to Larry and me, their expressions showed inquisitiveness, but they said nothing—two older people contemplating children who'd crossed the ocean. After a while, the man tipped his hat to us, smiled, and said something in French. His wife put some coins on our table to pay for our drinks and they joined the foot traffic outside before we could protest.

By evening we were on a train crossing the German frontier. I had never traveled by rail before, and the experience thrilled me. We rolled out of Luxembourg City's valley over a wide plain of farm and pasture, across the border into Germany, and then into the narrow confines of the Mosel Valley. We detrained at Konz, a small city west of Trier at the confluence of the Mosel and Saar. There, we caught a regional train to a tiny platform in the Saar Valley at the village of Kanzem. The vineyard there rose behind the lonely concrete shelter in straight rows up the flank of a steep hill. Here it was, like on postcards and pictures in books, but now I witnessed it with my own eyes. The air, cool and damp and clean, lofted off the Saar River, which ran lively and quick beneath a bridge beyond the train stop. The village seemed at rest—the streets and lanes empty, the houses' windows beginning to glow as evening set. We made our way down a narrow two-lane through farm fields. It had rained that afternoon; farmhouses and Bauernhöfe shimmered red and gold under the setting sun.

The Saar Valley widened to the hills surrounding the small village of Wawern. As we approached town in the twilight, the settlement began with a row of old, crooked houses that had settled in odd angles through centuries. They stood close on one another, sharing garden walls and trellises. Engraved cornerstones and door lintels indicated these houses were older than my country. Across the street, the vineyards of the famed Wawerner Herrenberg rose steeply to the forested hilltop 600 feet above.

We strode past tall, thick walls into the courtyard of a stucco-and-stone house with a steep slate roof. I stumbled on the cobbles and felt dizzy. The grounds were well tended, and the house freshly painted. A tall, quiet, and dignified man in his mid-fifties, invited us into the foyer. Josef Frick managed the Wawerner Herrenberg vineyard and its cellar for Weingut Doktor Fischer, a famous winemaker in nearby Ockfen. I couldn't believe my luck. I'd tasted the estate's wines in Kansas City and was delighted to meet a man who worked for such an august establishment. But Josef seemed so humble for the keeper of a famous vineyard. He wore solid work boots, knee breeches, and an army-green sweater. We climbed the stairs to the family apartment on the second floor. As we entered, Josef's wife, Marlies, greeted us with a smile. She was a good-natured woman of about fifty. After our chilly hike, the warmth of the house and her friendly handshake made me drowsy.

I remember bits of that evening. Night had fallen. We entered a small dimly but comfortably lit kitchen-dining room. At one end of a small breakfast nook, a large multipaned window looked out over the front drive and the garden between the house and front wall. Utensils hung neatly on hooks above the stove and sink. We ate hearty, dark bread, steaming potatoes, and chicken soup. The wine, which Josef produced from his own small vineyard, was flowery and flinty and soothed my rattled nerves.

The language was incomprehensible. Larry interpreted. He explained to Josef and Marlies I was the friend he had told them about. I heard the words "Kansas City" and "Missouri" and my name. Through Larry, Marlies asked innumerable questions: What motivated me to leave everything? What was I looking for? Where was I going to stay?

On our train ride earlier, Larry and I had talked about the possibility of my going to the wine school in Geisenheim. I knew of the renowned institution and thought attending might be a good idea if I was to make my living in wine. Larry had done some research before I arrived. I'd need a year's internship at a winery to qualify for entry, he said. Even before we reached Kanzem, Larry had begun to tutor me in the lines I would need to ask vineyard owners and managers for an internship. Now with Josef, I faltered through a few of the German words I practiced with Larry that day. *Ich bin ein Americanischer Student. Ich möchte in der Weinbauschule in Geisenheim immatrikulieren. Dafür brauche ich ein Praktikum* . . . Josef laughed good-heartedly at my effort and then told Larry about some wineries on the Mosel and Rhein that might take on an American student as an intern. By the end of the night, my trajectory, at least for the time being, was set: I would travel Germany's wine regions with the goal of landing an internship and attending the wine school in Geisenheim.

After a long chat with the Fricks, Larry and I trudged narrow stairs to the attic—a vaulted room where roof timbers stretched to the peak far above our heads. At one end, a door opened into a small chamber. There, a nightstand with a lamp stood next to a single bed. Marlies had laid out a pallet for me to sleep on. Larry and I sat on the sill with the window swung open under a wide eave. A violent storm had passed earlier, and the air was still now. Light rain pattered on the roof. The shaded lamp lit the room in a comfortable yellow glow and played on Larry's face like an Eduard Manet painting. The fields below spread out underneath us in the dark. But for the sounds of the rain and a slight breeze rising in the distance, the scene was silent. Here and there the lights of a house or streetlight shone. The air smelled vegetal and heavy in the chill of the wet night.

I climbed into my pallet under a feather bed with a big, soft pillow. Night settled in around me. The smell of age hung in the air. I blinked and it was morning.

Fog lay over the fields in the distance. I shivered and rubbed my arms. A vague hangover made my head feel stuffed with sand. Trees lined the road, which wound away from the village through wide fields. Silage piles covered with plastic and old tires slumped here and there between the swatches of newly plowed ground. Back from the fields grew stands of trees with large hills all around. Even the birds kept silent.

Larry left me to go downstairs. I sat a moment on the windowsill and wondered what I was doing. The sense of discovery filled me with excitement. At the same time, an anxiety heavier than I'd ever known lay on me. Sadness overwhelmed me, and I cried for a long time. I ought to turn back now, I thought. I'd come this far, and that was noteworthy. I understood Kansas City and could start over there. But even through the dread and tears, I knew it was too soon to return. There was too much ahead.

I gathered myself and went downstairs and took a seat in the breakfast nook and stared out the window. Marlies made us thick, black coffee and brought out *Brötchen*—small bread loaves—and ham and cheese slices. I wanted to say something in German but felt self-conscious. Marlies smiled and said "good morning" in English when she set down the homemade jam. Fog rolled down the vineyards beyond the wall that enclosed the courtyard and driveway to the ancient house. I'd never seen such a gathering of grapevines before. I'd been to Missouri vineyards, but they were isolated stands of vines on what were otherwise farming operations. This vineyard stretched the length of the village and then some. The house was quiet, and despite my sadness, I felt a calm serenity through my depressive funk.

Marlies sat down and through Larry began to tell the story of the house, which was also a winery—a *Weingut.* The cellars below the original house were built in 1077 and had belonged to an order of the priesthood that controlled the lands of the village, the farmlands we had walked through, and the vineyards. In feudal times, serfs' strips—pieces of land each family worked in cooperation with other serfs—reached up out of the valley into what were now the forested hills opposite the vineyard. The abbot and friars administered the vineyards and fields for the benefit of the house and the bishopric of Trier. Over the centuries, feudal bonds dissolved and the land came into freehold and rent. The present house was built in 1722. The Napoleonic reforms of 1806 confiscated the remaining church lands and distributed them among the villagers, some of whose families had worked for or rented from the abbot for centuries.

Marlies indicated the house's many rooms had belonged to the monks and friars. She took me into a large dining room, once the center of apostolic and social life in the monastery. Large windows looked out two sides of the room. She pointed at the house's backyard inside the wall that surrounded the property. There, she maintained a meditation garden like the one the monks would have used during their daily prayers. A gravel path wound in rectangles around low shrubbery. Fruit trees lined the path. She'd set a bench at one end of the garden and said she'd spent many hours there crocheting or knitting as her children were growing up. Sometimes, she said, that bench was her only time of peace in a busy household.

We went back into the breakfast nook. My face felt heavy and melancholy overtook me. I looked at the narrow street and wide courtyard behind the walls. Outside the vineyard's neat rows, no lines ran straight. Everything seemed unimaginably old. It was all clean and trim, and even what was left neglected seemed to have order and purpose. I thought of Kansas City. The straight lines of my hometown had been neglected. Yards in my neighborhood were overgrown. Neighborhoods fell apart after fifty years.

* * *

The sun burned away the fog. After breakfast and our long chat, we drove to Saarburg, an ancient town on the Saar River under steep and jagged hills blanketed with grapevines. Underway, we wound through the great vineyards whose wines I'd drunk so deeply when I was in Kansas City. I stared up at the Ayler Kupp, a great flank of vineyard under which the picturesque little village stood. I tasted again the wines of the great vineyards called the Scharzhofberg and the Wiltinger Kupp as we drove by them. I couldn't believe I was in a world I'd only ever imagined and until a few weeks before never thought I'd see.

In Saarburg, it struck me really for the first time that I'd left everything. The path before me was uncertain. For all its fascination, the world around me was unfamiliar. I felt despair. I stood in an artist's shop, looking out a window into a deep ravine where a sprightly creek cleaved Saarburg. The series of falls below me fed a slough that wound around a curved building. Waterwheels that had once powered a gristmill now turned for tourists.

I began to cry again. Maybe it was fatigue or a hangover or depression that caused the confusion and the tears. Great sobs erupted from deep within my chest. Fortunately, there was no one in the shop, and Marlies had walked outside. After a long while, I recovered myself and dried my face. Nothing, I thought as I squared my shoulders, was going to stand in my way, not even me. I didn't know what I was after, but whatever came next had to be better than what I'd come from.

We walked around the fairy-tale town of plaster and timber houses set one on the other. I found Marlies to be a wonderful, open woman with proper manners and a cheerful countenance. She was kind and helped me with my first words of German. As we walked, Josef impressed me as a big man with a quiet but strong persona. He strode with a pride I have always envied and never felt for myself.

The next day, Josef drove us to the train stop at Kanzem. Larry and I sat on the bench in the concrete shelter and talked about my extraordinary first days in a foreign country. I contrasted the new world I experienced with my own. Buildings of timbers and plaster lined Saarburg's and Wawern's streets. Nowhere stood a house made completely of wood. The Fricks' kitchen, its stove, and the refrigerator were tiny compared to those in my apartment. The streets were narrower, the cars smaller, and the houses older. I felt as if I discovered something all the books I'd read in school could never reveal.

Larry convinced me I should buy a special youth ticket good for any train in Germany for a month—a *Trämpermonatskarte*. We took a train to Trier and tried to purchase one there, but the clerk there told us the rail company, Die Deutsche Bundesbahn, had changed the rules earlier that month. Such bargains were only for German youth and students. Larry thought to go down to a station in a smaller town where the clerks may be more amenable or may not have read the train company's bulletins. Sure enough, in Merzig we bought the cheap youth card without issue. I watched my precious dollars, converted to Deutschmarks (DM) at a bank in Saarburg, cross the counter. But now with the month pass in my pocket, for a while, at least, I wouldn't have to worry about where to lay my head. Trains and train stations would be my home.

We took a train back to Trier and another to Koblenz. Leaving Trier, the train climbed up out of the Mosel valley and sprinted across a plain of heavily forested volcanic hills called the Eifel. When the train raced back into the river valley at Bullay, I kept my face plastered against the window. The fabled vineyards of the Mittelmosel climbed the faces of slate cliffs first on one side of the river and then the other. I watched men and boys high above the river working the little plots of vines on the steep, rocky cliffs. Teetering on precarious rock walls, they seemed small as insects.

At Koblenz, we waited for a train down the Rhein to Frankfurt. The Koblenz station sat in a squat and sturdy building of limestone and slate. An arched window let light into the vaulted great room where a series of doors let out onto a set of platforms under metal awnings. An sold his wares inside the front door, and a little gift shop operated nearby.

Off from Koblenz, the train took us through a land with architecture as solid as Germans themselves. The tall buildings of the center city soon faded into two- or three-story stucco houses with steep slate roofs. The dwellings had small backyards and stood nearly adjacent one another, and often connected. We sped by *Kleingarten*, land divided into little parcels with vegetable and fruit-tree gardens people from the crowded city maintained. Soon, we traveled into smaller towns and between their more pedestrian structures.

Our compartment contained six seats in a car with similar sections its whole length. We sat in one with an older couple, who kept to themselves as Larry chattered away about what he'd been doing since he left Kansas City. Soon, the train rolled into the Rhein River Valley.

I'd heard of this magnificent stream but had never seen a picture of it. The immense vineyards of the Rheingau rose from the banks of the river to the tops of the great hills and cliffs above. We made several stops in a row at towns whose names I recognized from wine labels: Lorch, Assmannshausen, and Rüdesheim. Larry pointed out Geisenheim as we sped by and said there lay my future.

We detrained at Frankfurt. The station sticks in my mind after all these years. The massive terminal with its ticket counters and shops spread over what seemed a mile. Rounded, steel-truss roofs stood over the lengths of dozens of trains waiting and slowly departing and arriving. The train sheds captured the noise of the crowd and the locomotives in a tinny cacophony of humanity and metal. People scurried everywhere. Larry and I were on our way east and in no hurry. It didn't matter which train we took. We dawdled and wandered, looking at the lengthy schedules in big glass windows at the end of every track.

We walked out of the station and ducked into a bakery across the street. The glass cases held all kinds of treats new to me. Besides varying kinds of bread loaves, the cases were filled with Brötchen and *Feinbackwaren*—cakes, strudels, and cookies. I bought an *Amerikaner,* a large cookie iced on the bottom, half in white, half in black. Larry told me the pastry was named for American soldiers, whose black and white units liberated Germany from the Nazis.

Outside stood a food stand, a *Schnellimbiss.* I chose a hot bratwurst on a brötchen and side of thick fries. I duded the sausage up with hot, spicy mustard. I did as Larry and chose mayonnaise for my fries, something he said Germans preferred over ketchup.

I was young and the world about me was new. Ordinary things took on new aspects and meanings. I turned to the glass-and-metal city roiling beyond the station.

This was Germany! I said to myself, a land I'd seen in a hundred movies and television advertisements. I'd never imagined I'd be here. This was the stuff of dreams.

* * *

Inside the airplane cabin, the balance of things changed almost imperceptibly. We had begun our descent into Frankfurt. The confusing gauntlet of customs—in both senses of the word—awaited us. I rubbed the ache from my writing hand and stowed my pen and journals. I found Virginia still asleep and Nick shifting uncomfortably in his seat. I stroked his hair until his eyes opened. He stretched himself awake and grimaced. He didn't need to say it.

"Drink some water, little man," I said. "It'll make you feel better."

I look back on that plane trip now and am glad Virginia and Nick had to be on their own for a while. I realize now those seven or eight hours were the most productive of my life.

CHAPTER FOUR

IVO AND MARTIN

Despite being moody, I felt the excitement of being back where part of me always belonged. Nick was in good spirits after his flight and was jacking around in the passport control line. He sang, poked at Virginia and me, and ran around in circles.

"These are serious people," I said. I was exhausted and the border agents were as good an excuse as any to shut down the frenetic activity my son gets into when he's tired. "They don't take jokes or playing around very well."

"What's their problem?"

"They don't have a sense of humor," I said. "They have single eyebrows that go across their whole faces."

The passport-control agent scrutinized our passports with a dour look. He didn't smile. He had a unibrow.

We breezed through customs. We stumbled into the terminal and into a world I knew by heart. Gliding down the escalators to the front doors, we climbed aboard the bus that would take us to the airport train station. We rode ten minutes to a glass-clad building shaped like a long, upside-down basket. It was beautiful in the way all train stations are—functional, efficient, and meant to be inhabited for a very short time. The intercity express's sleek profile and sharp nose resembled the futuristic trains I'd seen in magazines when I was a kid. Compared to the Amtraks that lumbered through

Kansas City, the train made it seem as if Europeans lived in the future.

We couldn't get out of the train station without buying something. Every gift shop or convenience store gives Virginia and Nick the opportunity to shop. I've become accustomed to their affinity for new things. But jet lag and lack of sleep left me sour. I sneered and snapped at them. I fidgeted as the time to board the train neared and they were still in the shop. "Come on, people," I said. "We need to be on the train before it leaves the station." They didn't seem to care much. Virginia shot me a look and went back to perusing what seemed to her and Nick exotic goods.

I walked out to the train platform and looked down the tracks. I shook off the agitation and recognized what was happening to me. My mood had swung low and I felt the presence of darkness over my shoulder. A breakout depressive episode was sneaking around the edges of my medications. In these situations, I've learned to accept the oncoming depression. If I ignore it, it will take me down. But if I admit changes in outlook and emotion are coming, I cope better. I took a few deep breaths and detached myself from what I thought was a frivolous waste of time. There will be another train, I told myself. We'd get to Ivo's without my worry and henpecking. I hung on, knowing that despite medication, this would affect me. I oughtn't let it happen without my consent. And besides, we'd find connections again with some of the best, most loving and open people I know.

Patience restored, I knew I would benefit from their shopping and we'd have good noshes for the train ride. They'd be happy eating exotic treats. When we boarded the train at the last minute, the relief I felt was overwhelming. The 110-kilometer trip from Frankfurt to Montabaur took twenty-five minutes. We moved smoothly at over

150 miles an hour. The effect was electrifying. The speed intoxicated me, and the heaviness that plagued me abated some.

We detrained at Montabaur. Ivo, a smiling character with a bright-eyed, mischievous look, walked up through the station entrance. He's about five foot eleven and round in the belly with broad shoulders. His balding pate and slight beard and moustache made his friendly and open personality even more so. I'd seen him every time I crossed the Atlantic, six times since I first left in 1986. He and his wife Andrea had come to stay with my daughter Sydney and me in our two-room house for a week in 1997. When Virginia and I got married in Kansas City in 1999, they attended the wedding, along with Udo. The five of us, including Sydney, went on our "honey-moon" together—a weekend at a state trout park in Missouri. Virginia, Sydney, and I visited him in Koblenz in 2000. Ivo and I often talked on the phone, but I didn't see him again until 2011, when I went to Germany to see my good friend and compatriot Joachim, who was dying of brain cancer. On that trip, I'd spent two days with Ivo and Andrea in Koblenz. Now, Ivo looked rounder and grayer than when I first met him in 1986. He walked with a confidence he didn't used to possess.

We've gone through our lives separate but connected. I reveled in his graduation from the university in Freiburg, where he had earned his doctorate. I celebrated, though from afar, his marriage to Andrea. He saw me through my changes, from sobering up and going to graduate school in Wyoming to my careers as journalist and ironworker, and then through my own PhD studies. We talked to each other at least once a month over the telephone, recounting as we could the vagaries and joys in our lives. Despite his physical changes, his personality—open, gregarious but also defensive and complicated—masked the years.

We all gave him big hugs, and Nick told how the trip had gone so far. "We were on a plane for something like a day. Then, we came into this big airport where we got on this train that went really fast." He talked about the treats his mom had bought for him and mentioned that he heard the language his dad spoke on the phone sometimes while he watched cartoons in the living room. I was surprised. Most of the time, he is shy and reticent. But in this moment, he couldn't stop talking.

"Now, we go," he said, when Nick had finished his story "We have much to catch up on."

When we arrived at Ivo's house in Koblenz, it was a rainy mid-afternoon. I was glad of it. Dark weather calms me, somehow protects my raw nerves when depression descends.

Ivo's three-story stucco house stood in a line of similar residences. The builders constructed the house in the style of 1950s German residences—solid, sturdy, and unassuming. It stood on a narrow street that wound up from the bottom of steep, forested ravine from the Rhein about a mile distant and 200 feet below. The people who built this house meant it to last. The walls were thick and the foundation substantial. Windows opened out of the house's common areas, bedrooms, and kitchen and suffused the spaces with natural light.

The peace and stillness of a gentleman scholar filled Ivo's house. The living room, a bright open space, led to a darker, wood-paneled room whose walls were covered with books and art. The whole place had sweeping spaces and simple furnishings. Along the walls of the living room hung several of Martin's photographs and paintings. A simple piece of rice paper done in Eastern calligraphy read, "I have enough." It hung in a frame behind a rocking chair next to a simple floor lamp and a wood-burning stove.

Nick and Virginia were tired but far from exhausted. I felt muddled, considering the sleepless transatlantic flight and the oncoming depression. Jittery and anxious, I wasn't ready to take on the world. I needed rest. We talked and ate—whole grain Brötchen, sliced sausages, fruit, cheese, *Quark* (a fresh cheese somewhere between cream cheese and yogurt), and cordials Ivo mixed with homemade fruit nectars and fizzy water. The eats were a blessing after airline food, chips, and candy bars.

Food fatigue settled on me. I eased upstairs to lie down in Ivo's guest bedroom, where I slid off my shoes and pulled a thick feather bed to my chin. The sound of the rain dripping off the eaves came through the glass door that was opened a crack. I thought again of the first time I'd met Ivo in February 1986. I'd been living in Trier for about three months.

* * *

Larry and I'd spent most of the first few weeks of my Germany adventure together on trains. When I became surer of myself, I took off on my own for a month tramping around the Mosel, Rheingau, and Pfälzer vineyards, knocking on two or three or more doors every day and spending nights at train stations and on trains. On one round, I circled back to Trier from Worms and then to the Frick's for a weekend. The following Monday, I headed back to Trier and lucked out. I walked into the Bischöflichen Weingüter (Episcopal Wineries), a maker of famous Rieslings whose vintages I knew from my wine days in Kansas City. The director, a short Austrian who knew some English, hired me on the spot. When I had trouble finding a place to live, he introduced me to the people at the state school for winery and vintner apprentices, where I secured a small room.

After I started working, I spent most evenings and weekends alone. My little ten-by-twelve-foot room stood under the roof in the fifth-story attic of the school. It had a bed, writing table and chair, and a standing wardrobe. A sink and toothbrush holder inhabited one corner. A bathroom with shower stood at the end of a short hallway past two other rooms like mine. My dormer window opened to Egbertstrasse, a block lined with two- and three-story slate-roofed houses. A couple of shops hugged the corner. I spent hours at the open window, watching the lights come on the evening or staring up beyond the roofs to Petrisberg, a large, wooded hill that rose a hundred meters above the neighborhood.

I shifted up my window-sitting with the view across the narrow hallway from my room. The vista of my new city looked out over the rail line and across the Palastgarten, a park that opened up in trees and green to the commercial heart of Trier. From the window, I could take in the ruins of the great Roman baths at the garden and look down toward the Roman basilica, the tall churches at the city center, and across the river to the cliffs and wooded bluffs beyond.

As I watched the neighborhood and the great city that seemed so quiet from my vantage point, I wondered how I'd meet the people behind those warmly lit windows. Finding a stable group of friends eluded me. Sometimes, winery and vineyard managers invited me to their houses on holidays. Other interns at the winery took to me. Wolfgang, a tall, gangly kid whose family owned a vineyard in Kasel, a village near Trier, befriended me. An English woman who spoke fluent German, Carmel, comforted and helped me a great deal with the language. Monika was a working woman who lived near the vineyard where she'd worked with me in the harvest. This little core of people made the first lonely and depressed days in Trier more bearable. Occasionally, on Friday evenings, Carmel, Monika, Wolfgang, and I sat in the warm confines of the small brewery that stood a couple of blocks from my room—and outside in the atmospheric biergarten when the weather was amenable.

The winery internship paid 500DM (about $250) a month. Monthly rent for my room at the school ran 210DM. The price included a light breakfast on weekdays, usually coffee, brötchen, and sliced cheeses and meats—part of which I made into a sandwich for lunch. I budgeted enough to buy nonperishable food (I had no refrigerator) for evenings and weekends. Each week, I also purchased an English-language paperback from a bookstore in the Brotstrasse, a narrow, dark lane that wound through street-level shops in slate-roofed houses with apartments in them. My drinking moderated. Though I drank every day and was frequently tipsy, I was rarely pass-out drunk except for a couple notable occasions. I couldn't afford it, and somehow my new life made it easier to stay out of the weeds with drink. The few Deutschmarks left in my pocket each week afforded me a pack of cigarettes, and a half-liter beer and plate of fries at the brewery or a bratwurst at a Schnellimbiss on the weekends. I bought liter bottles of plonk wine from the winery to keep myself company on lonely nights and weekends.

The internship took me from the cellar to the vineyard and back again, depending on the season and work demands. The labor outdoors with the vines suited me and absorbed manias and helped me through depressions. I started at the winery with the harvest well underway. I spent days learning how to cut grapes without slicing my fingers. I was out of shape for the steep slopes, and we worked our way from bottom to top, returning to the bottom to harvest uphill again. Taking turns with the other men, I carried a large plastic drum on my back, gathering buckets of the other workers' grapes and hauling the drum down to a trailer with an auger in the bottom that would shove the grapes into the de-stemmers and presses at the winery.

In late fall after harvest, we pruned the vines of their previous year's growth, leaving two new canes, each with ten buds, for the coming year. We raked the prunings into piles and then, each of us with a pitchfork, lifted the bundles over our heads and carried them to a fire below, around which we kept warm. That winter, the winery workers found the poor American kid coming to work underdressed. Over time, they and the Fricks provided gloves, warm hats, and sturdy coats. They also gave me wool socks and well-fitting work boots.

When winter set in, we tied the pruned vines to the wire trellises that spanned the vineyard from top to bottom. Spring arrived and we planted new vines, each one not more than a Riesling bud grafted to a stick of American grape rootstock. (Wiry, tough American-variety rootstocks have been routinely used in Europe since the early twentieth century against the root louse, itself an import from the States, which devastated the original, softer European-variety roots in the nineteenth century.) We sprayed newly sprouted vines with fungicide in hand-pumped water packs on our backs or with long hoses snaking from a wagon with a large tank that held premixed solution and whose pump was powered by a tractor. We plucked excess growth from the vines through the spring and summer and cut the vines back when they overgrew the trellises. A vineyard manager administered the operation, the goal of which was to produce the ripest, richest grapes possible. Summer brought endless rounds of labor, such as chopping weeds, spreading fertilizer, and strewing groundcover—mulch and chipped wood and stall leavings we picked up from the horse barns at the riding center above the vineyard.

Even in the middle of winter, when the morning frost stuck to my gloves and the wind swept the warmth right out of me no matter how I'd bundled up, I relished the work outside in the sweeping valley above the little stream called Avelsbach. There, Wolfgang and I worked with several journeymen who took up the more skilled, machinery-operated labor in the vineyard and left us to tasks in the steepest parts of the vineyard, where most of the work had to be done by hand.

Deep in the cellars, the work was less good to me. A vaulted cellar lined with barrels was a romantic vision of the wine business to me. But the labor there was tedious and repetitive. My hands ached, awash in cold water from hosing out the wooden barrels or wine from the barrel taps. We cleared musts—fresh juice—with unbearably loud centrifuges. We started fermentations and transferred newly fermented wines to tanks and barrels where the last vestiges of fermentation completed. Then, after the wines had gone still, we siphoned or pumped them back to tanks and barrels we'd cleaned. Meanwhile, we moved wines from concrete and stainless-steel tanks, crawled in, and scraped off the wine crystals. Then we hosed the tanks down with cleaning solution and rinsed them. We filtered wines we pumped up to the bottling-and-labeling line in the winery above. Then, we packed bottles in cases for shipping and for special, smaller orders.

The Kellermeister kept meticulous records for wines from particular vineyards. Differing divisions of the ecclesiastical community owned various vineyards throughout the Mosel region. Each parcel benefited a different entity. Each wine had to be vinted and bottled separately, a dizzyingly complicated job. I worked in the cathedral's vineyards. But under the same roof, the winery pressed, fermented, finished, and bottled wines for the Benedictine convent, the seminary, and the priests' retirement fund, along with other small convents and monasteries. During my first days in the cellar, I took cues from the teenage apprentices and learned the work by mimicking them, not understanding their heavy Platt dialects. I came home from the cellar cold and achy.

Because I was alone, I filled my evenings writing letters home and drinking cheap wine. I read and napped. To work out the restlessness I felt, I walked. Evenings and weekends, I wandered aimlessly. Luck and a good sense of direction brought me back to familiar surroundings, and I made my way home. Sometimes I took a map of the city and made it my goal to walk every street in the town center. I hiked through the vineyards south and west of Trier or through town for upward of nine or ten hours. Walking staved off the feeling of utter loneliness but also worked off the mania and carried me through the guilt that lying in bed, steeped in depression, caused in me. It kept hunger at bay, as well. In part, I walked to induce good sleep. After a few months, I knew Trier better than the neighborhood I grew up in.

I walked in all kinds of weather. I'd trod Trier's streets from where I lived in Petrisberg and up through the Olewiger Tal, the valley behind my room, back up over the wooded plateau rising above the town. There sprawled a French garrison, with its gray barracks and service buildings laid out in neat rows. Trier was still occupied territory in the mid-1980s, a remnant of the Second World War and the Cold War. French troops trained behind razor-wire fences with large signs that warned against trespassing, "*BETRETEN DES GELANDES STRENG VERBOTEN.*" I'd walk down into the center of Trier, through the market piazza, and then up the Palaststrasse and past the fourth-century, six-and-a-half-story Roman basilica. That such buildings, consistently occupied for 1,500 years, existed was unimaginable to a kid who came from a country where the oldest building in his town dated back only 150 years. I often stopped to touch the basilica walls just to say I'd laid my hand on something people built a millennium and a half ago.

The footpath away from the piazza before the basilica took me toward the ruins of the Roman baths. Trier was home to several such baths over time, and the most notable were the *Barbarathermen*—Barbara Baths—which I found to have the most romantic name. The ruins there were little more than humps of grass and stone a wrought-iron fence enclosed. The *Kaiserthermen*—Imperial Baths—though, were well-preserved, even rebuilt, ruins that gave the visitor a firm idea of the scope and workings of such an operation. Slaves and lower-class Roman citizens tended fires that warmed the floors of the baths through elaborate tunnels. Those same tunnels transmitted the warmth and smoke of the fires beneath the floors and also heated water in grand basins through the complex.

This walk, which I'd made more than a dozen times in my first year in Germany, took me through the Palastgarten, where I often stopped for a long rest under the lindens. On sunny days and days when it was warm and clear, I people watched. University students sat in circles discussing class subjects and the worries of the world. The old and young lay around the park in various states of undress. Topless women and nearly naked youths shocked and amazed me and gave me a feeling I was in a more cosmopolitan and less prudish world than the one I'd come from.

From the Kaiserthermen, I crossed under a roadway and the railroad tracks to the corner of the winery apprentice school that housed my little room. The great swath of the building stood on one side of what had been the old Roman circus, where chariots once raced and competitors bested one another in various track-and-field events. The houses across the street with their steep roofs and tiny gardens spread out over the center stripe of the arena. And up behind those houses on the next block stood the other side of the circus.

Behind my old neighborhood at the foot of the Petrisberg, the Trierer Löwenbräuerei served its beer and food in a lovely tree- and vine-draped beer garden. In summer, I sometimes spent Friday or

Saturday evenings there with Wolfgang and Monika. Carmel and her roommate Carla often joined us. Dark wood panels lined the restaurant, which glowed in candlelight. The smells of roasted meats, frying potatoes, and fresh, bracing beer seduced what little money I had out of my pockets. Most weekends, I used evenings after my walks to type long letters to people I knew, and those I hardly knew, on a cheap but sturdy East German Erica portable for which I'd traded a student five Deutschmarks and a warm hat. Between reading and writing, and drinking about a bottle or more of wine, I filled the evenings after work with long stares out over my neighborhood as the daylight dimmed and the lights came on in the houses.

Winter nights came early. In December, I often walked in the dark from my room down through the Palastgarten and down Brotstrasse to the pedestrian area in the center of town. In that great plaza rimmed with shops and churches and timber-and-plaster apartment buildings, stood the *Weihnachtsmarkt*, or Christmas market, a cluster of wagons where merchants sold *Glühwein*—a hot, spiced red-wine drink that tasted like melted gold—and handmade crafts. A toymaker peddled wooden toys, and food vendors provided all sorts of good German delights—brat- and currywurst, fries, strudel, marzipan treats, and cookies. A band played in the center of the affair, and Christmas lights hung everywhere. The effect at night was warm and welcoming, especially for someone like me who needed people around him even if he didn't know how to start a conversation with them.

On Christmas Eve 1985, I was in a manic state. I spent twelve hours from predawn into the evening dark marching paths through the vineyards south of town. It was bitterly cold and snowing. I'd brought nothing to eat or drink. I felt the steep hills in my legs and back. The chill shot through me from my hands to the nape of my neck and into my chest. Regardless, I didn't turn home. I kept moving to push the cold out of my bones. I'd determined to walk the nine kilometers to Konz and back through the vineyards, not taking one street or sidewalk along the way. I stopped once late in the afternoon and watched the towns of Trier and Konz in the valley, separated from me by hundreds of rows of vines falling steeply to the highway below.

When I arrived back in Trier, I wandered down to the Weihnachtsmarkt, hoping to surround myself with that warmth once again. I looked forward to the chance to see Monika again. I was falling in love and thought she might be down at the market.

My heart stopped when I walked into the plaza and found it completely empty and silent but for a couple walking their dog. The whole Weihnachtsmarkt had folded up and rolled away. I plunged from great heights into the abyss. I traipsed the plaza, looked into shop windows, and cried, trying to let no one see. Then I wandered again among the old houses with their windows filled with yellow light. I gazed with longing into shop windows, where every sort of ware reminded me how poor I was and how few people I knew. I walked for more hours, coming home finally around midnight, when I got good and drunk before the advent of the lonelier day of Christmas.

I was lucky to have Wolfgang, Monika, and Carmel as acquaintances by the middle of February, and I'm sure I put them out sometimes with my needy ways. I still felt lonely and was thinking of ending my Germany experiment and heading back to Kansas City. Unwilling to face my failure, I fell into a deep depression and contemplated suicide by leaping from my window. Doggedly, afraid of death and despairing of human companionship, I walked.

One night, I rambled again up through the vineyards and then to center of Trier, where I went to a Schnellimbiss I liked. It stood next to the cathedral off the Domfreihof, an open square, on a street called

Sieh um Dich—in English, "Look Around You." The cathedral's spires rose up sixty meters above the square. The crenellated Liebfrauenkirche stood beyond the cathedral. Solid three- and five-story buildings, all of one front, walled in the square. Sieh um Dich continued past the cathedral as a narrow lane, wide enough for foot traffic, between high, stucco walls for about a block and a half until it ran into a larger street.

The man who ran the *Imbiss* was a hardworking Turk whose professional bearing, white apron, and stovepipe hat gave him the look of a chef. I stood in line, waiting my turn, when the man in front of me bought what looked like a thick hamburger. I didn't hear what he said it was, but I wanted one. I hadn't had a burger in months. I imagined it with heavy, spicy German mustard and a side of fries. I looked around. A friendly, round man stood at one of the stand-up tables on the sidewalk in front of the Imbiss. He smiled when I met his eye.

"*Was isst der Mann?*" I asked the man at the table.

"*Was?*" he said, as if he hadn't heard me.

What I said in German could mean "What is the man eating?" or "What is the man?" My German by that time was simple but halting. I'd learned well by aligning signs in shop windows with the goods they signified. I assembled sentences with the help of the people at the winery and vineyard. But in that context, the friendly man at the stand-up table didn't know exactly what I was asking. I fumbled around to explain myself, not knowing what I'd gotten myself into. After a minute or so, he realized what I wanted and told me the burger-looking thing was a *Wurstkloppse,* a kind of meat lump made from the leavings of the chopping block and slicer. He said I really didn't want a Wurstkloppse knowing what it was made from, but I had my mind set. When my turn came, I ordered one from the Turk and turned to the stand-up tables, which were all taken. The friendly man invited me to join him.

He spoke English well and introduced himself as Ivo Rauch. I told him in faltering German and in English where I worked and how I got there. He said he apprenticed at a stained glass–restoration firm, but he'd been to the university and had a degree in art history. He was on his way to a house near the city center to meet with friends to discuss sharing a new apartment. He invited me to walk with him.

We ambled slowly through Trier's pedestrian plaza. Conversation came easily, and his friendliness seemed sincere.

"To tell you the truth, I'm very lonely," I said after a while. "I'm thinking of leaving my internship and going back home."

"Don't do that," he said. "That's silly. You work at one of the most famous wineries in Germany. Friends will find you soon enough. Spring is coming. Germans really open up with the weather."

On that spittle of hope, I dismissed leaving again—for the moment, anyway.

"Since you don't know many people," he said. "Let me take you to meet my friends. One of them has an attic apartment in a building off the pedestrian zone. They will like you. We are meeting tonight to talk about living arrangements in a new apartment we're taking."

All of them were open, warm people. The dim room filled with smoke and we sat at a table crowded with glasses and wine and beer bottles. They shared their food with me, brötchen, sliced sausages, and cheeses. I didn't know it, but this was the beginning of a lifelong friendship with Ivo and three of his roommates. One of them, Stephan, was a theologian studying at the university. The others, Martin and Udo, were apprentices at the stained glass–restoration firm. A fifth, Michael, also studied theology at the university. They were all very friendly. Conversation turned from their new living arrangements to me.

"It must be scary leaving everything to come to a place where you didn't even know if you would have a place to stay," Stephan said. "How do you do it?"

"I don't know," I said. "I just did it. I don't think I put too much thought in it. Life was miserable. There had to be something else."

"Do you know what you want to find?" Udo said.

"Not really," I said. "I just know that I hope to go to the wine school in Geisenheim."

"How are you finding your new home?" Martin asked.

"My room at the school is fine," I said. "It's homey, you know, just the right size for me. But the first months have been hard. I'm very lonely."

Michael slapped me on the back and said with a smile. "Not anymore, American. Not anymore."

"You're welcome at our new house anytime," Ivo said. They all looked over their drinks and nodded.

We became fast friends. I had the run of their new apartment, which occupied a second and third story in a house in the Saarstrasse, a lively avenue of shops and apartment buildings a ten-minute walk from my room. They even gave me my own key. On weekends, I often had the house to myself. Ivo and Martin knew each other from Koblenz and traveled home together. Udo returned to his native Reutlingen near Stuttgart on weekends and long holidays. Stephan and Michael were often gone to friends and family. When they were home, they stayed in their rooms busy with their studies. I watched television and listened to Martin's record player—two luxuries I didn't have in my little room. I sometimes overnighted by myself at the apartment after a long walk through Trier and the adjoining countryside. When the boys were home, we ate together and chattered and watched movies. They welcomed me any night of the week, and I took them up on their hospitality, eating dinner and having after-work coffee with them. For weeks at a time, my little room served as the place where I slept and changed clothes.

Ivo had listened to me when things were good and in the darkest days before I quit drinking in 1990. After I sobered up, he was a constant font of encouragement. He always opened his house to me.

Being in his home once again made me feel as if all the years led us right to this moment. I fell asleep, listening to Ivo and Nick joshing around downstairs. I had a glorious nap.

* * *

Later in the evening, after I rejoined Ivo, Virginia, and Nick preparing dinner, Martin arrived. It was good to feel his presence again. After Martin and Ivo finished their apprenticeships at the stained-glass firm, Ivo went on to develop a reputation as an authority on stained-glass restoration. He contracted with churches and businesses to catalog and restore windows, and Ivo hired the companies that specialized in the restoration. He oversaw all the work with a small staff.

Martin had begun serious work as a painter while in Trier, using his room in the apartment as a studio. We spent hours together while he sketched and painted, discussing creativity, art, and artistic endeavor. As an artist, he was far more developed than I was as a writer. All I'd ever really wanted was to be a writer but lacked the discipline and knowledge of process. He, on the other hand, knew art was work and hard work was going to get him where he wanted to go. He was also much calmer and meditative than I was. My inner life inhabited only a small part of my conscious mind. I didn't have much self-awareness. I covered up my alcoholism with a desire to own a vineyard. This wasn't completely disingenuous. I liked working with vines. But beyond a vague desire to go to the wine school in Geisenheim, I lived for the moment—I couldn't foresee a real future the way Martin did for himself.

I'd witnessed Martin's changes over the years. He attended art school in Düsseldorf. His painting resembled his mentor's then became more personal to him, more concerned with quiet moments. Themes of loneliness, contemplation, and inner searching dominated his work. His lithographs, engravings, and intaglio prints came to possess the quality of a true master who's accomplished at his craft and takes himself seriously as an artist. When he discovered the camera obscura—a simple box with an aperture in one side that projected an image on the other—he found he could make photographs resembling his painted work. From there he took the natural step of combining his camera obscura photos with painting, and he's remained with this form and abstract painting ever since. I keep a wall of his work in my house. I look at those seven pieces, which include an enigmatic self-portrait of him at his easel, every day. The work haunts me.

Now he was constructing his greatest piece, a camera obscura built of two shipping containers, one stacked on the other, and clad black plates that made the whole assembly reminiscent of the monolith in *2001: A Space Odyssey*. He planned to place the camera in front of the grand cathedral in Köln (Cologne), where he lived. The public could climb stairs to the top shipping container and see the plaza on a translucent screen. The whole endeavor entailed the use of welders and riggers, transportation specialists and, of course, Martin himself.

When everyone had settled, we fired up the barbeque and Martin took over as head chef. He grilled onions, eggplant, firm fresh cheese, kebabs, steaks, and potatoes. Virginia and Ivo made a big salad, sliced fresh bread and tomatoes. I set the table on Ivo's back porch, which opened onto a long lawn hedged in on two sides with tall evergreens. The back of the yard led to a large orchard of full, tall, unpruned apple trees. Horses grazed under the trees. The evening had a chill and the sky remained closed, which was fine with me, fighting as I was the depression looming over me. We sat at the outdoor table and passed the plates of food. A shelf behind us held wine and juices, bubbly water and drinks made with concentrated essences of fruit flowers Ivo had concocted himself. After a while, we sat back and watched in silence while the horses fed on the fallen apples.

After dinner, Martin and I talked a long time about our varying social universes.

"As an academic, I've never felt completely comfortable in academic circles," I said. "My dirty fingernails make me feel like an outsider." I took up with the ironworkers' union after we adopted Nick in 2007 at the end of my PhD coursework and spent time building bridges and buildings. I could walk in that universe and speak its language. It was part of the working-class background I came from.

"I know what you mean," he said. "Different classes and backgrounds demand shifts from one code to the other. I've found people stay in one class because of work and family and friends and breaking out of that class—finding the code—only happens with self-awareness and hard work."

"Being a writer has its difficulties, too," I said. "I'm always uncomfortable with writers unless we talk about our craft, of aesthetics, and of the personal insides it takes to be a writer. But I've always felt inferior to other writers and reluctantly let my work out to them."

"I felt the same way when I started as a painter," he said. "For many years. I felt minor to others with education, profession, and higher social status." He looked out from his chair on the patio toward a horse grazing by the back fence.

"I suppose," I said, "that comfort in different surroundings with different people comes after long experience and learning."

"I've become comfortable with other artists," he said. "Each of these universes you run in—the ironworker, the academic, and the writer—demand different languages, bearings, and actions. You just need to put yourself aside and go forward without thinking of what others might think of you or your work."

"I still have a long way to go."

"Not as far as you think," he said and turned and smiled at me. "So, there, *Pappnase*, ease up. You'll be fine. I know . . . you know you will."

* * *

I woke early the next morning and walked down to Ivo's study. I knew Nick and Virginia would sleep late and give me time to write in my journal. The depression I felt creeping up stood beside me like a ghost. I admitted its presence and took measures to keep it from welling up inside me. I breathed deeply and prepared myself to hold on, as that is sometimes the only way to deal with it. Hold on and know it passes. Writing felt good, almost lyrical in the silence and calm of Ivo's space. I wanted the same kind of peace in Kansas City. I wondered, with all the needs and distractions of home, if I could ever achieve it.

After a while, I put on my shoes and walked down to a trail that led through the wheat fields above Niederberg and the vineyards in the Mühlertal valley, which fell into a dark crease in the plain. The day was clearing, and puffy clouds let sun peek through. The breeze off the fields chilled me, but walking made the blood flow into my head for the first time since we'd climbed on the plane. Except for the wind in the wheat and through the branches of isolated trees next to the trail, the only sounds were the whine of tires on pavement and the crunching of my shoes on the dirt track. I walked away the negative energy building inside and kept going for a couple of hours, down into the Mühlertal and to the Rhein below, then straight up the steep hill on Arenbergerstrasse. I kept thinking of my suicide attempt. With the great life I'd been given, what would that get me besides dead? These manias and depressions come but they always end. They always end. It was something I needed to remember.

The whole time, despite the turn in my mental disposition, it felt good to be back in Germany.

* * *

I reflect again on that evening with Ivo and Martin. Our conversations went in hundreds of different directions. I felt fulfilled being with my friends again. Even better was that Virginia and Nick were getting a lot out of it. The other day, Virginia told me I have such wonderful friends and there is something in me that draws good people into my orbit. I kissed her and said, "You and Nick."

CHAPTER FIVE

COMING HOME

AN UNCERTAIN TREMOR of déjà vu hit me as Ivo parked the car in front of the Koblenz train station. It produced a kind of vertigo I've only ever felt when returning to familiar places and finding they are either much bigger or smaller than I recall.

The station had loomed large in my mind. The reality was more moderate. Thirty years before, I used the Koblenz station as the main exchange point from intercity trains to the regional coaches that took me to and from Trier on my rounds of the country. It felt smaller but no less familiar. I experienced again the excitement and despair that plagued me as I traveled the wine districts in search of a paid position at a winery. A little of that hopelessness stuck to me still. I tried to shake it off. With my family in tow and trains to catch, I had neither the time nor energy to indulge in depression.

The sun shone full, and the heat of the day radiated off the platform. We entrained on what used to be called the E-train (*Eilzug*), an express train that stopped at a few larger towns between Koblenz and Trier. Where E-trains used to be a dumpy collection of open-seating cars, this train possessed a modern flair. It sported two-storied cars with scenic views above and track-level seating below. The cars gleamed with glass partitions and comfortable seats. We took the upper story, so we could see over the bushes and trees lining the tracks. Ivo stood next to the train after we boarded. He waited, smiling and waving from time to time. We'd see him again in a couple of weeks but leaving him was still sad. As we pulled away, he walked next to the train until it sped along too fast for him to keep up.

"I really love Ivo," Virginia said, once she settled back in her seat. "I'm still mourning Andrea. It's not something I think I'll ever get over. It feels like unfinished business."

"Yeah," Nick said. "I never knew her, but I'm sorry for Ivo. He's such a great guy. He has such nice things."

"What do you mean?" I asked.

"Well, he has all those books, sort of like you do, but they are set up like in a museum. His house is so quiet. And he has all those cool pictures Martin painted. The whole place is, well, just peaceful. And Martin . . . his English is funny but he tries. He's a nice guy. You have such good friends."

"Thanks, Nick."

He opened a package of chips and looked in as if they were out to get him. He's a very picky eater and would rather starve than try something new. At Ivo's he ate bread and cheese but, even then, he piddled over the foreign-looking food. We talked him or, rather, begged and cajoled him into eating the sliced sausages. He nibbled and grimaced but ate some, assuaging Virginia's constant worry over his nutrition. I feared he wasn't going to fare well at Josef's and Marlies'. Trying to get Nick to eat the food she made—which wasn't going to be his normal mac-and-cheese or pepperoni pizza—would be a chore. After several morsels and considerations, Nick decided the chips were all right.

When I was first in Germany, I'd traveled this stretch from Koblenz to Trier dozens of times as I returned from wherever I wandered to stay overnight at the Fricks' or to my tiny domicile in Trier after a weekend in Koblenz with Ivo and his parents. The trips melded together in memory. I recalled specific places, scenes, and feelings but not the precise times I'd seen these sights. I watched them all materialize again. Between my first forays into the German landscape through my second stint in the Vaterland and into my many visits, this stretch felt like the way home.

* * *

Memories of euphoria and of absolute darkness streamed through my mind. The first month in Germany in 1985 was so uncertain. Larry and I traveled from Kanzem through Koblenz and outward to Kaiserslautern, Mannheim, Munich, and Regensburg. We spent time in Hamburg and Freiburg. Several times, we took a long night train just to have a place to sleep.

Before we parted ways, Larry and I stayed with his friends—students and workers all over southern Germany. I recall one student in Regensburg who put us up for the night. We arrived at the station late in the evening. The old market was a noisy conglomerate of students and revelers. Light from fires set in low burners danced against the brick and stone. Outside the busy town center, the night was serenely quiet. We wound our way through narrow, empty streets and tiny alleyways. Atmospheric dimness, even darkness, lay on the residential districts. I slogged along behind Larry, who was doing better, mood-wise, than I. For days, we'd only napped on trains and snoozed on park benches. I was happy when we arrived at Larry's friend's apartment and I slept without dreaming. Larry's friend had to wake early and get ready for school. I remember being resentful as he made his coffee and sack lunch. The burble and pop of the coffeemaker kept me from getting more shut-eye. Can't he see I'm trying to sleep here?

Though my early travels are packed with peculiar incidents and comic situations, with boundless energy and deep depression, perhaps the strangest trip on this trans-Germany train ramble was to Berlin. Larry and I crossed the border at Helmstedt-Marienborn on a rainy day. The countryside spread in dark green fields and pastures at the frontier. Villages appeared on the hills and valleys in the distance like phantoms. I watched a small, drab car, likely a Lada or rickety Trabant, trundle down a long narrow road through the fields and wondered how different the person in the car was from me. I'd grown up hearing horrible stories about communism, communists, and life under the East German totalitarian regime. At one time or another, I'd been taught all East Germans lived in fear and oppression. They were backward and uneducated. The government punished all self-expression. I watched that car as the train stopped on the tracks and guards with their oversized officers' caps boarded our car to check passports and transit tickets. There were no stops between Helmstedt and West Berlin. The officers asked questions in German, and Larry answered. They looked at our American passports and our train passes with deadpan faces. After an uncomfortable and officious moment, they stamped our passports and moved on. I looked back after the car. It had disappeared.

West Berlin impressed this child of the Cold War as an alternate reality. It possessed simultaneously a shabbiness that worn-out American cities have and a lively bustle marking a modern, flourishing metropolis. We'd learned in school that Berlin was a capitalist crown jewel in the middle of communist darkness. The city I experienced held none of that promise but instead occupied a gray area between my childhood vision of it and a starker reality. Military forces still occupied the city. West Berlin allegedly showcased a free-market fair of self-expression and consumer consumption. But the capitalist West subsidized nearly every aspect of the city's commercial life. American and West German government money underwrote everything from the city government to the stabilization of prices for everyday items and food. The occupying troops were another source of income from the state. The Wall divided the city's great sprawl. West Berlin had a cramped and anxious feeling. No one could enter or leave, except in certain, highly controlled ways. The East Germans built the Wall, allegedly, to keep the capitalist invaders out of their country. Everyone knew otherwise.

We stayed at a private-school dormitory in the city's Alt-Tempelhof quarter with Larry's acquaintance Lukas Deptios, an Indonesian student. He wore white suits, colorful shirts, and spit-shined shoes. He carried a cane. He joked all the time as he led us around the winding streets of West Berlin like a seasoned tour guide. Checkpoint Charlie, the Olympic Stadium, the Zoo. I'll never forget the Potsdamer Platz, a no-man's-land seemingly forgotten by the West Berliners and disowned by the East but present in the consciousness of each. The Wall ran right through the old intersection of streets from prewar Berlin and over streetcar tracks in the savage, post-industrial waste. A few homeless people camped in shanties and plastic sheeting next to the Wall. Graffiti, much of it weather-faded, splattered the concrete.

The beer from the grocery near Lukas' place was cheap, and the food at the school was good. Larry went off to visit friends, and I stayed back with Lukas and his classmates. We bought enough beer for all of us, plus some. I drank all the extra and got good and ripped for the first time since coming to Germany. I woke the next morning to a terrific hangover. It made me forget the darkness and depression I'd experienced since before I boarded the plane to Luxembourg. Sick as I was, the hangover felt comfortable. For once in my insomniac train ramble I found myself in territory I knew in one of the strangest places I'd ever been.

Later, Lukas, Larry, and I walked over to the Wall. I'd experienced nothing to that time more dreamlike. It ran up against buildings and divided residential blocks like a ship cleaving the ocean. Elaborate graffiti covered its western face. Raised platforms allowed tourists and military men alike to climb up and get a view of the *Todesstreife* (Death Strip) beyond the Wall's humped top edge. Guards in a tower in the middle of the strip watched us through huge binoculars. They wore pea-green uniforms and carried automatic rifles. Two men with dogs and machine guns patrolled a paved road beyond the barbed-wire fences, tank traps, and spiked steel grids called *Stalinrasen* (Stalin grass). I imagined myself getting across the no-man's land and climbing over a fence to land on those spikes. I'd never seen anything meaner.

Though it was right in front of me, the whole scene—the towers, the Death Strip, the fences, and Stalinrasen—might as well have been as far from me as the moon. The world beyond the Wall was gray and alien. The buildings and streets spread through the eastern city much like those on the west. But a smoky, factory-like atmosphere clouded the scenery. On the West, people thronged through the streets and traffic moved in a frenzy. The streets east of the wall were empty. Alexanderturm, the great radio mast built to show the East's technical prowess, towered over the city. Its stainless-steel-and-glass ball set 650 feet above the ground turned like an all-seeing eye keeping people and machines in check.

Larry went his own way after about ten days of our sojourn across Germany. I had no deadlines but the end of my month pass. My only errand was to knock on winery doors anywhere Germans grew grapes. I slept in stations when I'd missed last trains out or wanted to board early the next morning. One night after a string of days when I'd catnapped on park benches and aboard trains, I walked out of the station at Mannheim at midnight. I'd had my fill of schnapps and beer and felt the pull of sleep. But other overnighters and revelers made the place too noisy for shut-eye. I lit out and sacked out under the first bridge I came across. Below, a little stream bubbled. The night was dark, and I had nothing but a cigarette lighter to lead my way. I climbed down past the bridge rail and bushes and set my meager camp—a plastic groundsheet and sleeping bag—next to the abutment. I heard the traffic above for a few minutes and came to late the next afternoon.

I visited girlfriends, too. The Luxembourger whom I met on the plane, Monique, invited me for a weekend at her family's farm not far from Echternach on the Luxembourg-German border. The farm had belonged to her family for generations. Her brothers and father worked like animals to keep the place up. Their fields spread out over a plain and into a stream valley. They had corn and beans, but also livestock and fallow land. The farmhouse straddled a meadow beneath a large, heavily wooded hill. The great humped slate roof rose over the building of pale-brown stone. The whole place possessed the weight of age and, to me, an aspect I'd seen in romantic pictures of the European countryside.

The first afternoon I came to visit, Monique's mother, Mainsy, sat in the house's drawing room. Dark wood and family heirlooms surrounded us. She made us tea and brought out cookies and cakes. She was glad to have an American as a guest. She spoke flawless English. Monique and I listened as she told tales of growing up on her family's farm and weekends she spent taking in life in Echternach—Luxemburg's oldest town and the biggest in the area. She sometimes traveled to Luxembourg City, particularly in the days following the war. It was, she said, the largest city she'd ever been in until she went to Paris when she was in her twenties.

Mainsy then told of the American soldiers who liberated Luxembourg in World War II. She was a young girl when an African American regiment came through the farm as the Germans retreated.

"The Americans were kind men, gentle, with a good deal of character," she said. "My family hid in the cellar when the soldiers came over the hill. But I was caught out in the barn. I was climbing the ladder to the loft when a soldier yelled at me to stop. I froze and looked down at the him.

"I had never seen a black man before. He smiled in the kindest way and motioned me to come down. He offered me cigarettes and gum. He took me by the arm and joined the other soldiers, who'd opened the cellar door, their guns ready. It was very tense and time passed slowly. But when they found my family had no weapons, they climbed down and handed out chocolates and cigarettes. Those Black soldiers were the first Americans I ever met."

My romance with Monique had begun almost from the moment we stepped off the plane. It lasted through my first tenuous months of travel and into the period after I'd settled in Trier. She visited me there for day trips and shopping. One winter Saturday afternoon, Monique told me she was afraid she was pregnant. Terror paralyzed me. I didn't know what to say. We were walking up a side street by the Trier train station, near where she'd parked her car. The sun cut through the cold day. Leafless in the wind, the trees seemed to shiver.

I spent the next day walking toward Konz and back up through the vineyards home. What would I do if we had a child? I was ashamed and berated myself. How could I have let this happen? I couldn't abandon Monique to her fate or leave a child fatherless. I'd take responsibility and support Monique as well as I could. Regardless of my wishes, Monique, I knew, would be the final arbiter of whatever occurred next. Looking back, I realize I was more grown up about the situation than I realized at the time. I decided against getting married. That would happen, I determined, after we established a lasting relationship, and then if the slightest whiff of love transpired.

We spent anxious weeks waiting to make sure. When Monique found she wasn't pregnant, I cried. I couldn't believe my luck.

Before the pregnancy scare, though, I'd acted like a man-child with little accountability. A woman in Giessen, Sabine, allowed Larry and me to stay on her floor. Later in my travels, even while I carried on with Monique, Sabine and I struck up a romance. She was a lovely woman with deep red hair and fierce, dark blue eyes. She always seemed tremendously depressed and anxious. But when she smiled, it was as if the sun had come out. I visited her several times, and each time she acted as if it was a burden to have me in her house. Simultaneously, she behaved as if she never wanted me to leave. We made love furiously and often. After, she scolded and berated me for wanting only sex from her, which couldn't have been farther from the truth. When I was there, she fussed over having to cook for two people. She harangued me for unpacking and then told me to leave my stuff out since I was staying the night. When time came for me to leave, she made me promise to come back. This sort of confusion went on for the weeks I spent on the trains by myself. Such a confusing relationship made me nervous, but I kept coming back. Being with a woman, feeling a warm hand on a naked shoulder, was more temptation than I could resist.

At the time, I easily fell for women who slept with me, even though they may have wanted to sleep with someone, and I happened to be the guy. Sabine had certainly wanted to sleep with me. When I landed the internship in Trier, I called her several times. She made it clear after a while she didn't want to hear from me again if I wasn't going to visit. I couldn't visit. I had no money and a tiny income from the winery. After a while, I was busy with my job and found friends. My priorities changed. Sabine and I never saw or talked to each other again.

The towns and people of that month I traveled alone, except for the few I mention here, rush by in memory. They exist in a blur of overnights in train stations and train coaches, nights stolen here and there in the houses of strangers. Except for Trier and Koblenz, the train stations waft by so I can no longer distinguish the difference between Merzig and Wittlich or Hamburg and Bremerhaven. The people's personalities drift from one into the other.

For all the adventure on the train through other parts of Germany, I always celebrated returning to the Mosel Valley. Maybe it was the promise of staying with the Fricks or my growing knowledge of the region. I always found Mosel vineyards more intriguing and comfortable than the vast farms and plains outside the area. Detraining and knocking on winery doors gave me purpose. While it was enlightening to travel through unfamiliar countryside and visit strange and new cities, I felt most comfortable in smaller Mosel towns, where walking and getting around was more manageable, the landscape familiar. More than once, I entered the Mosel Valley happy to be returning.

* * *

On the train now, I contemplated the scenery along the river that was as familiar as my own neighborhood. The track turned out of the Rhein Valley and departed Koblenz along the Mosel. The bridge over Winningen spanned the valley, a concrete strip that monolith pillars supported more than 450 feet above the river. Vineyards grew up the steep bluffs on one side of the river, and their little towns occupied bottoms on the opposite bank. A few picturesque villages stood in the middle of the vineyards reaching down to the river. I marveled again at the tiny plots on the bluffs far above and set behind hand-built walls of slate. Here and there winemakers tended vines, perched on walls like eagles in their aeries. They moved slowly and carefully as astronauts. The jagged bluffs fell down to the rail tracks and then off into the river through more vineyards bankside. The lushness of the straight rows of vines and the brush denoting abandoned vineyard niches contrasted with the bare, dark slate of the bluffs they grew on.

The train ride again reminded me of the names I was once so familiar with in those early days of train travel: Winningen, Kobern-Gondorf, Löf, Moselkern, Müden, Treis-Karden, Pommern, Cochem. I had searched many of these places for an internship but found only the larger, more famous wineries had room to take on new interns. Once, a winemaker at a famous but small winery in Bernkastel-Kues invited me in for a long talk. He took me into a dim sitting room filled with family photos and heirlooms. A large window looked out on the picturesque bluffs and vineyards above. He brought out coffee and cakes.

Fortunately, he could speak English and had traveled to the United States with his wine business, as much of his stock went into export.

"I would love to take you on," he said, "but can offer only a small room in the attic, food, and no pay. I'm sure this is romantic, yes? I would think so if I was an American, or even if I was a German. Living in an old *Bauernhaus* and working in these vineyards high up on the cliffs is the stuff you make dreams of."

He paused and lit a pipe and continued. A grandfather clock struck two. "You would fit right in with my workers and family, you have the right personality. But you don't want to be stuck without pay. What will you do on weekends? There is nothing here for a young person who's not a tourist. You'd find your way, *ja*, but it would be lonely, and you would be bored." He cleared his throat and rubbed his hands together. He leaned forward and laid his big, muscular vintner's hand on my arm. He squeezed and brought his hand back to his pipe.

"I'll take you on if you don't find another position," he said. "But I want you to try bigger companies. They pay benefits. You'll get insurance. I can't do that. I'll keep you in wine and food—and plenty of fun and wurst at the wine festivals." I wanted to take him up on his offer immediately. But he demurred. "Better to continue looking," he said. "You will find something, and we will always be here."

The train now passed a familiar point, something I remember because it showed me how difficult building in this narrow, steep valley was. The cliff at Cochem bulged toward the train, and huge bolts, steel plates, and chain-link fences kept the slate from falling from many meters above. A spittle of imagination and memory clung to each village, vineyard, and bluff. I felt again the sadness and anxiety of the young man who had traveled this stretch.

* * *

Virginia and Nick busied themselves with books and devices. They looked out the window from time to time, but the landscape held no fascination for them. They could not distinguish the old from the new or the differences between Kobern and Gondorf or Treis and Karden. They didn't notice the way the vineyards shifted from one bank to the other—always facing the south and west—around the river's tight bends. I wanted to impress them but understood we were in territory from my past, my memory and mine alone.

As we approached Trier from the industrial districts of Ehrang, I felt as if I were coming home. We passed various landmarks and buildings I remembered from times past. Emotions rushed back—the joy at landing my first German job, the shock and dread of Monique's pregnancy, my shame and guilt at carrying on with two sensitive women at the same time, the occasions I'd traveled to visit friends in Koblenz. I remembered the mania escalating late one summer afternoon, well into my internship, after I'd visited Ivo and his parents in Koblenz. The day promised a beautiful evening, and I figured I'd walk at least part of the way to Trier. I left the D-train (a slow train that stopped at every station on the route from Koblenz to Trier) at Longuich, two stops before Trier, hell bent on walking the Mosel back to town. I had no idea where I was or how to find a walking path, if there was one, from there to Trier. I carried a small duffle with some clothes, no water, no food. Little did I realize miles lay between the two towns.

Into the evening and toward dusk, I hiked along two-lane, shoulder-less roads far from the river. I wound up walking, I estimate today, about twenty miles up the Ruwer Valley and back down toward the Mosel through tiny villages famous for their wines. The longer I was at it, the angrier I grew, more determined to finish the job. I walked faster with wider strides until I was almost running. At one point, a car pulled up and the driver asked if I wanted a ride. "*Nein!*" I shouted, "I got myself into this mess." By the time I stumbled into Trier North, night had fallen hours before. My feet were blistered and bloody, my legs rubbery, and my heart pounding out of my chest. I arrived home around midnight, exhausted and regretful I'd treated myself so roughly. I drank until I passed out somewhere toward 3 a.m. I don't remember the next day.

At Trier, Virginia, Nick, and I had little time to poke around. Our train for Kanzem was scheduled to leave fifteen minutes after we arrived. I implored Virginia and Nick to stay on the platform and away from the gift shop. I had to get a look, however brief, at the city. Of course, I'd seen it dozens of times. The last time I'd been in the station and in the city was in 2011 when I visited Joachim in Berlin and taken a side trip across the country to spend five days with Josef and Marlies in Wawern. On that trip, I'd taken a half day for myself in Trier and walked familiar streets that felt as if I'd never left them.

I ran down the tunnel below the platforms and came up into the station. Darting across the interior and out front, I looked back on the postwar-era station with a huge clock above the entrance. People bustled down Bahnhofstrasse and past the collection of tourist shops, restaurants, and bars. Trier was a tourist haven with Roman ruins, ancient churches, and cultural attractions, including a symphony and lively theater life. Much of the town had been bombed flat during the war, but postwar reconstruction replaced many of the buildings in the center of town in prewar and Middle Ages style. Church congregations and government agencies reconstructed church roofs and steeples. The Roman ruins—Trier was once the capital of the Roman western frontier—had been restored. The city's damaged housing stock had been replaced.

The view outside the station jolted my first memories of the town. One night when I was traveling by myself, I had planned on overnighting in the Trier station but felt bold enough to go out for a drink. I wanted to stay close, so I could get back in the station before it closed. I stopped in at a bar in front of the station and drank up a good deal of money. The patrons took interest in the American with a backpack. They began buying me drinks. Before I knew it, the station closed its front doors and turned out the lights. A panic pulsed through me. Where would I stay? It was already midnight and I had no idea where the youth hostel was. I was also tottering drunk. A

Luxembourger in work clothes befriended me and told me not to worry. He'd take me to Wasserbillig on the Luxembourg border. There, I'd could sack out on one of the train-station benches and get back to Trier in the morning. "It happens often enough," he said in English.

He was drunk, too. We careened through the night, running up over curbs and zigzagging through roundabouts. At Igel, he drove to the center of town and skidded to a halt at a sandstone column dating to AD 250. "Here . . ." he said with a hiccup. "Here is something you won't see from one of your trains. It's Roman. It marks a grave." We bumbled around the two-story column in the dark. "Touch it, American," he laughed. "It's very old. As old as your Indians." I ran my hands over the pedestal and swayed a moment, trying to comprehend its age. We then drove across the bridge at Wasserbillig, slowing to a stop at the border station. The sleepy guards had little interest, it seemed, in a drunk behind the wheel. They let us through, and the man dropped me off at the station.

I took up on one of the benches outside. The watchman came around after I'd climbed into my sleeping bag. He said something in either Luxembourgish or French to me, then tipped his cap. Given legal sanction, then, I closed my eyes.

Before dawn, the same watchman nudged me with his nightstick and said something again in a language I didn't know. He asked if I spoke English. "You can stay here," he said. "But you have to sit up now. The station is opening. Do you know where you want to go?" I told him Trier. "The train leaves in one half hour," he said.

I secured my gear. Deep blue and orange dawn broke above the town. Church bells tolled 6 a.m., and except for their tones all was silent. The station lights popped on and I saw the agent open his window. I bought a ticket and waited on the platform for the train. My head was full of cotton, and my back ached. I still have that ticket to Trier.

* * *

As they travel, a sensitive person absorbs people and places. Time doesn't erase them. I know now the many people I met and places I saw for seconds or minutes in those first few weeks are as important as those fixed in memory. Three decades later, I lie awake at night sometimes and a face or scene comes back to me—a vineyard here, the face of a bluff there, child sitting quietly next to a grandparent and holding a teddy bear in the middle of a busy station. I remember a quick conversation on a train with a teenager who was glad to meet an American. Searching memories' origins and trying to place them in the time line of experiences and events, I often recall the specific incident and not the context. Obscurity or absence in memory doesn't undo the way they tangled into personality or experience. They appear on empty nights in a restless head. All the time they remind me who I was.

* * *

For a few minutes, I stood in front of the Trier station watching people come and go and traffic back up along the Bahnhofstrasse. The weight of responsibility weighed on my shoulders. I wanted to make it back in plenty of time to the platform where Virginia and Nick were waiting. When I arrived, the two of them looked bored, standing among our baggage. The train was running ten minutes behind. But knowing we wouldn't have to rush to get aboard eased my anxiety.

Nick was still poking around in his bag of chips he bought in Koblenz.

"So, how long is this next train ride," he asked.

"About ten minutes," I said. "Josef will pick us up at the stop and we'll be home in no time."

"Home?" he said.

"Yes," I said. "Home."

CHAPTER SIX

A LOST FRIEND

THE DEATH OF my good friend Joachim haunted my daydreaming while we were underway.

The train out of Trier toward Saarbrücken sped us past ruins of the Roman baths and through my old neighborhood. I searched for the building where my old room was. Again, I peered out the train window into my memories. I tried to say to Virginia and Nick, "Ivo, Udo, and Martin lived just down the street here." "I hiked through these gardens to get to their house." "I used to get on the train at this station, Trier Süd, on weekends when I went from the boys' house to go to Wawern." They stared out the windows at trees and bushes rushing by. They saw industrial waste and the deteriorating old Konz rail station. Soon, though, we sped out of the city and into the rural Saar River Valley. We passed tiny postcard villages of Filzen and Hamm perched on vineyard hillsides above the river. Great arcs of land rose from the curving stream. Vineyards blanketed the hillsides in thousands of straight rows and millions of vines.

Within a few minutes, we arrived at the platform at Kanzem, where Josef was waiting. He was a tall man, fit for his eighty-five years. His piercing eyes darted cheerfully beneath a leonine gray and black mane. He smiled a mischievous, knowing smile that made me feel welcome. The sun shone full and warm on the vineyards climbing into the sky behind the platform.

Instantly, the three years since I'd seen him last disappeared. Josef's not openly affectionate. But I'm not one to hold back and I gave him a hearty embrace. Virginia first met Josef in 2000 after hearing about him from me through the years. She also gave him a squeeze. Nick, too, tight with his affections, shook Josef's hand. Josef looked surprised at our warm greetings, as though we were bringing him out of his shell.

"So, young people," he said in German. "Did you have a good trip so far? I hope you're ready for a few days at home."

* * *

It would feel like our home within a few hours. When I was working in Trier, I spent weekends with the Fricks in the old, stately Weingut. Marlies kept the attic room in clean sheets and dried flowers in a vase. She referred to it as my room. She always left me sweets or fresh bread to munch when I put my bags up. Often, I entertained myself in my room reading, writing in my notebook, and lounging on the low, single bed. I sat on the windowsill, stared off into quiet nights and woke early to watch the sun rise.

Marlies and I often walked through the village and up into the vineyards when she wasn't busy at home. She always stopped at a point above Wawern and made sure I took in the sweeping valley spread before us. The village snaked along its two roads. In the distance rose a forested hill as high as the one we were on. On the other side lay the village of Ayl, and above, the vineyard for which the town was known.

Josef and Marlies treated me as if I were one of their children come home for a few days. They had me at the dinner and breakfast table. Sometimes, in the late afternoon, they plied me with coffee and served cakes and cookies. I always departed Wawern with sadness, thinking I might not return.

Then, one night in November 1985, I called to see if I could spend the weekend in Wawern. Marlies apologized. Josef had lost control of the family Volkswagen on a patch of ice and crashed into a tree. From what I could understand as I stood in a telephone booth on the end of a bridge over the train tracks, Josef had broken his back and was in the hospital. He would be there several weeks.

After the phone call, I stood in the booth trying to absorb Marlies's story. My German was still rudimentary. I didn't get all the details. Josef could be dying, for all I'd understood of the conversation. I felt helpless and dreaded another solitary weekend. As I walked toward home in pools of streetlamp light, I tried to imagine what my life might mean without the Fricks in it.

After the turn of the year, Josef was back on his feet, and the Fricks had me over again. I returned about once a month to overnight or stay for the weekend. Marlies had me hoe the garden, fix things around the house, help her in the kitchen. Josef showed me his operation, and we often stood in the ancient cellars beneath the house tasting new and old vintages. He kept his cellars and machinery spotless, his workspaces open and free of debris. Wooden barrels of 250, 500, and 1,000 liters each lined the cellar's thick, vaulted walls. Everything in its place.

In April 1986, we stood together over a 250-liter barrel. He'd carefully siphoned out two small glasses of cloudy must. The cellar was dim and smelled of wet stone and fermentation. He asked what the wine was and when it was harvested. I guessed it was the 1985 Riesling *Eiswein* he and his workers must have harvested in early December after a hard frost. The frozen grapes gave up the most concentrated sugars and other dissolved solids that did not freeze, leaving ice behind in the press. He patted me on the shoulder and told me I was learning well. The wine had the sharp acid and heavy sweetness of a late-harvest wine, and the spunky, yeasty nose and fizz of fermentation. The must was so thick and sweet it fermented slowly, continuing long after other wines from that year had been bottled.

I had seen Josef as the active manager of the vineyard and known him through his retirement. In the early 1990s, he and Marlies moved to a house they'd built in the 1960s and rented out in another part of the village. Being free from work, he remained an active man. While working for Doktor Fischer, he'd received a parcel of land beneath the Wawerner Herrenberg for his own use. He grew his own vines and made wine from them for decades. Vineyards require hard labor year-round, particularly where good Rieslings only ripen on steep ground. As Josef had aged, he replaced the grapes with apple, peach, quince, pear, and apricot trees. Marlies made the fruit into jams and jellies, and Josef took part of every harvest to the local distillery and had it made into brandies. Besides the vineyard-turned-orchard, he kept an extensive garden in the small yard of the new house. He maintained a few heavily bearing grapevines of different varieties on the property. They gave him juice to bottle and for Marlies to make jellies.

* * *

We drove with my family through Kanzem. Josef explained to Nick, through me, "When your dad walked through this village the first time, most of its life revolved around farming and wine. But the vineyard and winery business has changed. Corporations took over vineyards that individual winemakers once tended. Now, artists have shops. Potters and ceramics artists have their kilns. Some of the old weinguts are studios. Galleries take up barns and old houses. Professionals who work in Trier live here now."

"What happened to the winemakers?" Nick asked.

"They took their money and moved away," Josef said. "Their sons and daughters now work for those corporations."

Josef looked resigned to the changes. We drove out onto the flat plain between Kanzem's vineyards and Wawern's. Farm fields blanketed the valley. Virginia and Nick sat in the back seat asking questions I translated as best I could, regretting once again drinking my way through German classes in college. I speak German to my friends once a month. I read articles in *Der Spiegel* and novels in German. My fluency would return in a few days, but now I had difficulty. Some of Virginia's questions stumped me. It wasn't my first taste of translation; that had happened plenty when we'd stayed in Germany or when our friends visited us in Kansas City. But it has become more difficult with age.

In Wawern, Marlies met us at the door. "Oh, Patrick, we are so happy to see you. Virginia, how are you? This must be your little man." She hugged each of us warmly.

At 81, she was fit and had the shine of outdoor exercise and daily activity on her. We sat at a dining table on a veranda that was a small courtyard patio. The house wrapped around the terrace on three sides, and a retractable awning fluttered above. She brought out mineral water and fruit juices. She asked questions about Virginia's work and Nick's school. Nick showed his twelve-year-old shyness at first, but after a few minutes, Josef draped his arm around the boy and indicated with a smile he was interested in what Nick had to say and he shouldn't hesitate. He soon began to ask Marlies and Josef about the house and the village.

Virginia and Nick marveled at the house. Marlies collected wall hangings and souvenirs, precious ceramics, and statuettes. Tapestries, rugs, blankets, pictures, ceramic masks, and gifts from the many international students who stayed with them over the course of fifty years covered every inch of wall on the patio, as well as the tops of sideboards, armoires, and tables in the house. The objects represented the bright colors of the rainbow. The effect was not one of clutter. The myriad keepsakes instead expressed her personality and sentimentality without flamboyance or gaudiness.

After naps, we walked the road to the old village toward the cemetery. The day was warm and humid. We passed the village synagogue, which once also served as a school and community center for Jews in the village. The synagogue was a two-story building about thirty feet square. It stood at the center of a small plaza between a farmer's house and the building that had once held the town hall.

We strolled up to the crossroad where the old Weingut stood behind its stucco and brick walls. We continued toward the cemetery, a square of orderly, marble-enclosed terraces at the edge of the old village climbing up from the road into the vineyard above. A small chapel stood at the cemetery's gate, and the gravestones formed neat lines on the terraces. Puffy clouds obscured the sun, and a warm breeze flowed down from the vineyard. Joseph and Marlies had seen three of their five children die. Joachim's twin sister, Ruth, died when she was a baby. The Fricks' oldest son, Markus, succumbed to leukemia when he was sixteen. We filed in around his stone. And now Josef and Marlies had installed an expertly engraved and small marker for Joachim.

* * *

Joachim and I met at the Weingut in 1986. He'd come home from a semester exchange with Clark University in Worcester, Massachusetts, where he studied economics. "You two will get along, I just know it," Marlies had often said to me in the months leading to his arrival. I came from Trier on a Friday in early May. She introduced me to Joachim. He was about my size, medium height with broad shoulders and sturdy build. His hair was fire-red. He wore a beard and moustache on his freckled, smiling face. We fell into conversation easily. A few minutes later, I felt like I'd known him my whole life. We snuck cigarettes at his room's open window. He told me of his studies and what he wanted to do. I told him the best I could of my plans, which I was still hatching.

He caught up with Josef, Marlies, and his sister Barbara at dinner. When dishes were washed and put up, Joachim and I hiked down from the Weingut to the Saar canal, about a mile and a half. I've always had a penchant for walking in the dark, but Joachim was hesitant. No streetlights lit the way between Wawern and the canal. We felt our way along the footpath running next to the road. At the canal, we stood above the boat locks, listening to the night. Joachim and I bantered for a long time, the vault of stars rotating above. A warm breeze blew down from the uplands above the river.

"So, what do you think you want out of this life in Germany?" he asked. "I mean, I know that someday I'm going to teach economics. I've been very lucky to get scholarships from the German Academic Exchange Service. I have graduate school ahead of me. What's in this for you?"

"I don't know that I know that yet," I said. I had a handful of pebbles and was dropping them off the top of one of the locks, listening to see how long they would take to hit the water. "I really didn't plan any of this. I mean, I came wanting to work in a vineyard, but I'm not even sure of that. I think that was just something Larry put in my head."

"You don't want to work in a vineyard?" he said.

"Oh, yes, very much. I love the work and I can see myself doing it for a long time."

"But?"

"But I more or less went along with the tide. I'm enjoying it now. It was hard at first."

"I have often found myself doing things I never imagined. You are in that boat."

"I'll go to school in Geisenheim," I said. "That much is clear to me. Otherwise, I have a job now and am living well and have met friends."

"And now you have another," he said. He patted me on the back.

"I haven't told anyone," he continued. "I am in love with a woman, a German here in Trier. She sent me a note shortly before I came back, saying she was leaving me. I expected to return to the relationship when I got back." He fell quiet and began to cry.

"Listen, Joachim. You will be all right. You will find that perhaps there's someone more suited to you." I didn't know what else to say. I told him about Monique and the fright I'd sustained. I recounted the first time I'd fallen in love only to have the woman end the relationship because she'd met someone else.

"I suppose you're right," he said, wiping his eyes and straightening himself up. "She didn't . . ."

"Deserve you anyway," I finished the sentence. His mood lightened. We continued our walk down the Saar and back up toward the village, laughing and joking with each other.

We walked together a lot at night, both at the Weingut and when he came to visit me in the States. Often, we'd light out from the Weingut and through the woods up beyond the village, and over the hill toward Ayl. The silent and dark woods enveloped us like a womb.

We whispered to each other and ambled slowly across the empty forest floor. It was so dark we couldn't see our hands in front of our faces and navigated toward the light coming through the edge of the trees. From the tops of the hills of the Herrenberg or the Ayler Kupp, the villages of Ayl and Wawern looked peaceful. Not a soul moved along those streets. We'd sit for hours among the grapevines, smoking and talking. We traipsed across the old wetlands in Wawern on sodden, squishy trails. Back at the Weingut, we'd have to scrape the mud from our shoes and carry them silently up the stairs to our rooms. We walked in all kinds of weather. Sometimes, he'd come up to my room in the attic. We'd sit on the windowsill smoking cigarettes, drinking beer, and talking of the women we knew and what we dreamed of for our futures.

Over the years, Joachim often visited the United States. As a professor, he taught summer seminars with undergrads and graduate students at Syracuse and Clark universities, where he'd gone to school on international scholarships and maintained close connections. He came to the States to give papers at international conferences. He'd arrive early and meet me somewhere for a weekend or more of travel. We'd hiked, camped, and fished in the Snowy Range west of Laramie when I was in grad school from 1991 to 1993. Later, he and I met at Syracuse and took long drives around Lake Ontario, through Toronto and then down through the Adirondacks. In summer 2001, Virginia and I landed at New York's LaGuardia Airport, rented a car, and picked him up minutes after he'd arrived at John F. Kennedy Airport. That trip took us through New Jersey and into Pennsylvania, where we spent the night at a decades-old resort hotel with an expansive porch and lobby, deck chairs and swings. We spent the next days driving through New Jersey to Princeton and then into Connecticut before we delivered Joachim to his appointed destination.

At one time or another we'd walked at night at Niagara Falls, in the mountains in Wyoming, a stretch near our cabin in the Adirondacks, and the lonely, lovely streets of Delaware Water Gap, Pennsylvania. We once walked a golf course from the first hole through the eighteenth at night. The moon was out, the grass heavy with dew. There was no sound but the squeak of our shoes in the grass. Sometimes we talked all the way along our walks. Many times, we strolled in silence, each other's company enough.

When I was in Laramie earning a master's, he visited two years in a row. One night, we were camped out on Douglas Creek in the mountains west of Laramie. We picked our way along the road without flashlights, listening to the sneers of mountain lions and the shuffle of porcupines in the grass near the ditch. The moon shone full, and my eyesight at night was quite good. Joachim was less sure, anxious and nervous about being in the dark, away from the fire. But I talked him through it, telling him if he felt he couldn't go on, we'd come back. He stuck with me and stumbled along the road down to the North Platte River. The silver moonlight on the hills and peaks and sound of the water combined with the wind in the sagebrush, he said, was beauty he'd never experienced.

The next evening, we stood by our picnic table alone up there in the woods. We faced the creek, where earlier trout leapt past my face as I cast my fly. At once, we turned around and found a man standing behind us. He had a full, white beard under a slouch hat. He wore breeches hung from suspenders. He had sturdy boots.

"Hello, men," the man said. "I've been trapping these woods for decades. Want to see some pictures?"

Joachim and I looked at each other with hitched eyebrows. How this stranger came up on us so quietly puzzled us. I looked for a car or ATV but didn't see any. Joachim shrugged his shoulders. The man rolled up his sleeves and pulled a set of snapshots from a pouch he carried over his shoulder. "This here's a passel of coyotes (cah-yotes) I trapped up out of the North Platte bottom down yonder . . . and here's a bear I got outta here last year . . . these is some beaver I got right out of Douglas Creek up in the flats above here . . ." He said he'd been a trapper for several decades and knew this stretch of woods "the way most people know houses on their own street."

The trapper told us stories of his exploits—a close call with a moose in rut, a mountain lion he had to pull out of a coyote trap in an early-season blizzard. We asked where he sold his furs, how much money he made, and why he preferred trapping to other work. "Hell, Forest Service don't pay nothin'," he said. "Plus, you gotta have a college degree. I ain't got one."

Our conversation lulled, and Joachim and I turned back toward the creek. After a few minutes, we realized the mountain man had disappeared as quickly and quietly as he'd come, like an apparition. That night, Joachim hesitated to take off with me. "The trapper said something about bears," he said. "I didn't come to Wyoming to have a bear eat me." I convinced him the bruins were less interested in us than berries and bugs, and we made a five-mile trek in the dark down from the creek along the North Platte and up into the highlands.

When we came down the mountain the next day to go to the hot springs at Saratoga, we rolled through the middle of a cattle drive. Men on horses with six-guns herded cows down the road. They signaled us to move up through the cows slowly. Heifers and steers surrounded the car. Dust settled on the windshield and I had to turn on the wipers.

"This is the real West, then," Joachim said. "Like on *Bonanza* and western novels. Here, within the span of a weekend, I get to meet a trapper, just like you see in movies, and then run through a cattle drive."

"Welcome to Wyoming, Joachim," I said. "There's no telling what you'll see. Maybe if you stay a little longer, we can go to a saloon and see the sheriff."

* * *

People were amazed at the relationship Joachim and I had. Our rapport never knew the separation of time and distance. Sometimes, we wouldn't see each other for years, but then in a few minutes were finishing each other's sentences. We might spend a few moments catching up before we talked as if we'd never been apart. Frequent phone calls and letters, then e-mails kept us in good contact. There were often times when I was thinking of him and he'd call. He said that the same happened to him. In all, it was the closest friendship I ever had. He was more like my brother than just a good friend.

In mid-2010, brain cancer of the worst, least-curable kind struck Joachim. When he got sick, he knew the seriousness of what he faced and, if he displayed hubris, it was in his belief, at least at first, he could lick the disease. The cancer had set on him over the course of a couple of months. At the German Institute for Economic Research in Berlin, he directed a long-term microeconomic study of social mobility in Europe. He'd worked at the Institute and on this study since 1989. At first, he didn't realize his growing inability to read indicated anything serious. He thought he'd become distracted and focused even harder on his work. But then his sight, particularly in his right eye, began to dim. He began to run into things, stumble at odd moments, and feel weakness in his right side. When he went to the doctor in early fall 2010, he found a virulent form of brain cancer, glioblastoma, rapidly advancing through the back of Joachim's head. By October he'd already had two rounds of surgery and started chemotherapy and radiation therapy.

One day, I was in a park playing with Nick. I felt something was wrong and made plans to call Joachim. At that moment, his wife Christine texted me and asked me to call right away, day or night. She said it was urgent. I waited until Nick found some playmates, so I could have a minute on a park bench and concentrate on listening to and understanding German. The evening was cool and overcast and twilight was settling as I dialed Christine on my cell phone.

When she told me what Joachim had been through in the previous month, I couldn't speak, and it seemed as if my world had stopped. In the next days, I made plans to visit them in Berlin over the Christmas semester break. Virginia knew how significant this trip was for me, and Nick sensed something important was happening. I'd have left immediately, but my classes were well under way and we were nearing the end of the semester. Besides, I'd have more time to spend with him over the break. The next months, I called Christine at least once a week. I spoke with Josef and Marlies every couple of days. I waited anxiously to depart on January 3.

When I arrived in Berlin, Joachim was in rehab for the day and wouldn't be out until later that evening. Christine took me for a driving tour of their part of city and to the Wall memorial where we looked out onto one of last remnants of the Todesstreife. We took a long walk together in the snowy strip where the city had built a large playground on land once part of the Wall. She said she was truly happy I'd come and Joachim was eager to see me.

Toward evening, we drove to the rehab center where Joachim spent his days. He walked out of the clinic slowly, using a cane. He looked as if he'd shrunk a little. His hair had thinned and, though he looked drained and tired, he greeted me with his signature smile. "I'm so glad to see you, old friend," he said, giving me a hug. He felt fragile, almost brittle. "It means the world to me." We rode through the winter twilight on wet streets, negotiating tangles of Berlin traffic to their quiet neighborhood in Alt Reinickendorf, a quarter in north Berlin. He and I sat in his comfortable living room past his bedtime, which was quite early, as physical and occupational therapy took a toll on him. Christine had gone upstairs to let us talk.

He told me what he'd been through. By the time I talked to Christine in October, infection had set in at the surgery site and swelling effectively ended his ability to speak, hear, and talk. It looked like the end. When aggressive treatment of the inflammation brought back his senses, he believed he'd been delivered from the grave.

Then, I told him I had to be honest.

"Joachim," I said, "I have to ask about what we Americans call 'the elephant in the room.'" We were speaking German.

"You want to know about how I feel about all this," he said slowly and with determination. A slight smile spread across his face. "I knew you'd ask."

"What will happen if you beat this thing?"

"I've received an offer from the University in Trier to join the faculty in the economics department. The Institute made a counteroffer and set up an academic appointment at Berlin Technical University, where I can now direct graduate theses and dissertations. They offered me a bigger salary. The position is not as prestigious as that in Trier. But I had to ask myself whether I want to go to Trier from a city I love.

"The most important thing is my family," he continued. "The girls have their friends here. Christine loves living in the city and she has a fine position in Pankow (a suburb of Berlin). In the end, it is a decision we all make, and I think, unless the terms of the Trier position change, we will stay in Berlin."

"What happens if you don't get your abilities back, if you wind up permanently disabled?"

"We'll have to see, won't we? I'll be alive, anyway. That's a start."

"What happens if you don't make it? If the tumor comes back or new cancer spreads? I'm afraid I'll lose you."

"Listen to me." His ice-blue eyes twinkled in the soft light of the living room. "After my first operation to remove the tumor, the swelling cut me off for three weeks. Three weeks. I couldn't see, hear, or talk. Nothing. I was alone and isolated. That was when I died. The isolation was hellish. I had no idea what went on around me. I couldn't even feel if anyone was around. But I was conscious, fully awake. Do you know what that might be like?"

"I can't imagine," I said.

"It was like death, I think," he said. "It was death. That's when I died for the first time. I consider myself lucky. Rare is the man who gets to die twice in his lifetime."

"Joachim, I'm selfish. What will happen to me? What will I do?"

He laughed. "These are questions that pass between friends who've known and understood each other for a long time. Good for us. If I were in your position, I'd ask you the very same thing."

He paused a moment and took a deep breath. "Every day I have between now and the next time I die . . . well, each represents a lifetime. I want *you* to feel that. I have what I know, and what I know right now is tomorrow I'll go to rehab and try to gain more strength. I'll do the puzzles and my language exercises. I'll come home and take a nap, as I did today, and then you and I will spend another evening together. Who knows what happens after that? You are here with me. That's what matters."

I was inconsolable and told him so.

"Patrick, brother," he said, "I've learned to live every day as if it were my last. We continue with the therapies because there's a chance. That's what I hold on to. If it doesn't work out, then I'm off to the next great adventure, you see. You must try to be with me on this. We have each other right now. Everything that's happened to us has led us directly to this conversation."

He took a deep breath and looked at me knowingly. "I'd like to take a walk with you through the park." His neighborhood backed up against one of the immense parks for which Berlin is known. "It's dark, your favorite time. But I'm more night blind than ever. So, let's just sit here tonight and wait until next time." He smiled and patted my hand.

I was happy to be with my friend, to talk frankly with him about what would happen to us. For the next week, while he was in the clinic and Christine was at work, I toured Berlin on foot and train and bus. We sat evenings and watched soccer matches. We ate chocolates and talked with Christine and their fourteen-year-old daughter Katharina. His other daughter Anna was on exchange with a family in Uruguay. We looked at pictures she'd sent home and more photos from family vacations and of times he and I traveled together in the United States. We discussed his accomplishments at the Institute, which were many. His optimism never flagged. When he went to bed in the evenings, I hiked miles through the park, the streets of Alt-Reinickendorf, and then out along where the Wall once stood. The nights were bracing but not bitter. The moon was up that week, and I made my way through the forests and parkways without help of the flashlight Christine sent me from the house with.

To watch my once-vigorous friend move slowly about his house, work though his German and English vocabulary worksheets like a grade schooler, and talk to him about mortality made me sad, even despondent. At the same time, his will to get back what the cancer had taken from him—his ability to speak well and the vivacity of his limbs—kept me going. He had an easier time writing English than he did German. The cancer grew in the area of the brain where the childhood or first language was centered. The second language inhabited a different part of the brain and was unaffected. Every night, he asked me to help him with German grammar. We took short walks that exhausted him. He treated my visit as one of the greatest pleasures of his life.

The days I spent with Joachim, Christine, and Katharina were heartbreaking and dreamy at the same time. I felt the weight of loss and reveled in my friends' presence. Though I hoped the treatments would work, I knew, inside, the cancer would take him. Only a tiny fraction of glioblastoma patients survive more than a few years. Most die within weeks or months.

My departure was a rough one for me. I knew I'd never see my friend again. Trying to set things in my memory, I held him for a long time. I looked him in the eye so I would remember his spritely gaze and interminable smile. When I returned home, I talked to him weekly but couldn't shake the grief that haunted me. I told him about it, and he said to me more than once, "I'm not dead yet, so don't think of me that way. But I know you will." When I went into my usual seasonal downturn, my anxiousness over Joachim's impending death brought on depression deeper than I'd ever known. This culminated in the dysphoric episode during which I was going to hang myself. I was intent on keeping the incident from Joachim until he asked me a week or so after I left the nervous hospital if there was something wrong.

"I can hear in your voice you are in one of your depressions," he said. "You didn't try anything silly, did you?

"Yes. I did. I was going to hang myself a few days ago and spent a week in the hospital."

"Thank God you came to your senses," he said. "I hope they set you straight. I wouldn't know what to do or where I'd be without you."

In August, neurologists found a second tumor near where the first had been removed. He went into serious decline and died on December 16, 2011. Christine tells me the two weeks I spent in Germany that January were the best time of Joachim's last months.

* * *

Virginia, Nick, the Fricks and I now stood over Markus's stone and Joachim's marker—his ashes are interred in Berlin. A warm breeze floated off the vineyard above and smelled of cut grass. The Fricks kept the site in flowers and low-growing evergreen plants. A few candles in red glass containers with pointed metal tops stood among the green. We were quiet, and maybe the warm breeze and the silence got to me. My memories of Joachim and the way I'd felt cheated in his loss welled up in my chest. I felt anger again, much like when I called his parents, knowing Joachim had died that day, to see how they were. It struck me again how the little things seemed to matter the most: the postcards I wrote and didn't send, the emails I should've written, and the phone calls I should've made but didn't.

I take that more seriously today than ever. When I think of someone, I remember that ache when we stood in the vineyard at Markus's gravestone and Joachim's marker. I call or write as soon as I can. I send postcards from trips we take as a family.

I still miss my friend and wish I'd had more of him while he was here.

CHAPTER SEVEN

THE FRICKS

I STRUGGLED. HEAVINESS dogged my shoulders and turned to deep melancholy. After we returned from the cemetery, we sat to a dinner of Sicilian soup, bread, and boiled potatoes. Everyone was in good spirits. I was quiet and reflective. Conversation moved from reminiscing about Joachim to our lives in Kansas City. We talked about Nick's schooling, what was going on with Sydney and her life, and what Virginia did as a nurse in the oncology unit at her hospital. The conversation did nothing to assuage my declining mood.

Translation was taking a toll on me. When I left Germany the first time, I had good working knowledge of the language. My German had improved over the years, both from communicating with my friends and reading the novels of postwar writers and magazine articles. But translation always demanded muscles I didn't develop for many years and which are still weak. I speak German without thinking in English. This is due, I think, to learning German outside of books and translations. Virginia talked to the Fricks of infinitely complicated and colloquial things. They demanded the same kind of complex communication with Virginia and Nick. Too many voices, too many different things to keep track of, assailed me until I could hardly understand what anyone said in either language. Toward the end of the day, my mind was mushy, my mood depressed, and jet-lagged body weary.

Beneath depression, I rejoiced in being here with what I considered my families. When I finally lay down in the basement apartment on the huge, firm bed, voices crisscrossed in my head. Virginia and Nick fell asleep immediately. Silence filled the house. In the glow of a night-light, I considered the room. Roots of a grapevine adorned with colored glass drops floated in a corner. Markus's paintings of furry-footed horses—like Clydesdales—hung on the walls. The horses were all in motion, running, something Markus couldn't do in the last years of his life. Riders wore thick horn-rimmed glasses of the kind I'd seen him wear in photos from his youth. Family pictures through the years hung around us—smiling children and beaming parents. A handwoven rug made to look like an American flag, decorated on another wall. Vases and tureens, ornate pillboxes and handmade artificial flowers stood on the wide windowsill. Everything in the room spoke of friendship and connection to other people. Some were gifts. The Frick kids fashioned others—school art assignments, mother-and-son and mother-and-daughter projects.

What did I do to deserve such good people? I was a drunk. I'd been in the suicide business long before I tried to hang myself. I'd wrecked cars, relationships, and lives. Twenty-four years later, everything was different. I never meant to marry or have children, and now I had both. My daughter, Sydney, was now working and living her own life. Marlies and Josef were closer to me than my own parents, and Joachim had been my closest friend and soul mate. Virginia made me grow up and take responsibility for things I'd often neglected as a benefit of single life. Nick came to us when he was four and half and made me a father again, which had its own rewards. I couldn't help but think of how these people had formed me. Their faces flashed through my mind. I was learning I wasn't the recipient of so much good but a participant in something wider and bigger than myself. I had no right to change that by suicide or any other means.

* * *

I awoke the next morning after eleven hours of solid sleep. Sunlight seeped through the closed roll-shutters. My face and limbs felt heavy, and my inclination was to stay tucked in. I stared at the ceiling and struggled to right my mind. Virginia slept soundly next to me. Outside of her breathing, the room was still. The house was in a newer part of the village much quieter than the older village down the road, where I used to hear people talking, shoes clattering across cobblestones, and tires swishing down narrow streets. Here, there was no sound.

I hoisted myself out of bed and forced myself to dress. I peeked in on Nick in the next room. He sprawled across the couch, wrapped in his blankets. He slept on his side and I could see his face in the dim light. Scratching his nose, he stirred a little and settled back into his comfortable nest.

After a quick breakfast, Josef and I drove through the older part of the village and past the old Weingut. We left the road and rolled up a grassy byway to his parcel of land. He handed me a couple of plastic pails and opened the fence into his orchard. The sun came and went behind the clouds. The trees grew thick and full and layered the ground below in perpetual twilight. He scooped up a handful of yellow plums (*mirabellen*) from the grass. His hands were stout, vintner's hands, old beyond their years but strong and lively.

"Ach, ja!" he said, beaming at me. "See here, these are the ones." He held a plum up in his fingertips. "Full, ripe, and juicy, without blemishes." He popped it in his mouth.

We searched the ground and chose the best fruit. He bent at the waist, his legs straight, his hands expertly sifting out the finest plums. When we'd picked up what we could, he retrieved a long shaft of wood he kept in the orchard for shaking trees and jostled the branches. Mirabellen fell like rain, and we resumed filling our buckets.

I ate plums whole—mouthfuls of sunshine. I sucked the pits clean and rolled them around with my tongue until I couldn't accommodate more. I spat them out and filled my mouth again and again.

After a short time, we'd packed our buckets to overflowing. The tree still hung heavy with fruit. Plums covered the ground, and we couldn't move without mushing them into the soil. Despite our five full pails, it looked like we'd harvested hardly anything at all. We left the buckets under the Mirabellenbaum and walked up to the peach, apple, and pear trees. All were unripe, except for a few peaches that yielded easily to our touch. They melted in my mouth. My eyes rolled back in my head.

I walked up past the peach trees to the end of Josef's land. The strip wasn't wide, but it was long. Vineyard grew on three sides away from the grassy road where the gate stood. Vines swept up the steep incline of the Herrenberg. When Josef grew his Rieslings on this parcel, he produced enough wine for household consumption and for gifts, with enough left for the cellar. He caused a village scandal when he ripped out his vines and planted the orchard. He pruned sparingly, which resulted in big trees with tons of fruit. On two sides of the plot, he trained apples and pears onto the old grape trellis. Their short, angular arms hung heavy and lush.

He wandered through dappled sunlight that fell through the trees, testing fruit with a squeeze here and a shake there. He looked contented. Through my depressive fug, I still sensed happiness to be in this beautiful place with my old friend. He asked me questions about home, and we talked about gardens and his orchard and trees.

"You don't seem yourself today," he said, popping another Mirabelle in his mouth.

"It's just a thing I go through. Jet lag and such."

"No, I can tell it's your depression. But stay up and around. You'll feel better this afternoon?'

"Probably."

"Listen, I don't have much time left, you know" he said.

"Ach, Josef, I know, but don't say that."

"Why not? It's true and you're an adult," he said. "I've lived a good life, I think. Marlies and I've raised four great children. Markus was a good kid and headed somewhere before the cancer. Barbara (who was several years younger than I) owns her own business school in Trier. Bernd built a long and successful academic career in economics, like Joachim." Bernd was Joachim's older brother and vice president of the university in Paderborn. He'd become a well-known expert in industrial relations and sports economics. "What more can a man want?"

I was silent, looking at him. He smiled.

"Come on, *Junge*," he said, wrapping his arm around my shoulders. "Life has been good to me. It's being good to you. Virginia is a very smart person, and I'm sure she's a good nurse. She has many good things to say about you, I bet. Nick, well, he is a special lad. You should be proud. When you're my age, and you will be, you'll also look back on a full life."

He slapped me on the shoulder. "Now, we have work to do."

* * *

We spent the afternoon making Mirabelle preserves and jam. I pitted the plums with a device that seeded the fruit with a little plunger. Marlies dropped plums in a large pot and added pectin. The fruit was so sweet she didn't need sugar. Nick wanted to be a part of the relationships he saw so ripe and full around him and worked to show it. He and Josef gathered jars and lids from kitchen cabinets, shelves, and from the garage, where Josef kept a large pot of boiling water on a hot plate to process the jars of preserves and jams. They worked well together, each directing the other by finger-pointing. Then, Nick helped Josef and Marlies in the kitchen while Virginia and I scrubbed lids and jars. Nick stirred the boiling fruit and assisted in bottling and processing the jars of jam. He set the table for lunch, and fetched water and coffee. We stacked up some fifty pints of jam. Marlies would make dozens more in the coming weeks. She would give away most of it in presents, keeping enough for her table.

Virginia and Nick sat quiet after the jam-making, reading on the porch outside, while I brought out lunch. I'd forgotten how much we ate when I visited the Fricks. It seemed we ate all the time. Every morning we had bread with jam, eggs, milk, and fresh butter. Afternoons, Marlies made something hot—soups, meat, *Knüdel* or *Klösse*, cooked vegetables, such as carrots and beets from the garden, and stews. Every meal had some meat—salami and cured ham, bratwurst, and once pot roast.

Poor Nick. His food portfolio is very narrow. This comes, in part, from his experience as a small child. My sister went down the meth hole long before she became pregnant with Nick. After he was born, he lived with her for two and a half tumultuous years. Many days, from what we can gather, she left him in front of the television with chicken nuggets and macaroni and cheese while she carried on her drug habit and the other addictive behaviors in the bedroom. He found making a fuss over food garnered his mother's attention. Food also served as the most effective way to wring care from my parents during the eighteen months he'd lived with them before Virginia and I took him into our home. When he arrived at my parents' house, he refused to eat anything but sugar cereal, processed chicken nuggets, fries, and canned green beans. By the time he joined us, he'd widened his tastes to include pepperoni and salami. He showed visible stress when confronted with new foods.

Now with the Fricks, we'd convinced him to try everything Marlies put in front of him as a courtesy. He did yeoman's work. He tasted it all faithfully, and even avoided grimacing as he usually did when he faced unwelcome food.

After soup and bread, Josef lay on the porch swing for a nap. Jet lag dogged me. The heaviness in my shoulders and mood persisted. Virginia understood when I said I needed to take some time on my own and retired to the basement, leaving the Fricks and Dobsons to their own.

* * *

From dealing head-on with manic depression, I knew too much time with people allowed both depression and mania to creep up uncontrolled. Once either is firmly set in place, managing the illness becomes a matter of enormous self-control. I didn't want to get into a situation where I was judgmental and testy, which can happen both with mania and depression. I've learned to take a break from people and think things through. Writing about fears, worries, instances of selfishness, and dishonesty in my journals staves off incipient depression and helps me to avoid manic episodes. Physical activity absorbs mania and eases depression but doing too much can exacerbate both. Deep breathing and quiet meditation help. Getting enough rest was another part of the puzzle.

Staying on medications was essential. They treat symptoms most of the time. My regimen includes an anticonvulsant and a mood stabilizer. Too much of any one drug produces side effects: weight gain, lethargy, apathy, high blood sugar, and sleeplessness. I'm happiest on enough to balance me most of the time. I still feel dips and heights but less severely than if they went untreated. In times of stress or change, serious mania and/or depression threaten to "break through." Generally, mania is less of a recurring problem than depression, which can sometimes be as light as mild melancholy for two weeks or as critical as outright lethargy, deep sadness, and feelings of worthlessness that beat me down for months. The family trip, while a great pleasure, stressed me. I felt the responsibility for these people in a land where they didn't speak the language and couldn't orient themselves. I had to keep myself in check.

I went to the basement and took time to write in my journal. Away from the needs of translation and care of Nick and Virginia, I sat for a long while letting thoughts roll through my mind uncaptured. Solitude dampened the melancholy threatening to tip into deeper depression, at least for the moment. Finally, I laid back and read until my eyes closed and took a long nap.

Later, when we sat down to coffee and cake, I noticed the way Nick and Josef got on. They had taken to each other from the start and communicated in artful ways. Josef, I'm sure, showed a great deal of interest in Nick initially for the sake of Virginia and me. But by the end of our first day with the Fricks, Josef had Nick out in the garage working on a birdhouse project. He showed Nick how to use a handsaw and then let him go at a couple of pieces of wood with a little fatherly oversight. As the days passed, a deeper connection revealed itself. Both felt joy in the presence of the other.

We strolled that afternoon through the forest above the village. Nick and Josef walked ahead. Though they couldn't speak the other's language, they talked to each other as if it didn't matter. They chattered along, gesturing, raising and lowering their voices to show emotion. Josef pointed to various things and told Nick the German words for them. Nick did the same thing for Josef, indicating the English names of trees, grass, fence posts, and other objects.

* * *

When we returned, we set to the business of the evening meal. Marlies planned dinner that night for us and my old friend Paul Legill and his wife, Violette Weber. They lived in Schengen, Luxembourg, on the Mosel riverfront at the borders of France and Germany. Paul's family made wine from about five and a half hectares (about thirteen and a half acres) of vineyard his family had owned for six generations.

Paul and I attended the wine school at Geisenheim together. He was a tall broad-shouldered man with a mop of curly blond hair and a gentle, friendly bearing. We struck up a friendship right away. We lived in small apartments in that housing-starved area of Germany. His was nothing more than an attic room in Rüdesheim, the town bordering Geisenheim on the west. He could barely fit all of him in it. I inhabited a small studio in a former hotel in nearby Aulhausen above Rüdesheim.

Fortunately, Paul had a car, and occasionally he drove me the eight kilometers (five miles) from the wine school to my place. We spent evenings together when time and studies allowed. I often met him at a small bar near the train tracks in Geisenheim for a couple of pints of beer. Dark, wood-paneled walls surrounded a small bar and a few wooden tables. The music was sedate and the lighting spare. We sometimes ate bratwursts or currywursts when I had the money for such things. Occasionally, Paul bought me a dinner and drinks when I had no cash to spare. He helped me with German, and I with his English.

After a few weeks in Aulhausen, I'd drummed up work with the village winemakers. After school, I rode my bike—on loan from the hotel's owner—from the school at Geisenheim, which sat at the riverbank back home, five miles and 150 meters above the river through some of the most famous vineyards in the Rheingau. I then spent evenings walking or riding my bike up and down the steep village street from one winemaker to another. At one, I oversaw the presses where workers deposited newly harvested grapes. After I started that process, I hurried to another winemaker to clear musts for fermentation. I supervised the schoolkids who harvested grapes after school in another vineyard, and then started fermentations at another winery.

In between, I snuck in some study and drank.

The life I'd chosen for myself, in which I worked hard, studied, and stayed drunk—as well as cycling through mania and depression—was exhausting. I was lost, flustered, and always broke. My health suffered, and I lost over thirty pounds in a couple of months. As winter approached, I barely had enough energy to keep up with my responsibilities and often slept through class.

Paul made my stay in Geisenheim bearable. His empathy and spirit inspired me when I didn't think I had anything left. And after a while, I didn't. After a rally of mania, I fell into deep depression and gave up and returned to Kansas City, heartbroken. There, I faced more dissolution and despair. I enrolled at the university and worked at a nearby restaurant, barely keeping grades and rent together. I binged outright every night. I was sick, and my liver bulged beneath my rib cage. My kidneys hurt all the time. I lived for a while with my aging grandmother, ostensibly to help her around the house. But really, I was sponging free rent and a place to study. When my grandmother's health deteriorated, I took my own apartment and let relatives move her to assisted living. I had so few contacts and friends I didn't need a telephone. I lasted a week in my new place before I landed at the door of an AA hall.

* * *

Paul stuck with me throughout those dark days. With letters and phone calls, he encouraged me and supported my efforts to get and stay sober. I'd since visited him in Luxembourg nearly every time I went to Germany. Now he and Violette sat at the same table with the Fricks. Marlies cooked a sumptuous dinner of several courses. As the sun set and the candles glowed, I listened to Paul and Josef talk about wine, the business, and what Paul was trying to do with his vineyards and his efforts to sustain and grow his market, including expanding his sparkling wine selections and adding brandies and liqueurs. His winery took up the space of a double garage, with another section of a building serving as his lager and wine-tasting room. He had a steady clientele, and his wines consistently won awards from the Luxembourg government and several wine cooperatives and industry magazines.

I translated their conversation for Nick. Violette spoke good English, and she and Virginia were in deep conversation. Virginia had met the Legills first in 2000. It wasn't hard to imagine this woman I'd married, who had a bubbly and open personality, would get along with Violette, a sympathetic and talkative person. They also had much to converse about—family, work, home. Everybody around the table made conversation that covered many topics over the course of the evening—family, our conjoined pasts, and what we were into today.

Marlies brought in a vegetable soup made from Josef's extensive garden and salad with a bright-tasting vinaigrette and walnuts and cranberries. Pot roast with onions, carrots, potatoes, and celery was the main course. After the entrée, she served tiny bowls of sorbet, and then a special sweet cake topped with whipped cream. We ate and kept eating.

We sat for hours. Josef brought a couple of different vintages to the table. Paul and Josef talked to each other in formal German and with a great deal of respect. These journeymen discussed the cellar and vineyard management, how the business had changed over the years, and what the year might bring in harvest. Virginia and Nick knew the trouble I put into my own grapevines at home and, through the chatter between Paul and Josef, better understood the effort it took to grow grapes at scale. I could taste the wines they talked about—Riesling, pinot blanc, pinot gris, pinot noir, gewürztraminer, auxerrois.

Josef and Paul drank moderately and enjoyed what they tasted, always with the knowledge that Paul and Vio had to drive the twenty miles back to Schengen along a narrow, curvy two-lane country road. They lingered long beyond their bedtimes. Violette was a concert violinist and had students in the morning. Paul would be in the vineyard early. He was sure he'd spend a tired day at his work, but he said it was well worth the time to see me, my family, and the Fricks, again.

After they left, we all stumbled to bed that night. I had a few minutes before I fell asleep to think about the relationships I'd made over the years with all these people, my wife, the Fricks, the Legills. How had a person with such a troubled past come to make such good friends? Despite depression and the withering self-criticism that comes with it, I knew something in me fostered or influenced these relationships.

I realize now how seamless our evening with Paul, Vio, and the Fricks had been. Through me, Josef and Marlies had invited the

Luxembourgers so they could know my family and me a little better by being a part of the conversation. I understand that Virginia and I do that as well with Sydney's and Nick's friends. Maybe I learned that from Josef and Marlies over time. It also makes me realize Virginia's right about me attracting good people into my orbit. I'm slowly accepting that.

CHAPTER EIGHT

SAARBURG AND TRIER

OUTSIDE OF FRIENDS' visits, our routine at the Fricks' went something like this: We woke around 8 or 9 a.m. A light breakfast consisted of coffee and bread with butter and Marlies's jellies and jams. We ate fresh figs from Josef's tree at every sitting. In the mid-morning, we sat again for coffee and a light sandwich or bread and fruit, perhaps vegetables from the garden. A walk through the village or drive into a neighboring town that had a grocery store took up the next few hours until we sat to a stouter lunch, usually of bread and a soup Marlies concocted from Josef's garden vegetables. A rest of about an hour took up the next part of the afternoon, after which we sat to cake and coffee. We'd hike in the woods above the village, walk in the farm fields, or trip up through the vineyards to take in the magnificent vistas of the valley and hills. In the evening we ate a larger dinner of cooked meat or sausage, fresh salad, and cooked vegetables—always potatoes fried, braised, boiled, and baked—and followed up with watching television news or reading.

Nick put his best face forward and engaged enthusiastically in the activities of the house. In part, he's that kind of kid. When given a chore, he didn't complain or hesitate. The tasks around the Frick house kept him busy. He liked seeing new things and learning new skills. He enjoyed the praise and smiles Josef gave him with a job well done. He and I helped Josef in the garden, hoeing, mowing, and picking vegetables. Working in the basement, we finished projects Josef had begun and straightened wine bottles in his extensive cellar collection. Nick had me read the labels, some in Old German Gothic script. The bottles spoke from all the German wine regions with many from the Mosel. Nick wondered at the very old, unlabeled Rieslings whose corks were covered in mold—a 1936 Wawerner Herrenberg, a few bottles of the same vineyard from 1959 and 1976, some 1976 Kanzemer Altenberg, and a 1986 Oberemmeler Hütte. We cleaned tools in the garage and tore rags Josef used to tie up his garden plants. Nick also helped me participate. When the darkness is on me, I don't feel like doing anything. But I felt the obligation to get in and get my hands dirty. Being with Nick and Josef motivated me when all I wanted was to sleep.

* * *

On our third morning, I woke and made my way around the room, careful not to disturb my mates, and trudged upstairs. Today would be a big day for them. I dreaded what was coming but knew the best way to deal with it was head on and at full speed. Marlies already had coffee ready and the table on the terrace set with stout bread, sliced sausages and smoked meats, and her homemade jellies and jams. I thought, as I sat there, I had to accept I was, in fact, in a full depressive episode and it would likely stick with me for the duration of our trip. I drank coffee and picked at my food, staring out across the valley and the town. Cloud shadows played across the distant, towering vineyards.

The Saar River greatly affected the lay of the town. It was in the Mosel, Germany's oldest wine region, with enology and viticulture reaching back to the invading Romans in the last centuries before

Christ. The Mosel wine region, as a geographic designation, encompassed the Mosel, Saar, and Ruwer river watersheds and lay at such northern latitudes (about that of Winnipeg, Canada) that vintners go to great lengths to ripen their grapes. This was especially true for the noble Riesling grapes, which made the best wines and for which the region was known. They took their character from the weather, where they were grown, and the soil they grew in. Rieslings ripened slowly and their wines vary greatly from year to year, region to region, often from vineyard to vineyard, and often from one side of an incline to another. The Mosel was also the steepest wine region in the world, with over 50 percent of the vineyards having grades of thirty degrees or more. (The steepest vineyard in the world was the Bremmer Calmont with an incline of 65 degrees.) Grape growers almost always planted the steep grades on the south and west hillsides and bluffs to capture the most sunlight, which also warmed the vineyard slate and sandstone. The stone gave up heat slowly and helped vines grow and the grapes ripen even on the coolest, cloudiest days.

So it was for Wawern as for the rest of the Mosel. I watched sunlight flutter across the great fields of vines and felt a warmth born of memory and affection. Despite my youthful desire to cloak alcoholism with purpose, I really did love grapes and grape growing. Labor in the fresh air always provided an outlet for my inner tensions and doubts. I remembered the way I lay down for a break in the sunshine. The black and red shale burned my back and then rendered off to a warm glow. The yellow-red light through my eyelids almost always led me to the noisy and unfettered borders between waking and sleeping. The rest those moments afforded me was often deeper and more refreshing than a drunken night's sleep.

As I sat on the patio reminiscing, Marlies sat next to me. She asked if I ever thought of Joachim in my workaday life.

"Every day," I said. "I miss him. Often long periods passed between our conversations. But I always had the comfort of knowing he was there for me. I don't have that anymore and it saddens me. I took him for granted and now he's gone."

"You and he were special together." She patted my arm and grasped my hand. "You were close like no one I've ever seen. You were truly soul mates.

"It is a terrible thing to watch a child die," she continued. "Joachim was unique. Always that smile. He saw good things even when times were rough for him. We're so proud of his achievements and the way he lived what we can call a full life. I think about him everyday, too. But we have you and thank God for that."

She looked toward the vineyards. While I'd often seen sadness in her bright eyes, they now possessed a tired resignation I hadn't seen before.

"I love you, Marlies," I said. "I feel closer to you than my own mother, the same way I held Joachim dearer than my own brother. If family is who we chose, then I've made good choices, despite the person I thought I was."

"I treasure that," she said. "Virginia, Nick, and Sydney are very lucky people."

"No," I said. "I'm the lucky one."

"Don't you think this sort of thing works both ways?"

* * *

After Virginia and Nick had breakfasted, the five of us made our way along a path through pasture and up into woods beyond the edge of town. The sun shone full and a few puffy clouds wandered through the blue. Marlies and Virginia talked, though Marlies knew a little

English and Virginia no German. Ahead Josef held his arm on Nick's shoulder, and they chattered away. I walked by myself, plucking blackberries along the fence lines. I picked flowers and rolled a stem of grass between my teeth.

We entered the woods on a forester's road at the top of the great hill where once Joachim and I'd walked at night to the magnificent vineyards that washed down past Ayl and onto the Saar Valley floor. The mature forest canopy cast shadow on everything below and had the hollow, echoing quality of a cathedral. Cuckoo calls pulsed beneath the trees. The forest exerted a kind of hush on all things in it, except Nick. He skipped ahead of us on the forest trail. After a while, he began to whoop and talk to himself.

Years before, Josef had bought a strip of woods where he built a small *grillhütte* for weekends and family gatherings. Marlies and Josef stepped carefully down the steep grade to the hut and its treasures below. I held Marlies's hand as we negotiated sharp turns in the trail. At precipitous stretches, Josef had hewn steps into the ground and supported them with tree limbs. At the hut, he'd captured spring water for a small goldfish pond. In the past, Josef had tended his bit of forest much like he cared for his vines and orchard. He cut away the undergrowth cluttering the forest floor and encouraged the oaks, firs, and elms to fill the canopy. Cedars punctuated the space between the forest ceiling and the ground. Around the hut and pond, wooden staves with names etched on them were nailed to the trees. These indicated trees the Fricks had "given" their children, grandchildren, and friends. Nick would soon have a fir of his own.

We arrived at the hut and Josef bemoaned the state of the structure and fishpond. As he'd grown older, he visited his outpost less frequently. His ability to tend his piece of the forest diminished. While forest floor was still free of undergrowth, the grill hut and fishpond had fallen to disrepair. Moss grew on the structure and some of the wood had rotted. The fishpond no longer flowed with spring water. Feral hogs had ripped up the water-gathering apparatus Josef had built at the mouth of the tiny spring up the hill. The pond itself had become a catch basin for rainwater, a sort of mosquito pond.

Josef missed the work he once undertook without physical limitations.

"Those days are gone," he said. "This place is a mess. Look at it. The hut needs repair." He shrugged his shoulders and looked resigned to the changes he had experienced with age. "But that has to be all right. We live well at home and have plenty to do there. Hopefully, we've made a good example for Barbara and Bernd and the grandkids. They can enjoy this with their families someday. When we're gone, Bernd will inherit this."

He already had bought Barbara a strip of forest next to his, and she, someday, might treasure that.

* * *

Later in the afternoon, after naps and coffee, we drove to Saarburg, a bustling town of about seven thousand. There, Marlies planned to attend a support group for parents whose children had died. Josef was a stoic and preferred to deal with these things on his own. He opted to take the Americans into town for a tour and an ice cream treat. We dropped Marlies at the meeting and parked where Saarburg's old fishing village fronted the riverbank.

Saarburg struck me again as a picture-book medieval town, the feudal ideal we learned about in school. Its castle stood on top of a high, pointed hill. A towering steeple rose over the church's imposing red-sandstone exterior. The town itself filled the valley around the hill and feathered down both sides of the Loh River as that small stream rushed to the Leuk and then to the Saar. Vineyards blanketed the hills around the town and farms covered the open plains in the valleys.

Crooked houses in the old fishing village stood directly on one another, some eight or ten feet wide in two squat stories. Virginia marveled at the houses where once fishermen lived. She'd never seen dwellings so narrow or houses so oddly shaped. "I'm used to big houses. How can anyone live in a house you can hardly build a room in?" she said. "It's all so cute, so old. Amazing."

It wasn't hard to imagine serfs working at their strips, the townspeople performing skilled tasks like blacksmithing and grinding grain. The streets of the old town center led to the castle. We strolled up the narrow, curving lanes past houses on whose lintels were hewn dates like 1721, 1690, and 1583. Some front doors opened two feet or more below street level, as paving and repaving had raised the street over the centuries. Tight corners hemmed in odd-shaped lots. Ancient walls, pitted and worn, enclosed tiny courtyards. The street suddenly opened on the market, down the center of which flowed the Leuk, a picturesque little stream running between concrete and rock walls and forming the waterfall in the center of town.

Saarburg has always been a magical place for me. The feelings from the first time I was there—a day off the plane from the States—flooded back to me. The river and old town hadn't changed in the three decades. I reveled in the air of stability, something I couldn't find in Kansas City, where an absence of five or six years would likely put me back into a completely different city. In Saarburg, businesses change, people move, but the city streets and buildings on them seem exempt from the ways American capitalism razes the old and builds the new in an instant.

As we walked, Josef was circumspect, but he enjoyed showing his guests around. He pointed out houses and old buildings to Nick and Virginia, and I did my best translations so far.

I ducked into the art gallery where years before at the small window looking down onto the waterfall I cried with such despair. Gazing through that window into thirty years of experience, I realized how far I'd come and how complicated my life had been. Memory and emotion overwhelmed me, and tears welled up. This time I wasn't thinking I was lost, but that I'd been found and knew exactly where I was. My family life was secure. I knew my immediate future. We were safe. The trip was allowing me to see who I had been and who I was becoming.

We walked up higher in the town. From cornerstones and lintels, we saw the buildings and houses grow older the farther we climbed. Nick and Virginia took off ahead, but I moved at Josef's speed, his gait slow but steady. His fitness impressed me. He neither grew short of breath nor slowed his pace as the incline increased. We exited the town proper and stepped up on the *Burgweg*, a foot trail leading upward to the castle ruins. Stone steps interspersed long winding stretches up the hill.

We drew closer to the castle, climbing above the lindens and oaks growing strong and tall below us. Down the hill's sheer slopes lay a crossroads where the old city's streets met roads leading out of town. Narrow strips of housing lined either side of the valley. Dense forest backed up against the homes, cloaking the neighborhood in a tranquility that didn't exist in the old city or on the Burgweg. On a flat run of the trail, we stared out over a sea of slate-tiled roofs of all shapes and sizes. Vineyards soared over the town on the hill across from us. The late-afternoon sun threw long shadows. Butterflies fluttered and bees buzzed in the wildflowers along the path. A breeze puffed gentle and cool against the long hike.

The castle ruin towered over the top of the hill among complicated walls and structures, now worn and tumbling into the forest below. Count Siegfried von Luxembourg had built the castle in 964, one of the first hilltop castles in Europe. Craftsmen constructed the structure with slate and sandstone they mined at the top and sides of the hill. Lords and bishops of Trier employed the castle for seven hundred years. They expanded the buildings and their walls until the complex covered the whole top of the hill in an area the size of about one and a half football fields. By the time the town of Saarburg was chartered in 1291, the castle had become one of the most elaborate in Germany. The outer walls were built right to the cliff edges and once stood twenty and more feet tall. The castle fell to disuse in the mid-1700s, and townspeople deconstructed the deteriorating castle complex for stone to build their houses. The town finally laid claim to the castle again in the 1860s and set to conserving what was left. Further improvements, such as the path and steps up to the hill, came later.

Josef sat down on the edge of the castle well. When it was dug in 1362, it reached sixty meters below the surface, almost to the level of the river. Nick skipped across the cobblestone courtyard and ran up the 107 steps to the top of the castle keep, the last and oldest of the ruins still standing. Virginia followed. Josef didn't seem tired from the long climb. He watched Nick skip up the steps. Depression has a physical effect on me, and from our sojourn so far, I felt dull and worn out. As much as I wanted to climb those steps with Virginia and Nick, I couldn't.

I sat down next to Josef. "It's good to be young," he said with a smile, looking up toward the keep. "I climbed those steps many times when the kids were little. There's not much to see inside, you know, but the view from the top is fantastic. I remember it and so don't need to see it again. I'll leave it to Nick to discover it for himself."

Josef and I turned our attention to the vineyards on the opposite hill. They caught the light of the early evening sun. He pointed at the vineyards.

"They aren't the best in the area but are still quite good," he said. "They ripen grapes and produce fine wines most years."

We stood after a while and walked to the edge of the castle wall and looked down on the roofs of Saarburg. Josef was quiet and looked deep in thought.

"This is a lovely town," he said almost to himself. "One of the prettiest, I think, in all of Rhineland Pfalz, and certainly of the towns on the Saar. It received some bombing during the war but there was little industry here so it came out fairly well."

Mention of the war turned his thoughts to his time in the Hitler Youth in the Mosel town of Mehring upstream from Trier. He sat on the wall and invited me to sit next to him.

"*Hilterjugend* was like Boy Scouts (*Pfadfinder*)," he said. "It was fun. We had uniforms and were proud to march in line and salute the flag. We pledged allegiance. It made us feel very important. We went camping and sang songs. The summer camp was in the woods and we slept in tents.

"Maybe my parents knew what the little moustache was up to. But as a youngster, I had no idea. The Hitlerjugend provided belonging and companionship, you know, a chance to get away from home. Later, when I found out about Hitler and what he had done, I felt cheated. Germany was the greatest country in the world, you see. That's what I grew up with. I was two when the little man came to power. Into my teens, we learned about the great German people, their accomplishments, the boundless things they still had to achieve. At the same time, we went to school. We helped in the vineyards when we got home and on weekends. We harvested grapes with our parents and friends. There didn't seem to be anything amiss.

"I remember when the bombers came. We were at the Hitlerjugend camp. We heard them above in the night. They never dropped bombs on us, of course. Little Mehring, my hometown, was much smaller than Saarburg here. There's nothing there to bomb. But we had to get out of our tents and shelter in the mess hall." He laughed. "It wouldn't have shielded us. It put us all in one place very close together. One bomb would have finished us."

Nick and Virginia joined us after their climb. The sun was setting in gold and purple beyond the hills on the other side of the town, leaving us in shadows. We made our way down the long incline toward the crossroads and then into town. We passed one of the last church- and big-bell foundries in Germany and looked in on the courtyard of what was now a museum dedicated to German bell making. Nick skipped ahead again, shouting and whistling. We talked of the fishing village, where we now were walking, and of how the fishermen once provided food for Saarburg. By the time we arrived at the car, the town had begun to turn on its lights. The path next to the river glowed, and people walked in twos and threes on the footpath. The Saar flowed silently next to us.

We left Marlies in Saarburg—she had arranged for a ride home. When we arrived at the house, we made dinner and talked outside on the veranda until Marlies returned. Josef enjoyed some schnapps distilled from his orchard fruit. The candles flickered against the night. Despite the dread the day started with, I admitted I was glad we'd spent the time together.

* * *

The next day, we drove into Trier to the flea market (*Flohmarkt* or *Trödelmarkt*). I was sluggish and slow that morning but looked forward to the trip. It would take me through old territory, past buildings and parts of town that still intrigued me thirty years later. The city of over 110,000 was more familiar to me than my own neighborhood. Josef drove up through Konz, across the Mosel and through the center of town. I remembered the sights, streets, back alleys as we left town and entered an industrial area. Beyond a long line of cars, people set their wares in a vast parking lot. Hardcore dealers had set up tents and elaborate rows of tables. They peddled antiques and old books. Others piled up their wares on a spot on the pavement. Some people sold whatever they found in their basements. Still others offered new items, such as toys, T-shirts and other clothes, and housewares.

As she set off down the rows of tents and tables, Marlies shopped with the wiliness of a bazaar trader. She picked up old picture frames and antique toys. She examined books and rifled hanger stands and boxes of clothes. She bid for items and made counteroffers, and then combined items as part of the sale. When the price didn't suit her, she put down what she had in hand and walked away only to have the owner make a new offer. We sauntered down one aisle and up another, Marlies horse-trading for small things here and there. "These knick-knacks will look good on the sill in the living room," she said in German. "This fabric will cover the couch nicely." She soon had a small armload of goods. Josef feigned interest as long as he could but after a while went back to sit in the car. We were at it for another two hours.

Nick turned out, with Marlies, to be quite a shopper. He found items and toys that interested him and compared prices. He didn't beg us to buy things but made clear what he wanted and the differences between quality of goods and prices between vendors. We bought him a truck and whirligig, and some small commemorative

coins for his keepsake shelf at home. Virginia and I w hands behind Nick and Marlies.

To get a break from my compatriots and clear my he at a bookseller, whose antiquarian volumes covered sever much of the ground around them. Two- and three-hund books stood among newer, out-of-print paperbacks and h lost myself in an early twentieth–century history of the dev the German Empire. The scope and complications in such cinated me. It made American history seem simple and dir colonies. Colonies turned into states. New states came into t various means and ultimately formed the nation I knew. Ra supported it all. No nation's history is simple. But centuries o intra-kingdom and duchy and empire relationships leading mation of a unified Germany in 1871 baffled me. The bre back with Virginia, Nick, and Marlies in good order.

What I like about Josef is his patience and contemplativ He had little to read or keep himself busy in the car. He c himself watching the people come and go. I wondered w through his mind. Memories, perhaps. Thoughts about his and garden, his kids. When we returned to the car and pac items in the trunk, he seemed completely at peace and very we'd had a good time.

We arrived home and ate a fat lunch of bratwurst (my f German sausage), potatoes, and fruit. Josef plucked and sl bunch of ripe figs. I went down to take a nap and slept deeply.

* * *

That evening, Marlies put on a formal dinner on the terrace for the ex-wife of Marlies's cousin. Though the relationship betv

arlies and her cousin was poisonous, Marlies believed once family, ways family. Ula was slender, with a pleasant upper-Mosel accent. er beau, Robert, was a dentist in Trier. He commented on our teeth. mericans always have such lovely teeth," he said. "It must be either e state of dental care or what you eat. But since I know most mericans eat too much of the wrong things, I admire your American entists."

"I don't know," I said. "I've seen some pretty crappy American eeth."

Fortunately, Robert could speak English and was good at translating. So, I retired from the conversation a while to write in my ournal, time for which had been precious in the preceding days. osef and Marlies had filled every moment for us, except naptime, which was an activity itself. Walks, trips to town, plucking fruit in the orchard, making jams, cooking. And we ate and ate and ate. Every day, however, I looked at my journal with longing and found a few minutes to make general and sketchy notes, mostly entries that helped deal with the depression dogging me. At the end of every evening, I tried to track the important conversations of the day but often found my eyes closing. My journal advanced a just few pages each night.

I rejoined our group on the patio, more to experience the feeling and atmosphere than to be friendly. It was our last night with Josef and Marlies before we took off to visit Udo in Reutlingen. After Ula and Robert left, I sat for a long time with Josef on the terrace, looking out past the candlelight, watching the dark fold around us. He wrapped his arm around me and patted my shoulder and went back to looking out at the night.

I appreciate Marlies and Josef taking us on these day trips and inviting Ula and Robert over so we could be a part of their

conversations. Marlies on some level wanted us to know her and Josef better, wanted us to be a part of their lives.

I also understand now that Josef and I had never been closer than in that wordless moment in the candlelight.

CHAPTER NINE

THE LAST RESORT

NICK APPEARED AT the door of the Fricks' kitchen. He wore his flat-brim ball cap, colorful T-shirt and long shorts, and boarder shoes. He'd slung his backpack over his shoulder and had his Superman rollaway in hand behind him.

"When does this show start?" he asked.

He looked ready to take to the road. The day promised train travel, and his experience on the express from Frankfurt to Montabaur trains had thrilled him. We planned to go from nearby Kanzem into Schwaben Land to Reutlingen. With Udo, we'd embark on a longer trip into the heart of France. While darkness blanketed me, I felt the promise of open road before us.

The Fricks drove us to the Kanzem train stop. The sun shone full and a warm breeze flowed down off the vineyard and over the platform. Josef squinted in the sun. He insisted on helping us with our things, though we were self-contained with shoulder bags and backpacks. We'd see him again in about a week, but it was important to him that he send his guests off well.

Josef's goodbye was quick and clean. His broad smile scrunched up his dark eyes. We hugged and shook hands. He took Nick under his arm and told him to absorb as much as he could. "It'll all be new to you," he said. "You are the witness." (*"Es wird dir alles neu sein. Du bist der Zeuge."*) He wished us a good trip and looked forward to seeing us again before we headed back to the States. Marlies, on the other hand, had mastered the long goodbye. Hugs and smiles, tears, more hugs. She wished us well and sent us off with greetings to Udo, whom she had never met but knew through me. Repeating how joyful our visit had been, she thanked us for spending our time with her. It didn't matter that we'd be back in a few days; she made me want to stay another day, week, year.

They ascended the platform and waited for the train with us. When we'd climbed aboard, we took seats where we could see the couple, standing arm in arm, waving. In many ways, Josef and Marlies had raised me. Thinking about how we were all getting older, I wondered with sadness what would happen to me when one or both of them die. The time will come sooner than I wish. I'll get a call or an e-mail from Barbara or Bernd. I will try to make it back for the funeral. But mostly, I'll be inconsolable because I am selfish. I want them there for me, always. I thought of Virginia and me in the future. Would we be so close? Would our home be as welcoming to guests and strangers? Would we sit with each other in silence, our company good enough? I hoped so.

Then, I thought any of us could get wiped out in a car accident or simple fall at home. Who knew who was in for a stroke or heart attack or aneurism? Would I have another go at hanging myself? Would I be the next of their children Josef and Marlies would have to see die?

* * *

We settled into our seats in the upper story of the train car. I fetched my book and Nick pulled his device from his pack. Virginia read a book on her phone. We rolled down the Saar valley, away from the vineyards and into row-crop country, a landscape of variegated rolling hills. Small towns swooshed by. As we entered the more industrial Saarland, the valley narrowed, and ravines grew deeper. Factories and mines sat in pockets chopped into bluffs and hillsides. The train followed the Saar's great curves. While our surroundings were turning industrial, the stream appeared more natural. Gone were streamside walks and concrete piers. Wetlands and reeds grew next to the rail tracks.

The valley broadened again as we approached Saarbrücken. I was already tired; I hadn't slept well on our last night in little Wawern. I felt the contradictory pull of depressive fatigue and manic excitement over new places, new vistas. Fear of missing the next conveyance grew as we closed in on the city. I felt compelled to stay sharp so we wouldn't miss our stop—which was silly because the train terminated in Saarbrücken.

When we arrived and stepped out on the train platform, I checked after the schedule at a kiosk for our next train. I couldn't find it right off, so I asked the first passerby, who smiled and pointed to a platform. We hopped on the train as it pulled away.

Six-person cabins ran the length of the coach. We traveled without reservations and had to find empty seats not already taken for the whole trip. Walking car to car, we looked at reservation tickets in little racks on each cabin's windows. The train was crowded. Finding no unreserved seats, we took what was vacant. I made note of an empty space in one cabin. Two seats were presently empty in another and Virginia and Nick settled into them. Virginia was nervous.

"What if someone with a reservation shows up?" she said

"Well, they might be irritated, but apologize. Come get me three doors down and we'll find other places."

Virginia beamed at her cabin mates and before I walked away was in conversation with a couple across from her and Nick. I smiled and walked to the empty seat I'd noticed before.

Five people shared the cabin with me. An older woman traveling alone read a book in the seat near the window. The man over from her stared at the scenery and fiddled with a string. Another man nodded in the seat next to me, his chin dipping to his chest. A younger couple across from me spent their time fishing around in their bags for things to eat. I'd have the chance to get a wink or two before we arrived in Stuttgart, where we'd change trains again for the trip to Reutlingen. I leaned my head back and closed my eyes. It disturbed me how grumpy I get when I'm tired and depressed. But right now, I had a couple of hours free of translation. I began to doze off. The young couple laughed and their chip bags crunched. The man next to me snorted himself awake and then settled back and began lightly snoring again. The train rocked and swayed beneath me, ushering me into sleep.

Between naps, I checked in on Virginia and Nick. I felt it my duty as the leader of this little band to make sure my charges were comfortable. I felt pangs of guilt for enjoying time away from them after having been with them almost constantly for the last week. Of course, when I looked in on them, they were fine. Yes, they knew where the bathrooms were. They understood how the headrests worked. I assuaged my conscience and then went back to my cabin and rested soundly.

When we finally arrived at Stuttgart, we changed trains again. A wide atrium opened over the well-lit interior of the train station. Passengers scurried by snack and coffee shops. A bakery filled the space with the smell of fresh bread. The hall opened onto the main pedestrian zone or plaza in central Stuttgart. Outside, the Mercedes Benz circle-and-star logo rotated like Stuttgart's hood ornament 170 feet in the air atop the square tower of the the *Bahnhof.*

* * *

When I visited Joachim in Berlin in 2011, I'd stopped for an overnight with Udo on my way to visit Josef and Marlies in Trier. It was a Sunday and I had an hour and half wait in Stuttgart for the train to Reutlingen. I took the time to visit territory I hadn't seen since 1985. The long, tree-studded plaza spread out cold and vacant from the station through the *Schlossgarten* (Castle Garden) to the Baden-Wurttemberg palace about a half mile from the station. As I strolled among the empty shops and cafés in the plaza, memories of my first wild train ride through all of Germany came back to me. I remembered the stark beauty of the palace and its gardens. I felt again the doubt and anxiety that'd plagued me on that first visit to Germany. I was so young and lost then, hoping someone, anyone, would employ me before my meager funds ran out and I'd be forced back to a home I felt held nothing for me.

Larry and I sat on the edge of the garden fountain, a wide and tall fixture whose water drained out of a large basin on top through the mouths of lions and down into the pool below. Cherubs danced around the base and gave stately, rococo wonder to the scene. Larry and I shared a piece of Gouda and some apples, typical fare for the traveling day. I was thirsty and we had nothing to drink. The clear, cool water of the fountain made it worse.

In 2011, I'd wandered the plaza between the palace and the fountain, seeing again through older eyes what I'd witnessed so many years before. My life had changed, gone through its seasons and twists. Between the time I returned from Germany the first time and my thwarted attempt to go to school, I lived in a small closet in a house some friends of mine rented. It was a sordid existence, the novelty of sleeping in twin-bed-sized cubbyhole wearing thin after a few weeks. I often stayed up much later than my housemates, drinking until I saw double. Though I lived with four friends, I was often lonely.

Their parties satisfied me less and less. I cycled through manias and depressions, alienating my roommates. My need for people diminished. They got in the way. They told me I drank too much. I didn't want to hear it. My alcohol habit, which had moderated in Germany spun out of control back home. I needed more and more to reach the oblivion I sought.

Standing now in the station with Virginia and Nick looking for our train platform, I realized how far I'd come in twenty-four years. In sobriety, life and manic depression had often thrown difficult, almost insurmountable obstacles my way. Jobs, mostly low-wage and unskilled, came and went. I graduated college with two degrees after ten years of on-and-off enrollment. Despite having a baby at home, I attended the University of Wyoming and earned a master's degree in history. Returning to Kansas City, I found my new degree gave me few prospects. I finally landed a job in the banquet department of a hotel and then moved into the engineering department when the boss discovered I could restore and refinish furniture. This kept my attention for a year, and then the days became routine, deadening. In a manic frenzy one afternoon, I decided to relieve the stress and change things up and planned a walk from Kansas City to Helena, Montana. In my feverish brain, this became a desperate gamble to find purpose and something to write about. I'd show my daughter there was something more to live for than the next paycheck.

I canoed back from Montana on the Missouri River. As I returned to my job at the hotel, I found I'd become a stranger in familiar places. The displacement jolted me, and I didn't adapt well. The friends I'd made since I'd cleaned myself up after years of hard drinking stepped in and helped me stick with my job and try to be a decent father. Doubt often riddled me with sleeplessness and anxiety. But I had something to write about. At the heights of mania, I freelanced dozens of articles for a local newspaper. After a year, I took my first full-time job as a journalist and was making a living writing—a dream come true. I've been writing ever since.

My family gave me a place in the world. My kids made me grow up. The trip to Montana, and many long journeys since, revealed life didn't change overnight or with a journey of self-discovery. It's a process, and a long one I do better at when I accept the lumps with the joys and see them all as part of what it means to be human.

* * *

Udo met us at the Reutlingen station. He's a tall, balding man with heavy features and thick glasses. Thirty years in his trade transformed his once-lithe hands into mitts. He was a stained-glass master and ran his own art- and architectural-glass workshop and studio. He looked healthy and happy.

Severe thunderstorms had pummeled Reutlingen with large hail several months before. It's as if the hail came right on time for Udo. When the storms hit, he was suffering burnout and the trauma of moving his studio to a new location. His business was at an ebb, and he feared for his financial future. The storm, while a disaster for Reutlingen, relieved him of worry about where his living was coming from. He now enjoyed business that stretched him in his trade, as people sought to replace everything from simple glass panes and roll-shutters to elaborate stained and architectural glass. The work paid bills and allowed him to build his reserves. With a buffer, he felt the freedom to focus on more personal and artistic projects.

* * *

Udo and Nick had come to know each other two years before, when Ivo and Udo had visited us in Kansas City. At that time, ten-year-old Nick, Udo, and I took a trip out West. Udo'd wanted to go to the Grand Canyon and see the Monument Valley. I convinced him our time was short and we didn't want to spend the six days we had driving. We'd do something equally stunning and a little closer in. Mesa Verde National Park wasn't the Grand Canyon, but Udo found the prospects of rough camping and seeing the ancient ruins interesting and new.

We spent the first night in a charming old motel in Lamar, Colorado, with a Spartan but atmospheric interior done in knotty pine and rustic lamps and furniture. The next day, we planned to make Mesa Verde but took a right turn into Great Sand Dunes National Park, where we spent much of our day hiking the dunes and touring the visitors center and museum. While Udo and I sat outside park headquarters, Nick scurried to the top of the dunes and tumbled down again, laughing.

By the time we were back underway, we faced getting into Mesa Verde in the dark. We could choose to take up for the night where we were or deal with the uncomfortable prospect of setting camp in the dark and under fatigue. Better to tackle the job in daylight and while we still had energy. Toward sunset, we pulled off the road to camp in a national forest campground. We had the place to ourselves. The closest campers were half a mile away, hidden in thick pine forest smelling of turpentine and wildflowers.

Nick's a camper, and he'll sleep out under the stars with me; I don't like tents much. Udo stood wringing his hands as Nick and I unpacked sleeping bags, tarp, and mattresses from the trunk.

"What's the problem?" Nick asked as he spread a large plastic groundsheet. He rolled out our self-inflating mattresses.

"What about a tent?" Udo asked. He looked at me with a note of terror in his eyes.

"Why? The sky's clear," Nick said, bending to his work. "It's not going to rain."

"What about the bears?" Udo asked. Bears inhabit that part of Colorado. Stories of maulings ran through his head.

"A tent won't stop bears," I said. "We'll lock the food in the car and make sure we've cleaned up good before we bed down. They shouldn't bother us."

"But what if they do?" he asked.

"We'll have to figure it out." I didn't know how to comfort him. I'd slept out with bears innumerable times—even been sniffed up on a couple of occasions—but felt a pang of anxiety for him.

Nick finished laying out our sleeping gear while I gathered firewood. As late evening wore into night, Udo adjusted slowly to the idea of sleeping in the open air. Only after we lit a roaring fire did he seem comfortable enough to take up his sleeping bag. He didn't wake until late the next morning.

We slept the next week under the stars at Mesa Verde, Hovenweep National Monument, and Arches National Park. High, gusty winds buffeted us in Arches. We'd spent the day driving and hiking the park's trails, sand-blasted and hot under an unforgiving desert sun. Night brought no respite from the murderous wind. The great plates of stone rising perpendicular to the earth provided us little shelter as we set camp in a sandy plaza-like clearing beneath them. After red-yellow sunset faded to starry sky, Nick climbed in the tent we'd erected—minus the rain fly—for the first time on the trip. I suggested to them that we tie T-shirts around our heads to keep the sand out of our eyes, ears, and noses. Udo said he was uncomfortable with anything around his face. I told him it was that or he wouldn't sleep for the sand filling his nose and ears. He thought for a moment and dug into his bag. He pulled out wonderfully light muslin scarves he'd brought with him for some reason. We all wrapped scarves around our heads like Bedouin and slept like champions.

In the middle of the night the winds suddenly stopped. The place fell dead silent and the quiet woke Udo and me with a start. Even without my glasses, I could see the stars as filmy points of light through the weave of the scarf. While Nick slept soundly, Udo and I looked up at the constellations, translating for one another their names in German and English.

* * *

Virginia had known Udo since he, Ivo, and Andrea came to our wedding celebration in 1999. Virginia and I had wanted to show off our Hispanic neighborhood and held the event in the Sacred Heart Catholic Church basement a hundred feet from our front door. A neighborhood restaurant on the next corner from our house catered enchiladas and rice and beans. Beer came from the neighborhood brewery. Neighbors played in a mariachi band. The whole block attended the wedding, along with our relatives and friends. For our German visitors it was an America they had yet to see. Udo, Ivo, and Andrea stayed in our six-hundred-square-foot house for the visit. We brought them on our "honeymoon," a weekend in a Missouri state trout park at Bennett Springs.

Once we settled into a spacious park cabin, Udo and I walked that night up around the hatchery. We kept going beyond the streetlights and out onto the dark highway. No cars passed. He was nervous walking in the night, but I convinced him there was nothing to fear. We hiked wordlessly in an alley of hardwoods under a starry sky. "It's beautiful," Udo said after a while. "I never walk in the night at home. Some friends of mine own a little cabin up on the Alb. When it's dark, I stay close to home. There's something magnificent about this."

Since then, Virginia had seen Udo in 2000 on our visit to Germany, and again in 2012 when Udo and Ivo came to visit us in Kansas City. They'd spoken by phone many times in the intervening years and exchanged Christmas and birthday cards. Udo had a great affinity for Virginia, and she for him.

* * *

Now, Udo put us up in his small, two-room apartment. The roll-shutters still had holes hail had punched in them. His sliding-glass door let out on a roof-top deck wrapping around two-thirds of the house, offering a view of steep rust-colored tile and black-slate roofs, steeples, and bell towers. The dark blue mountains of the Schwäbische Alb rimmed the entire scene.

The evening was still young. We piled into the camper van Udo had borrowed from friends for our journey in the coming days. Comfortable bench seats filled the space behind the driver. All the accoutrements for home-away-from-home camping were stowed under and behind the seats. A detachable compartment on top of the van held a tent that would set up over the top and down around the side of the van. Virginia and Nick found themselves a new and exotic environment. He poked around in the van's compartments and she lounged across the seats like an emperor.

We were on our way to visit my cousin Erik in Tübingen, a town adjacent to Reutlingen. The short drive took us down busy streets that wound through narrow valleys and into the heart of typical, unforgiving German traffic. Cars drove nose to tail. Drivers shifted lanes with only the quick flash of a blinker. People lined up, literally, bumper-to-bumper at stoplights. Udo navigated it all with a craftsman's skill. When we arrived in Tübingen, he circled a block, took a quick left then a right, dodged a light pole, and yanked into a parking space. He made it look easy.

The traffic's tense atmosphere lifted as we climbed out of the van. We met Erik at a predetermined spot around the corner from where we'd parked. He stood about five and a half feet tall and had shaved his head. He held out his stout arms and gave us all hugs, including Udo, whom he'd met several times through my visits over the years. Erik led us along the ancient streets of the university town and down into the city center, where a pretty little creek flowed in a concrete canal through the pedestrian plaza. We took tables under a canvas canopy next to the water. Conversation started of its own, without the kind of uneasiness that begins with, "So, uh, what have you been up to?"

The waiter didn't introduce himself by name but instead asked if we had preferences maybe he could help us with. Each of us ordered something German—bratwursts, *Käsespätzle*, schnitzel, potatoes, and green salad. The waiter then asked if he could get some drinks—beer, soft drinks, or water. "Our wine selection is second to none on the plaza here," he said in English. He waited patiently with his order pad. No flair, no show, just plain, good waitering. Poor Nick sat in a grump until the waiter offered, "The young man would like some chicken nuggets and French fries, perhaps." Nick lit up.

Tübingen and Reutlingen abut one another, and both are hilly, ancient towns. Reutlingen was more industrial and pedestrian than the cosmopolitan Tübingen with its five-hundred-year-old university. But Reutlingen was a year-round town. Tübingen suffered from its own prosperity. The university was founded in 1477 and became one of the centers of German intellectualism. It influenced the course of liberal-arts higher education at German and American universities. Its alumni included famous German scholars, writers, poets, and scientists. Johannes Kepler graduated from Tübingen in 1594. More recently, the university had graduated several Nobel laureates and a pope. Some twenty-seven thousand students attended classes, and the university had over ten thousand administration and hospital staff. Students constituted about a third of the town's population. As such, the town nearly shut down during holidays. In summer, when other towns held festivals and local celebrations, Tübingen remained quiet.

Udo's and Erik's conversation danced back and forth, as if the two couldn't talk to each other fast enough. Udo, who's usually reserved if not sullen around strangers and people he doesn't know well, became animated. He dug into Erik's opinions of their towns and the life in them and recent turns in German politics. With us, Erik stepped outside of his insular group of friends and his "scene," as he calls it, of punk rockers and barflies. Erik and Udo included Virginia in the conversation and occasionally asked Nick a question and kept him entertained. I stayed mostly silent, as I generally get in depressions, and listened to the socializing going on around me.

In the early 1990s, Erik went to school for a year at the university in Eutin. He came back to Kansas City after a year only to return to Germany in 1994 and try his hand at music and concert production and promotion in Tübingen's lively cultural scene. He managed tours for American punk and rock bands and owned his own record label where he produced American and German band records to sell in German markets. Most of his success came through trial and error, and many times he found himself living on the edge of financial collapse. As it was, the record business proved to be too hand-to-mouth. He started teaching English at a *Volkshochschule*, a sort of community college. Today, he works for wages and tips in a little club called the Last Resort, the latest of many such clubs and bars where he'd worked through the years.

Erik looked healthy and happy. His life had fallen into a comfortable routine. He worked at the bar five or six nights a week until 2 or 3 a.m. He went out with friends for a while after, and then home to watch television. He slept late in the morning and had most of the afternoon to take care of his daily and week-to-week necessities. He'd taken up with a good roommate—Erik could write a compendium of crappy roommates—and seemed to have settled into the life of a forty-plus-year-old bartender.

After dinner, Erik took us on a long walk through the town's picturesque streets. The houses and buildings in the city center came right out of the Brothers Grimm fairy tales and history books on medieval Europe. Ancient houses of timber and plaster towered over narrow and cobbled streets. Night was falling and our evening excursion grew more atmospheric. Our footsteps and voices echoed between the shop windows and then up into the night past the apartments on the upper floors. A few people, mostly young lovers and students walked slowly before closed shops and sleepy restaurants. Now and then, someone sauntered by with a dog. Otherwise, we were alone.

The conversation hinged on Erik's tour-guide efforts to show us where and how he lived. We arrived at the Last Resort toward the end of the night. The entrance took us down two flights of steps and into a small *Kneipe* where the bartender was glad to see us. His business had been slow. The place displayed a nautical theme with ship ropes and pictures of what you might see through a porthole—exotic destinations, desert islands, and ocean.

We had a soda, and then Erik walked us a little farther down the ancient streets and out onto the main boulevard. He looked sad, as if he really wanted us to stay longer. Since he worked nights, his day was beginning. He was off to another bar to see friends.

As he walked off into the night, I couldn't dodge the notion Erik hadn't really grown out of his punk rock days. The bar kept him in contact with the university and music scenes. They gave him purpose and meaning, and he looked the part. He wore band T-shirts, jeans, and hefty boots. He kept his wallet on a chain attached to a belt loop. Working for minimum wage and tips while approaching middle age must keep him awake occasionally. I think about being a college professor—an adjunct—and a minor writer in my fifties. What happens to us when we get old? Without retirement accounts and savings, how will we support ourselves? I'm fortunate that Virginia underwrites my obsessive writing habit and my inability to work a regular job. Erik doesn't have that.

I lie awake sometimes and think of my friend and my cousin. Their lives as bachelors are so different. Udo owns his studio and shop. Erik used to own his business but now works for others. Udo labors in an ancient trade that would possess a demand for his services until the end of his life. If his shop fails, he'll try again or find the work he loved in another workshop restoring and producing art, and architectural glass products. He is a master and an artist. But I worry about Erik. He's found himself in a business whose fashion changes quickly. He keeps working in the cultural scene whose members are growing old. He finds new students and patrons brusque and impolite. He bemoans the passing of the Germany he worked in when he was younger. The life he's chosen might provide him fulfillment until he became irrelevant to the scene, if he hasn't already. I'm not supposed to judge, but I hope the Last Resort isn't where he's destined to stay.

CHAPTER TEN

INTO FRANCE

UDO HAD PLANNED an excursion through France from Alsace to the heart of Burgundy for us. Our destination, the halfway mark of the journey, was a modern castle-building project called Guedelon almost in the geographical center of the French Republic at Treigny.

That morning as dawn poked through the hail holes in Udo's shutters, I didn't care about the trip. Nothing could make me care. Heaviness dogged me. I pulled the blankets up, thinking, my God, I must get out of bed, but I dread it.

Fortunately, everyone else slept at least until 8 a.m. When they began to rise, a sense of duty compelled me out of my cocoon. The world felt weighty, as if I were Atlas under the globe. I checked to see if I'd taken my medicine the evening before. I knew psychiatric meds didn't work that way. They build up, and I maintain a level of them in my body. Missing one day wouldn't produce a notable difference. Still, I counted my pills. I did, indeed, take my medicine. I would have to hold on. A stout cup of coffee lightened the load a little. I decided to don my best face and determined not to be a crank.

I had reservations. I feared Guedelon would be a Renaissance-festival kind of amusement park with gaudily dressed people fighting with swords, shouting "huzzah!" and devouring roasted turkey legs. I was also unsure of our accommodations. The trip would include overnight camping in our camper van. Except for nights on park benches and under bridges, I'd never been camping in Europe. Not even Udo had ever been camping in Europe. Nick and Virginia had no idea what to expect. There was a nervousness in the air about what we'd find.

On the other hand, my fellow travelers emanated a sense of discovery and curiosity. Nick and Virginia had never been to France. I'd only gone to Metz and Colmar to eat dinner and see some sights. I was ready to brave a faux-medieval amusement park to take in as much of the French countryside as I could.

* * *

After piling our goods into the camper van, we made our first stop at Udo's studio in an industrial, garage-like building in the middle of Reutlingen, not far from his apartment. We entered the shop and felt a master's presence. Here was the very definition of order. An astonishing barrage of light saluted our eyes. Sheets of glass stood in rows of vertical racks. Sorted by color, size, and type of glass, remnants and special squares and shards filled banks of drawers for various projects he was working on or that might come along in the future. He'd arranged his machines and work benches in neat lines. His tools hung precisely on pegboards, and he had more in dozens of drawers and cabinets around the shop. Art pieces he'd made for himself hung in a bank of windows admitting natural light into the studio.

I'd seen his previous studios. This one fascinated me no less. Cold and sharp, often dangerous, glass had the ability to transform space and time. The hands of the craftsperson worked magic with light. Udo transfigured ordinary sheets of colored glass into sublimely beautiful objects. While art glass was ethereal to sight and mind, the transformation from ordinary glass to art was a very rational one. On drafting paper, he laid out schematics and engineering details down to the last millimeter. Nothing was left to chance. He showed us the various kinds of glass and explained their best uses. He demonstrated his prowess cutting glass.

Udo's abilities awed Nick. The shop captivated him. He wandered among the racks and touched the sheets of glass in their stacks. Rummaging around the drawers of tools, he asked endless questions about Udo and his business. We reluctantly left the shop after about an hour, as we felt we had to press on.

* * *

The autobahn swept us toward the French/German border. Travel was tricky. Our camper van, loaded with four people, baggage, and camping equipment, confined us to the slow lane. The speed limit went sometimes to 120 km/hour (about 75 mph), but our hefty machine topped out at about 90 km/h (55 mph). Above that, it whined and rattled and bumped, making us think it might shake itself to pieces. Traveling north and west, we rolled through Stuttgart's industrial regions and into rural areas outside of the city. The autobahn ran us up and down steep grades as we left the Schwäbische Alb, the mountain range in Baden-Württemburg surrounding Stuttgart, Tübingen, and Reutlingen. At Pforzheim, we descended toward the Rhein Valley and Karlsruhe, in whose station I'd slept it seemed a hundred times when I was younger. The highway curved into the Rhein and headed south. The valley spread out wide and flat to hills rising in the east. Wheat and corn fields filled the space around the highway. We could have been in western Kansas on Interstate 70.

To travel with Udo is to move at the speed of Udo. He's quiet and lives a solitary, reflective life—almost that of a monk. The crash and bang of the autobahn was not his style. Traffic and its haste unnerved him. Cars passed us by the dozen. He was tense. He didn't whine or grumble, but his face scrunched. His shoulders crawled up his neck. He ached to get off the autobahn and onto the quieter two-lane highways—*Landstrasse*—in France. But we wanted to get through Freiburg and cross the border at Mulhouse where we'd turn straight west and head out over the two-lane after Belfort about forty or fifty kilometers into France.

Meanwhile, the day grew gray and the sky closed. The dour weather made the madness of the autobahn a little more bearable. We drove by thick copses of woods that made the plain seem wider and flatter. After Baden-Baden, we sped by Strasbourg on the opposite bank of the river. Behind us to the east lay the Black Forest.

* * *

I'd traveled this stretch of highway back with Ivo in 1993 when he was working on his PhD studies at the university in Freiburg. After the hectic frenzy of the autobahn, we'd driven into sleepy Baden-Baden and sank ourselves into the mineral waters of the ornate 120-year-old Friedrichsbad. Cloaked in linen, we progressed in seventeen steps from warm steam rooms to hot saunas, and then into warm pools of water, and to tables where Turkish attendants scrubbed our bodies with stiff brushes. We then plunged into an icy bath, and attendants covered us with linen sheets and left us to rest on comfortable beds in low light. Never had I been treated to such bodily delight. When we left the spa, we could hardly walk. We ate lavish gyros from a stand serving huge spates of food for little money. Drowsy and relaxed as wet noodles, we dawdled along a slower route back to Freiburg on two-lane roads through the Black Forest.

I was enchanted and intrigued. When I was a kid, people in my family spoke with reverence of the Black Forest. I imagined the thick woods of Red Riding Hood. My dad's mother, the daughter of immigrants, had relatives north of Koblenz, in Siegen, where she and her family sent CARE packages after World War II. At some point her relatives sent her a real cuckoo clock that Black Forest artisans had crafted. Heavy pine cone–shaped weights on chains powered the clock. Every time we went to Grandma's house, my siblings and I fought over who'd pull the weights back up toward the clock. A little bird popped out of the chalet-shaped clock and cuckooed the hour. The bird emerged for a single call at the half hour.

Grandma and her sisters inculcated in us an admiration for anything German. My mom's parents were also offspring of immigrants. They, too, presented us with a German ideal that included foamy beer, tasty bratwurst, and Oktoberfest. Their Germany was one of tour books and fairy tales. These influences are very likely why, when Larry called that dim night in summer 1985, Germany seemed so possible. I wonder now if he had called from other great wine-making countries like France or Austria, if I would have been so amenable to dumping everything I knew to start over.

The Germany I found was nothing like my grandparents and parents made it seem. It wasn't a place where the autobahn was speed limitless, men wore lederhosen and women *Dirndl*, and craftsmen labored for days and weeks on cuckoo clocks. The mythical forest lay not in one large, dense stretch of wild, dark woods as I'd been taught in home and in school, but in series of hills and valleys, many of which were farmed and grazed. It didn't look primordial as much as it did used and cared for. The real Germany didn't crush me with euphorically remembered tradition but encouraged self-discovery. The country awed and amazed me—the ancient streets, the old villages and their quiet town squares, and, where buildings hadn't been bombed flat, the ancient, timber-and-plaster construction. But it was thoroughly modern country, in some ways more modern than my own.

And I wondered about my family's history in Germany. No one spoke of or even considered that our German relatives might have participated in the rise of the National Socialist state. Our family's relation to the conflict was opaque, hidden. As far as I knew when I was a kid, none of our relatives served in the Wehrmacht, Luftwaffe, Kriegsmarine, SS, or Gestapo. I never heard that anyone in the Stahl, Bauer, or Bruns families belonged to the Nazi Party or supported it. Today, I can't imagine not one of our loving family took up with Nazis or served in the German armed forces.

* * *

Despite traffic, the van and Udo moved at their own paces as we drove from Baden-Baden toward Freiburg. We discussed deep subjects like philosophy of life, the afterlife, and the existence of God. I loved Udo this way. When he brought up complicated subjects, he forced the edges of my German fluency. He made me figure out ways around my limited vocabulary and reflect on how I was living my life. The conversation also distracted me from the heaviness I felt earlier and drew me out of myself when my instinct told me to retreat.

"What do you think happens after we die?" he asked, his hand draped over the steering wheel, his eyes to the mirrors.

"I imagine we cease," I said. "That's all. Puff. It's gone."

"That doesn't bother you?"

"Not in the least," I said. "What matters is right in front of us, our futures, our children's futures. We do good because it's the right thing. No one's forcing us. No one is in charge. We have to be optimists."

"I suppose that means we must give meaning to our lives," he said. "It's not really built in, not something to find as a treasure?"

"That's right," I said. "Meaning and purpose are things we strive for. Such a view also makes life more precious."

"In what way?"

"If we have this life and there is no other, then we have to make the best of what we have. We don't get a second chance."

"What you're saying is there's no afterlife bank account."

"I don't think so," I said. "It's not like I can save up my good works on a ledger to be drawn on like a retirement fund."

"I suppose I see things similarly," he said. "But I do believe there is a God."

"I didn't say I didn't believe in God. I think the jury's still out."

"So, you would call yourself an agnostic," he said.

"In some ways," I said. "But it's hard to divine. Some moments I conduct myself as a believer, other times an agnostic, and still other moments as an atheist."

"So, there's a range of understanding, you're saying, a kind of spectrum and not three easy divisions."

"Exactly. It depends on the situation, on the subject."

We'd had similar discussions over the years. In 2012, when we went to Mesa Verde, we had a week together to converse over such things. The wide-open desert spaces lent themselves to vigorous conversation and debate. He rarely left things to chance and admired my seeming devil-may-care attitude toward deadlines and most other things in life. He liked what looked to him to be spontaneity and eagerness to embrace new experience. In fact, fear ruled my whole life. These two aspects of my personality constantly warred with each other. Often, fear of not doing or undertaking a new task or adventure overcame the fear of doing it and I acted. Udo knew there was more to me than the carefree traveler. He knew of my suicide attempt and what it revealed about my mental health—a deeply serious side that could be destructive. But he liked the adventuresome side of me and wanted more of that for himself.

* * *

We pulled into Mulhouse for supplies at a large French food market. It sat in a shopping center that looked and felt very much like an American strip mall. The store was Walmart-huge, but it sold more than cheap crap. The French are known for their kitchens and cooking, and this store peddled everything a respectable French cook needed. The shelves offered items we Americans considered specialty and gourmet but that a decent French household would need every day. The bread and baked-goods aisle stretched the length of one side of the store and sold everything from the darkest rye to the humblest white bread—all fresh, crusty, and substantial. I counted forty different kinds and brands of cooking oils—olive, walnut, almond, grapeseed, sunflower, flax, rapeseed, and more. The produce aisle stretched, it seemed, for colorful miles.

In the store, we fanned out in three different directions. Nick moved slowly, thoughtfully. He doesn't rush, and he'll do whatever he can to avoid it. When he feels pressed, he goes silent, withdraws, and, ultimately, resists. Left alone, he takes his time, observes everything. The market intrigued him. Toys not so unlike what he'd find back home attracted him in passing. He pointed out things new to him and asked questions about kitchen utensils he didn't know in our house, such as tiny sauce whisks, automatic lemon and orange juicers, and egg slicers. He wondered at aisles of soda and mineral waters—so many different kinds and brands compared to the American market. This was not a new country to him, but a new world.

Virginia, too, had her speed. She looked at every item, divining its American counterpart. She loved the selection and the ways the store marketed the items. She's an impulse buyer and puts things in the shopping cart depending on her mood or the way a store or market presents it. She wanted to buy cosmetics, various kinds of food and drink, even toys for Nick. She trundled along, taking items off the shelf and reading labels. She spent a good deal of time in what we might call the health-food aisle.

But Udo is a no-nonsense kind of guy. He asked what we wanted and sallied forth, seeking the essentials—cheese, bread, milk, vegetables. He and Virginia hashed out what they needed in cold cuts and sausages. They chose various kinds of cured, smoked meats that Nick would eat and that would survive a few days in a cooler, particularly Italian and French pepperoni. While making our selections, we discovered we were dependent on Udo. I knew no French and Virginia's was limited to a few words and phrases she'd learned in high school. Udo's limited French would have to suffice.

We couldn't find ice for our cooler, in which we would store milk, vegetables, and cheese. Americans ice the hell out of everything. Europeans, on the other hand, don't much demand ice. Cold pop ordered in a restaurant came with one cube. Beer and white wine arrived at the table at cellar temperature. We asked and were directed to the gas station in the parking lot. But it didn't sell ice, either.

Udo didn't take it well. He wanted to be self-contained when we left Mulhouse. We were headed into the French countryside, where the availability of ice, food, and gas might be limited. In truth, Udo was as new to this game as we were. He'd traveled in France but mostly in Alsace and Lorraine, where life, while French, is still recognizable to the German. I could tell he was nervous and uncertain about the territory into which we were headed.

* * *

We sped out of Mulhouse without ice but with enough food to last. We again hit the French equivalent of the autobahn until Belfort, where we entered the world we'd live in for the next six days. The two-lane highway bounded out of town hardly wide enough for two cars. Essentially, where the pavement ended on the right side of the car, that was it. But the van felt good. It negotiated curves and took bumps with an easy motion.. It jerked not at all. The sound of the engine thrummed up through the vehicle. We were finally on our way.

The two-lane led us through the steep, wooded hills of the Haute-Saone until we reached Ronchamp, a tired little village. The town's grand tourist past had faded long ago. Empty storefronts and closed souvenir shops lined the highway. The sky closed and it started to rain. Udo pulled over and looked at the map, wondering how we were to get up the mountain of Bourlemont to Le Corbusier's (Charles-Édouard Jeanneret's) famous chapel, Notre Dame du Haut. At my insistence, he drove on. After a few minutes, we came on a road called, strangely in English, Chapel Street. The macadam provided barely enough room for two vehicles meeting. It climbed the steep incline in tight curves. Thick and lush forest, dark in the rain, draped the road. We passed old mining operations and ancient houses. Toward the top of the mountain, we drove out of the dark forest. The chapel appeared before us.

I'd studied Le Corbusier's groundbreaking chapel in my freshman Introduction to Art History class. I remembered it well so many years later. In the early 1950s, the Association de l'Oeuvre Notre Dame du Haut commissioned Le Corbusier to build the chapel on the site of a pilgrimage church destroyed in World War II. The Norte Dame du Haut was the third church built on the site, the first in the fourth century. The association and its attendant priests and nuns desired a building that reflected their efforts to remain relevant to the modern era.

I never gave Le Corbusier's work much thought, being, in my youth, a reactionary when it came to modern architecture. Much had changed in the intervening decades. Ivo, Udo, and Martin and their writer, artist, and sculptor friends introduced me to new forms and showed me the arc of art history. Their respect for the past and for modern aesthetics in art and architecture transformed me from a backward pedestrian into a sponge, ready to absorb whatever new and interesting abstractions I came across.

Now the Notre Dame du Haut took my breath away. The chapel towered over the top of the mountain, bigger and more majestic than I'd imagined. The airfoil-like roof and broad concrete sides spanned three towers, one much higher than the others. The roof reminded me of a nun's bonnet, as it was supposed to. When we entered the chapel, we found it intimate and close, like a cocoon. The place emanated a kind of reverent silence. Candles lit the interior. A ghostly, spiritual glow fell from colored glass set deep in the concrete wall. Each of the structure's three towers presented a separate apse with clerestory windows above. The largest apse wrapped the main altar and a bank of narrow, clear glass reaching from floor to ceiling. A small crowd of people, maybe twenty, joined us in the church. The chapel itself possessed weight, an effect of the dim light and thick concrete construction.

Just as we'd entered the chapel, a thunderstorm broke. We could feel the thunder but it hardly made a sound within. It was as if we were miles away from that storm.

While Udo, Virginia, and I sat in the pews taking in the church, Nick poked around. He wandered, examining each of the altars. He popped his head into the confessional at the back of the church. He tiptoed and didn't make a sound.

People entered the chapel not just to see this architectural wonder but also to pray. Ronchamp had been a sacred site devoted to the Holy Virgin for centuries. It took its place on the one of the many pilgrimage roads through Europe that constituted the Camino de Santiago, or St. James Way, which led to the shrine of St. James at the Cathedral of Santiago de Compostela in northern Spain. The interior of the chapel struck everyone, pilgrim and tourist, dumb and demanded reverence. Those who spoke whispered, adding to the overwhelming and worshipful atmosphere.

We wandered the grounds after the storm had passed. The gray sky dampened color and made the verdant lawn and the surrounding forest deeper green. We were as silent outside as we were in. We wandered the gravel paths out behind the chapel, where the bonnet roof drained into a basin of abstract sculpture. The Saone plains spread out below us in hues of green, and Jura mountains fluttered off blue and dark gray the other direction.

After we'd toured the chapel and grounds, we trundled back down the mountain. The forest grew dark in the late afternoon and branches hung low over the roadway, weighed down by the rain. The main highway led down through the Jura Mountains' valleys and up over enchanting, rolling hills. When we arrived in Vesoul, a city of 16,000 in the middle of Haute-Saone, the weather had cleared and we sought a campground for the night. Shadows had grown long, and we wanted plenty of time to get set up and have dinner before dark.

* * *

I had no idea what to expect from Eurocamping. Europeans have less open space and wide-open, unoccupied land than Americans. They are, however, avid campers, and over 10,000 campgrounds in western Europe attest to their enthusiasm. They pulled their trailers not with oversized, overpowered pickups but with regular passenger cars and small SUVs. Their campers seemed comically small next to their American counterparts. The European RV resembled more Udo's camper van or cars with small, boxy living spaces attached to them. In all, European campers, trailers, and RVs all looked cute and rustic compared to the big shouldered, portly waisted American versions of the home away from home.

There was little chance of sneaking off into a hedgerow and setting up for the night, as I'd done on occasion as I walked from Kansas City to Helena. Virginia, not a camper by disposition, detests sleeping on the ground. Nick had proven himself capable of camping wherever we landed and in whatever situation. He'd been out with me in state parks at tent sites with no hookups. We camped out West, where we had, at best, a fire ring. He'd also been backpacking with me in a national forest wilderness in Missouri, where we cleared our own camp spots in the middle of the woods at the end of a day's hike. Udo had seen us operate and had slept under the stars with us. But given a choice, he preferred a flush toilet and a spigot where he could wash his face. We had to keep Virginia comfortable and Udo within the civilized camping he liked. Anything but finding a place with clean bathrooms would prove less than adequate.

Udo's friends' camper van came with a thick, unwieldy guide to European campgrounds. It listed amenities, such as restaurants, bars, and even bakeries. As I paged through the guide, I imagined American RVers sought this kind of information in *The Good Sam RV Travel and Savings Guide* as they poked around the country. The guide, however, was ambiguous about where the campgrounds were and how to get to them. We tried to match the lines and road numbers in the guide's cartoon maps with our more sophisticated Michelin road atlas. Still, we couldn't divine where to go, how far to drive, or what to look for. Vesoul had a campground somewhere, we were sure of that.

We followed little "camping" arrows on posts studded with signs directing drivers to other towns and attractions. We wound up at a dusty campground outside of town and looked it over with indecision. The late-afternoon sky had cleared and the sun shone full. Humidity clung to our skins. The place sat in a floodplain next to a wooded creek and the campers stood in a worn field of sparse grass exposed to the sun. Some kids kicked a soccer ball around in the dirt between the campers and RVs. Udo's ambivalence, born of his shyness in the face of new things, made the situation worse. Where, exactly, would we set up among the other campers? We felt like strangers at a party who didn't know the house rules or anyone in attendance.

We wrung our hands. Usually, I'm the guy who breaks the ice in a situation like this. I swallow my pride and embarrassment and dive right in. But I had no French. I asked Udo to approach a couple standing next a trailer near us.

"I don't know," he said.

"Come on," I said. "These people don't know us. If we embarrass ourselves, we get to drive away and never see them again."

Udo walked up to the couple, head bowed, shy and apologetic. But he did spectacularly well. The man indicated the campground was full. Udo asked where we would find another. The man, through a series of complicated gestures and stiffly dialectic French that made translation difficult for Udo, indicated another campground lay some distance from Vesoul.

We drove around the countryside in circles for another hour until we found what we sought. Fields of wheat and corn stood on all sides of the campground's copse of trees and bushes. A closed gate greeted us and we couldn't find a proprietor. Beyond the gate lay a few campers and RVs in organized rows. A woman walked toward a bathroom/shower house we could see from the gate. At my insistence, Udo ducked under the gate and hailed the woman. Virginia, Nick, and I watched as Udo and she went through a series of animated gestures. After several minutes, Udo turned and walked toward us with a smile.

The owners were gone, Udo said, but the woman had given him a code to unlock the gate. We selected a site as far from the other campers as we could get. I ushered us into a spot sheltered against the rising sun, so we could have those extra minutes of sleep in the morning. The sky had turned sunset orange and purple. The wheat grew golden in long shadows. Beyond the fence on one side of the campground, a wetland spread beneath the trees. The humidity hovered around the saturation point and festooned a small lake at the center of the campground with foggy haze. Frogs burped in the wetland next to us.

Our site was a mown square of grass and tall hedges hemmed in on three sides, like the organized spaces of a KOA. It wasn't my favorite kind of camping, but we weren't in a national forest wilderness. My fellow travelers seemed to like it. I resolved to do the same.

Once we parked, the construction phase of our Eurocamping adventure began. Udo pulled a collapsible ladder from beneath the bench seats in the back of the van. When he assembled the complicated device, he climbed up, unhooked the fasteners on the pod that rode on top of the van, and pushed the container open. He unfolded a platform that ridged the top of the van. He then pulled the tent down over the side like a drape. With telescoping poles, we slowly erected our tent over the platform and side of the van. We struggled with zippers and Velcro strips. Virginia, Nick, and I would sleep atop the van on the platform under the canvas, and Udo'd make his bed on the van's bench seats. We assembled another ladder to climb up to the platform.

We learned as we went. At first Udo was in charge, since he'd practiced setting up the tent on his own in his driveway. He's a real German like that. He wanted nothing left to chance. But setting the tent up was obviously something that took practice. Virginia and I made suggestions. Nick emerged as the director of the operation, intuiting where things went and how they fastened and zipped together—"Hey, this pole goes into this hole!" "No, it looks like this zips into this." "The flap here goes with that one there." When we thought we'd finally finished, we found we'd missed a step or two. Nick waved some extra poles around like swords.

"But, hey, who's counting?" he said.

"What does it matter if we don't have Tab B slid the correct way into Slot C?" Virginia said, grabbing a corner and shaking the structure. "The thing will do for the night."

After we zipped all the zippers and fastened all the Velcro, we unpacked the cooler, our water bottles, and a few other things from beneath the bench seats. While I downed most of a bottle of water, Udo opened the hatch on the back of the van. He and Nick started unloading the folding table, chairs, and propane stove from their appointed slots. I could tell one thing put back the wrong way would ruin the entire operation.

The camping implements and accoutrements were miniaturized and sort of cute. Everything looked like it was made for someone Nick's size and height. Little folding canvas stools served as chairs, and the table with spindly legs was made of Formica and aluminum.

Another table held the stove with the propane bottle beneath. Udo lumbered like a giant among this elfin furniture as he chopped onions and mashed garlic. I cut bread with tiny strokes since the table wasn't built for two men with broad shoulders and workingman hands. Virginia towered over the stove, where she stirred a pot of boiling spaghetti. Nick wandered around the hedge, singing and talking to himself. Once this fiddling around with gear and food commenced, it continued until, somehow, dinner of spaghetti with red sauce and salad appeared.

Dusk brought whole new rounds of animal sounds to our impromptu dining room from the wetland adjacent to us. By the time we sat down, scrunched over the little dining table, we ate with flashlights to the music of the frogs next door. Crickets chirped in the hedge and night birds screeched above. When everyone had eaten their fill, the fiddling began again with washing up, stowing dishes in the chest from which we'd procured them, and putting the camp in some order.

When we'd finished, night had fallen. A bird squawked and others let go with primordial croaks in the wetland next to us. Frogs belched, cheeped, and whistled. Beyond the confines of the campground far across the fields a dog barked. In the windless evening, we sat back in the humid but cooling air satisfied we'd done our best.

After we'd crawled up the ladder and arranged ourselves in the tight space on the platform atop the van, Nick and Virginia fell asleep right away. I could feel Udo moving around in the van beneath us until, I supposed, he fell asleep, too. The salad smell of cut grass and the watery freshness of the wetland joined the odor of waterproofed canvas in our small cubby. The great yawps of a bird punctuated the night. It was otherwise so quiet I heard dew dripping off the trees onto the canvas above. The dark bulk I'd felt all day settled on me and

I looked forward to dreaming. Through my mental fug, I fell into restless sleep thinking how lucky we were.

And we were fortunate. There is little likelihood we will ever traipse off through the European countryside again. We may never again spend so much time alone with Udo. I ask Nick about his impressions of those first days of our romp through France. He tells me, while he was in the back of the van often playing on his handheld electronic game, he remembers the countryside, the campground, and the way our conversations flowed naturally. He says he wants to take up a backpack with me and walk through Europe, seeing what comes next. If not for our trip in the camper van, he says, he never would have thought being so close to me would be so comforting.

CHAPTER ELEVEN

GUEDELON

We woke and fumbled out of our perches. I usually eat breakfast standing up over the sink at home. But Udo, being more mindful, sits down as part of a sacred ritual and he won't be rushed. Years before, in the coming and goings of the house in the Saarstrasse, he would often make a full meal for himself and sit down to the table, while everyone else picked out of the fridge and the fruit bowl. At breakfast, he preferred muesli or some other cereal with milk, tea, and toast. For dinners, he didn't assemble things from the fridge. He cooked and ate meals purposefully while everyone rushed about. More than once, social activities had to wait until Udo finished eating.

So, it went with breakfast at the camping spot. He put out several kinds of bread and rolls we'd bought at the French market, as well as cheese, cereal, and fruit. I fetched butter and jellies from the cooler. Virginia set the table. We hunched again around the tiny table on our little foldout stools. We were polite, asking for and passing food around. We ate our fill, drenched in fresh coffee, tea, and, for Nicholas, milk.

While breakfast started the day, our eating almost ended it. I wanted to take a nap. My dull senses kept me from enjoying the morning. The light was too bright, the bristling activity around breakfast too much. Coffee had addled my nerves. I knew that should my mates cross me I'd have fallen into a withering fit. I ached to get away and avoid any confrontations. I knew that the only sure way to deal with depression was to get moving, breathe fresh air, and rejoice in not having my neck in a noose. Telling my group, hey, I'm going for a walk, I lit out at a brisk clip for the pond at the center of the campground.

In the clearing, fog was lifting. Unfamiliar birds sang and warbled in the trees. An almost perfectly circular berm contained the pond. Dimples and concentric circles indicated the owners had stocked it, an amenity for kids who wanted to try their hand at fishing.

The campground road looped me past an elaborate playground. Sites like our own radiated from the gravel path like spines and ribs of skeletal fish. I bid "hallo" to relaxed and sleepy people lounging in the sun in front of their campers and RVs. It wasn't so bad, this Eurocamping thing. It possessed a certain kind of charm and sociability. The place was mostly empty, likely waiting on weekend trade. I imagined the campground full, a family in every spot. Separated by a few feet and some tall bushes, campers had to consider their neighbors. The orderly campground layout demanded people behave themselves. Loud and boisterous adults would stand out. You could always tell where the children were.

The walk cleared my head and settled me down. Though I didn't look forward to spending the day in the van or taking the tour, I resolved to put my insides aside and consider my compatriots. Though I had tried to keep my downturn to myself, Virginia suspected something was amiss. Udo had already asked me about being distracted and distant. While he had often seen me in depression and mania before, he had little idea of the nature or course of my malady. My German friends all knew of my suicide attempt and trip to the hospital. But they weren't informed about all the complications of my illness. In former years, they'd ushered me through ups and downs, comforted me when the sadness and despair manifested themselves in crying jags and absences from their lives. Udo would certainly understand if I explained to him why I wasn't up for the tour, but he would have been gravely disappointed after all his planning and care.

I circled one of the campground loops a couple of times, firming my resolve. I felt the strength of my younger self, how I'd coped despite the drink and depression and mania. Back then, the only treatment for depression was, "What do you have to be depressed about?" and "No one in this family gets depressed, get out and play." As I grew older, I had to work. There was no time to dillydally or lay around in bed. I labored and drank harder. In Germany, it was easy to disappear on long walks through town and vineyard. I typed frantic and descriptive letters and wrote journal entries about what I'd found on my walks. I'd discovered more of Germany and myself due to manic-depressive illness than I would have without it.

We dawdled a while when I returned to the campsite. While we were reluctant to break free of our postprandial daze, the road lured us on. We had another night camping in front of us before the tour at Guedelon but didn't have far to go (about 320 km from Vesoul to Treigny). We weren't driving straight through. We'd stop to see sites that intrigued us and take breaks and eat lunch at some roadside pull-out or town square.

* * *

By the time we'd packed our gear, the sun had climbed to noon. Under the warm, wet blanket of depression, I chose to drive and distract myself. We wound through broad hills and wide farm fields heavy with hay and corn. Except for wooded thickets, the whole landscape turned yellow and brown, distinctly lovely in its nuances and hues. The sky spread without end over the plains and rolling inclines of rural Burgundy. Immense fields of sunflowers swayed in the late summer sun. Isolated farmhouses stood off the side of the road. The narrow two-lane wound through gray brick, stone, and plaster villages often no more than a knot of ancient houses with steep, tile roofs. Some displayed signs of life: shops with open shutters, geraniums and impatiens set in window flowerboxes, cars parked on the street. Others looked utterly abandoned and seemed as if no soul had stirred in them for many years.

We came to a halt in the town square of the small provincial town of Fayl-Billot. The shadow of a bronze statue of Napoleon stretched across our van. We wandered around the empty square and bandstand into a sublime park built around a canal, mirror smooth and covered with water hyacinth. Adjacent to the park stood a thirteenth-century church. We walked a narrow alley between ancient bulging walls and to the entrance. Eight centuries of supplicants had worn the floor's flagstones smooth and uneven. A crypt stood off to one side of the front entrance behind a crenellated wall of arches. Around the sarcophagus, statues of saints on platforms held up pillars that supported the roof far above. The old wooden pews squeaked when we sat in them. Ancient and smudged stained-glass windows dimly lit the church. Nick wandered around in the gloom and whispered he'd never been in a place so old. "I bet they had knights and queens and things when they built this place," he said.

Past Langres, the territory grew more forested. Breaks in the woods gave us vistas of plains, rivers, and vineyards as far as we could see. We dropped into the Seine Valley, where the hills grew larger and the vineyards even bigger and broader. Some looked as steep as those I had worked in the Rhein and Mosel valleys. I could see the transition from machine-worked rows to hand-tended vines due to their steep grades. The mechanically tended rows stood wide from each other, the vines trained on wire trellises; the hand-tended rows narrowed, and individual vines were trained on single posts.

We traveled through towns I'd been familiar with through their vintages. Chatillon sur Seine, Tonnerre, Auxerre, Chablis. The small and nondescript villages amazed me. Most were no more than tiny settlements standing under hills and great swaths of grapevines. The village of Chablis, a place with such a name, so world renowned, I thought, should be bigger, statelier, perhaps even more modern. It was a mere collection of houses and farm operations with a few wineries of famous name.

When I was a drinker, I knew Burgundy wines well, and as I looked out over the vineyards, my taste memory kicked in. I remembered the whites most clearly. Flinty Tonerre, sharp and fragrant Chablis, softer and rounder Chatillon. I didn't dwell on it but found it interesting I could actually taste a Tonerre first cru some twenty-four years after I'd put down the bottle.

At Touchy, the sky clouded and eased the edge off the day. We headed almost south though the forest and wooded hills toward Saint-Sauveur-en-Puisaye, a small town with a lively center. I lumbered the van into a narrow parking space and we headed up to the market. Two- and three-story buildings of whitewashed plaster formed narrow streets and hemmed in the town center. In the square, fruit-and-vegetable vendors shared space shoulder-to-shoulder with artists and craftspeople. Fishmongers sold their wares next to butchers, some of whom offered sizzling cuts from wood-fired and propane grills. The heady smells of the market—fresh-cut vegetables, bakery goods, searing meat, and flowers, lots of flowers—enchanted us. Shoppers, looking grave and determined, moved among vendors.

We hustled through the crowd, winding past the stalls and tents in a kind of conga line. A few bars and restaurants along the perimeter set tables out on the sidewalks. We eddied out of the human stream and took up chairs at a restaurant that looked friendly. We ordered coffee from a snappy waiter. He served each cup of wonderful foamy, thick brew with a pirouette and a cube of neatly wrapped sugar. He set a small pitcher of fresh cream on the table. We noshed bread we'd bought from a baker in the square.

The Saint-Sauvear bazaar made me think of decades before, when Udo and I went shopping in the Trier weekend market and crunched through fresh bread while drinking coffee at outdoor cafés. Not all of my drinking life or mental illness had been bad for me. These diseases had led me to Germany and to experiences like the Trierer market. I'd met friends like Udo and the Fricks. Manically pursuing life, I'd done and seen a lot. Alcoholism and mental illness led me in directions and to take risks I might not have taken if I'd been balanced and moderate. Remembering what Joachim had said, I thought alcoholism and manic depression led me right to this small table on the edge of a French town market. To this cup of coffee with fresh cream. To a family adventure turning into more than a relaxing time away from home.

* * *

We took off back toward the van after the market closed and the crowd began to disperse. The vendors drove their vans and trucks into the square and packed away their goods. We strolled through the town awhile. We were due at Guedelon the next day. Udo'd arranged an English-speaking tour of the castle construction site that started at exactly 2 p.m. We were a few kilometers from our ultimate destination and only had to find a camping spot for the night.

But there was no camping to be found. With Udo at the wheel, we followed the little arrow-shaped signs and wound up in dead ends. It disappointed us but we needn't hurry. Still, I could tell Udo was getting a little nervous. Virginia said she liked not finding a place right off and enjoyed the scenery. The campground guide didn't help us, except to indicate there were campgrounds around Treigny, several kilometers from Saint-Sauvear. The road wound through heavily wooded countryside. The day was clearing. Dappled light falling to the forest floor produced the effect of a Georges Seurat landscape.

I didn't mind the drive. But soon Nick became restless. In Saint-Sauvear, he'd sat at the table patiently, as if entertaining us. I could tell he was itching to get back to his handheld game console. In the van now, it preoccupied him and held his attention as we drove through another village or around another curve to another grand vista. Much of the territory we covered the previous day looked a lot like Kansas away from the interstate. Off the highway, beyond the edge of sight, often lay rolling hills and nuanced prairies. Although there was more to see, Nick found the back of the van confining and infinitely boring. Even the handheld device gets a little old, the games too familiar. After an hour, he put it aside and asked are-we-there-yet questions we couldn't answer.

We negotiated sharp curves and popped in and out of the forest shadows. We followed one campground sign after another. Finally, we ducked into places and met proprietors who told us in flat, fact-of-the-matter tones they had no room for us.

As we were despairing, we came across a place with one site left. The little square of grass and hedge allowed us only enough room for the van and our tables. This campground proved more elaborate than our previous one. It was near town, not situated in the middle of open farmland. Little weekend cabins, trailer-sized boxes, lined one side of the campground. I thought of myself with dread when I spied shirtless, potbellied, hairy fathers sitting on the porches of weekend cabins. Some fussed with their children as the kids ran in and out. Others drank beer and looked bored. A sit-down restaurant and bar stood next to the entrance, and we put in an order for fresh bread that would arrive in a baker's wagon in the morning. A kiddie playground, obviously for the smallest, youngest children, sprawled out from the restaurant deck.

The owner was a woman in her mid-fifties. She sat at a wooden table on the deck in front of the office, adjusted her glasses, and filled in papers. (The French seem to use a lot of forms and papers.) She took our money and gave Udo a handful of receipts. We asked if she had ice for our cooler. She shrugged her shoulders in a way that said, "Ice? What for?" This puzzled me. When an American car-bumper camper or RVer can't find ice, the world comes to an end. We had milk, cold cuts, and cheese to keep cool, we told the woman. The best we could do, she said, was to check in St. Sauvear. But we'd inquired and even tried to buy ice from a fruit vendor at the market to no avail. The man told us he would save his for the next weekend and needed all he had.

Ice was a hot commodity in France.

The unfolding process commenced. We made sure the van stood somewhat level with chocks under the wheels. Then the ladder came out and snapped together. We unloaded poles, straps, and fittings. Udo climbed up the toy ladder and popped up the top cover for the canvas. Agitated and flustered, my mood in the sink, I struggled with zippers, my hands shaking, while Virginia attached the roll-down pieces of canvas around the bottom of the tent. The process put me on edge and peeled away the relief I first felt when we found the campground. Virginia noticed my distress and took my hands in hers. She smiled. "You're going to be all right." She set up a chair and let me sit out setting up toy tables, stools, stove, and all the chests and boxes holding dishes and utensils.

* * *

The next day, we had plenty of time. I was glad of it. Neither my mood nor constitution was up for rushing anywhere. I anticipated the Guedelon tour with dread and wanted to sit in the campsite all day. Fortunately, we put the van together and then lounged around reading until close to the appointment Udo had arranged at Guedelon. I wrote for a long time in my journal, in part to record the previous days' events, in part to steel myself for the time ahead. Punchy and in the doldrums, I took a nap in the van before it was time to leave.

I ensconced myself behind the wheel to fight off darker thoughts. The day was hot and full sun. The drive was not long but enough to put my head on straight. We parked in one of the red dirt lots spreading out from one side of the site and walked the quarter mile or so through throngs of people. Little golf carts transported the elderly and disabled to and from their cars.

We waited in front of a wooden building with other tourists. Udo insisted on footing the bill and Virginia protested. This place interested him as a craftsperson, he said, a man who worked in an ancient trade and with his hands. People in period dress came out of the building at 2 p.m. and began to call in various languages for tourists to line up with them. The crowd divided up according to language: English, French, Dutch. One other guide spoke in what I surmised was Flemish.

Our little group lined up in front of a wiry man with a hatchet face. He was blond but had the ruddy complexion and tan of a person who worked in the sun. He wore a short-sleeved linen tunic and rough-fibered pants falling unhemmed to the middle of his calves. His leather, pointed-toed shoes wrapped up around his ankles. He spoke in a forceful voice and identified himself as a Dutch mason, who, when he wasn't giving tours, cut the posts and lintels for the doorways and windows of the castle.

Our first stop was a small mockup of the castle built on a concrete slab near the entrance to the grounds. With a pointer, the guide identified the various buildings on the site. He showed us the kinds of blueprints and primary sources the architects and workers used in their trades. He unrolled sturdy canvas prints of church windows featuring tradespeople and explained that craft guilds often sponsored stained-glass representations of their work for churches. Such pictures revealed various aspects of the trade, he said, as well as tools, materials, methods the laborers and artisans used for their work. Other documents included church records and sketchy, unfinished plans that existed from the period. Otherwise, he explained, the construction workers and engineers worked with archaeologists and historians to figure out exactly how the trades went about their business and with what.

My fears of this being a hokey Renaissance Fair put-on proved unfounded. There was no sword fighting, ale sloshing, or turkey-leg chomping. The tour was also not a round of "here is where we do this" and "here is where we do that." Instead, it was a comprehensive rundown of the castle's purpose, the intentions of the business partners behind it, and the trades and their practitioners. We walked over rough ground and through quarry dust. We climbed through holes in the castle walls and up narrow steps into dark hallways and into the great room of the castle itself. Nick even served as willing example at several points in the tour, when the guide demonstrated the measuring methods and ways individual workers leveraged their human strength to move heavy stone with relative ease.

The idea to construct the Chateau de Guedelon came to French entrepreneur Michel Guyot as he renovated the castle he bought in the early 1990s at Saint-Fargeau, thirteen kilometers from Guedelon. In renovating the Saint-Fargeau castle, workers tore away all the renovations and additions of the eighteenth, nineteenth, and twentieth centuries and came closer to the original castle. It dated to the reign of Philippe-Auguste, known as Philip II. During his reign, 1180 to 1223, Philip defeated the Plantagenet dynasty. He fought off Richard the Lionhearted and his successor King John, ultimately kicking the Angevins out of France. He then defeated and banished the Holy Roman Empire and other royals vying for French territories. Philip II also freed towns from church control and checked the power of the nobility, taking all lands of the growing French state under his command and out of the hands of his vassals. In the process, he granted new powers to an emerging bourgeoisie. He transformed France from a weak collection of lordships and small feudal estates into an all-encompassing nation-state and created the monarchy that would rule until the French Revolution.

To protect his new realm, Philip II built castles throughout the country. They all shared similar floorplans and siting. Guyot's castle at Saint-Fargeau was one of these. When he began the experiment at Guedelon, historians and archaeologists knew little about thirteenth-century building methods. As renovation of Saint-Fargeau proceeded, Guyot's architects and workers engaged in reverse engineering to complete their work.

Fired with the determination to discover the ways Philip's nobility constructed their castles, Guyot took on a business partner and envisioned a twenty-five-year project in which tradespeople would work with thirteenth-century technology and tools to build a medieval castle. They hired accomplished masons, carpenters, and blacksmiths and other tradespeople. Along with woodcutters, tile makers, basket makers, rope makers, and teamsters and their animals, workers used existing documents and other primary sources to build the castle. The construction site sat in a rock quarry from which the stone for Saint-Fargeau was cut. Guyot set up the construction site to make profit and educate the public, schoolchildren, and college students in an important aspect of French cultural heritage.

While the site had to make money, Guyot also wanted to keep his experiment academically and scientifically relevant. His board of directors, which directed construction through foremen and their journeymen, included historians, archaeologists, and tradespeople. Workers won all construction materials, save for the iron for door hinges and ornamental aspects of the walls and buildings, from the site itself. This meant the old quarry would again function as such. The wood for the carts and falsework for constructing arches and doorways came from the surrounding forest. The woods also supplied timber for the castle buildings' pitched roofs, stairs, and the scaffolding the workers used for construction.

Guyot and his partner were businessmen. They envisioned the site would sustain itself from tourist revenue and return a profit after a few years. Business went better than they'd ever dreamed. The first year, 1997, more than 30,000 visitors came to see workers quarrying stone and assembling the cuttings for foundations and walls in an empty field. The numbers increased as the castle and its walls grew. By 2014, some 300,000 visitors fueled a project with fifty full-time workers, a like number of interns and volunteers, as well as dye and cloth makers and a farmer who took care of livestock in a living-history village adjacent to the castle grounds. Volunteers signed on for extended periods and underwent rigorous training—you couldn't show up and start carrying stone. Guedelon also served as an outlet for putting at-risk youths to work, completing Guyot's vision for the social good the project should include.

As far as I could tell, we were the only Americans and German in the tourist crowd. Nick took up at the front of our group of Brits. He formed an immediate interest in what our hatchet-faced man was saying and the way he said it. Udo, Virginia, and I hung back in the crowd, letting Nick closely follow the guide throughout the tour. The information and sights took his whole attention for the next hour and forty-five minutes.

I watched Nick in this new environment. Normally shy with strangers, he displayed an ease and comfort I rarely see in him in these types of situations. Usually, he hangs back, observing the environment around him, assessing dangers and opportunities. When addressed, he looks away and answers in such a low voice people often ask him to repeat himself. This time, however, he stayed in front of the crowd. When the guide asked for volunteers for a demonstration, he ran up and acted as the willing victim. His participation meant he was paying attention, something that's not easily divined from the way he listens. He often looks as if he's miles away. In fact, he hears everything, knows all the time where the action is. The demonstrations engaged him. He was having fun.

After the official tour, we wandered. A living-history village fanned out into the forest from the construction site. Actors showed the everyday lives of medieval artisans, serfs, and farmers who would've lived next to the castle. Cloth makers worked their looms. The dye maker took common materials—plants and minerals—and crushed or soaked them into dyes she used to color the workers' clothes. Carpenters and plasterers built houses. Villagers kept donkeys, horses, and pigs in corrals and sties, and cooked some of the animals on-site into stews with vegetables grown nearby. The laundry with its huge kettles and busy attendants washed the workers' clothes. A group of blacksmiths, forge roaring, fashioned hinges and wall ornaments with loud bangs. Lime burners and rock crushers mixed the mortar for the castle walls. The effect was not that of Renaissance fairs back home but of a working village where people went about the serious efforts of medieval life.

We repaired to one of the roofed pavilions where site volunteers and employees sold food. While the living-history actors ate what they cooked in the village, tourists bought modern fare at stalls that sold baguettes sliced and filled with meat and cheese, vegetable plates, soda pop, juices, and ice cream. Visitors filled the tables beneath the roofs and chatted away in several languages. I looked closer at the details of the pavilion as I munched through a baguette with cheese and drank a cold pop. Everything was handmade, from the tables and benches to the supports for the roofs and even the roofs themselves. The refrigerated cases and pop and soft-serve ice cream machines bowed to the modern age.

I gazed at my little group of travelers. It struck me, now three days into France, how little we'd interacted with the local populations of the places we'd been. Guedelon was a tourist destination, separate from the people who lived around it. But the act of building a medieval castle, with the skills and ingredients castle construction demanded interested the tourists and kept them rapt. Visitors asked the workers at the site questions, and no actor or craftsman hesitated to engage the inquisitive. Unlike most tourist attractions, Guedelon didn't feel as if it was engineered to separate participants from their money. There was nothing but food to spend money on. The fare was reasonably priced, about what you'd expect to pay in a common French market.

What mattered most to me was Udo's satisfaction and that Virginia and Nick were enjoying themselves. Nick was able to see the workers' crafts and ask questions. Udo gained a greater understanding of the work involved with construction in the Middle Ages, something that would inform him at his own work. A trip to Guedelon might affect him for years to come as he restored church windows and lived among the ancient buildings in his town and others close to him.

* * *

About forty minutes from Guedelon, we found a campground near Clamecy. The place spread out from a central restaurant and family pavilion, replete with a children's playground and a building with washing machines and showers. Choosing a little spot of grass between large hedges that shielded us from other campers, we began our exercises with the camper van. By this time, we were becoming experts and setup didn't take long. Finally, after a long day, we sat around our camp at our little tables and chairs. The sun had set into our bones and we became sleepy before night had fallen. We were quiet, satisfied the trip, the reason we had come to France—besides, for me, just being in France—was a success.

Virginia says the Guedelon journey was one of the highlights of her life. She's proud of her little trouper and will never forget what a great companion he's become. Nick, for his part, appreciates still, now years later, the experience he had at the castle. It was, he says in his seventeen-year-old way, one of his most formative experiences.

"It sort of changed the way I look at the world," he says.

CHAPTER TWELVE

HOTEL DU COMMERCE

WE STARTED LATE. The clouds hung low and threatened rain. I was tired and grumpy after a restless night. The castle tour and our camping made me happy because everyone else had such a good time. But now I was in a grump. Depression's heavy fatigue lay on me and would, regardless of whatever else was going on. I grumbled through breakfast and humped around alone, not wanting company. I was short with Virginia and Nick. They asked me what was wrong and I harrumphed. I wanted more than anything to climb back into the solace of sleep. I had to get myself straight. Depression, I felt, was my problem and I ought not make it anyone else's, as hard as that is to do sometimes.

Once we were on the road, the weight lifted the farther I drove. I apologized to my mates and they forgave me. I resolved to accept my mental state and do my best to be a good fellow traveler.

The short distance to Clamecy took us again through heavy forest and then up into a series of rolling hills and into Vezelay. The camper van hummed along the roads and left me without much care about where we were and where we were going. My tourist self slumped in the seat, my mind working through the immense variety of sights and sounds of the previous days.

Tourists and pilgrims flooded the narrow streets of Vezelay. We parked at the base of the long ridge the village straddled. Udo wanted to see the eleventh-century Romanesque Basilica of St. Magdalene, which perched atop the mountain. Benedictine monks first inhabited the immense hill in the ninth century and still maintained an abbey at the crest. In the tenth century, crusaders transported the alleged bones of Mary Magdalene to the abbey, and in the eleventh century Pope Stephen IX confirmed the authenticity of the relics. Construction of the massive basilica continued for over two hundred years.

The relics' authenticity came under scrutiny in 1279 when church authorities discovered a shrine to Mary Magdalene in Saint-Maximin-la-Sainte-Baume in Provence. After the revelation, the Vezelay abbey lost support and the basilica began a period of neglect. French Huguenots, followers of John Calvin after the Reformation, sacked the basilica in the late 1500s and the church languished through the 1700s. Rioters in the French Revolution wrought further damage. A restoration began in 1840 under the architect Eugene Viollet-de-Luc and lasted more than twenty years. The present structure is one of the starting points for the pilgrimage of the Camino De Santiago.

Udo, the artist, took particular interest in the basilica's famed stained-glass windows. I had little concern with seeing any of it. I wanted to bury myself. The sky had cleared and the sun grated right into my bones. Traveling at close quarters with others also drove me a special kind of crazy. I didn't want to see them anymore, at least for a while. I wanted to lie back in the van, take in the sounds of the people and the market at the base of the mountain, and nap. Despite Virginia's insistence otherwise, I sent them off on their pilgrimage and lay down in the van.

* * *

Sleep came and went, and after an hour and some, my senses returned. The sky turned overcast, which helped. I shook off the slumber and lit out into the crowds of tourists and pilgrims. I knew if I didn't find my travel mates along the narrow street or in the basilica, they would wait for me until I returned. Or I'd return and wait for them. Or, maybe, due to the way I was acting, they wouldn't wait at all. I wouldn't blame them. It was a chance I'd have to take.

I pushed off up the hill. Houses and shops, filled with tourists, lined both sides of the steep street. I passed them all, challenging myself to make it up to the basilica at a quick clip. I'd often taken to such physicality when I was depressed. It was something I had learned when very young and dealing with the dumps. No matter how severely I was depressed, no matter how impossible movement was, I forced myself out into something physical. Something about bodily strain helped absorb the foul mood. Soon, my heart throbbed in my chest and breaths came quickly. The more I pushed myself, the better I felt. I followed the winding street, sometimes stopping to look at the offerings of the wine shops set in little bays of windows outside. I thought we ought to bring Josef back a good first-cru burgundy he might keep in his cellar and enjoy with guests.

As I neared the mountaintop, the ridge narrowed with no room for houses or buildings on one or the other side of the street. Rock and brick walls kept people from plunging down the bluff sides and into the vineyards below, which draped the long ridge and fell into the valley. Crews of workers walked behind tractors and trucks crawling along the lanes cut into the sides of the mountain through the vineyards.

The Benedictines first planted and produced the famous Vezelay burgundies made from Chardonnay, Pinot Noir, and Melon de Bourgogne in the tenth century, though viticulture in the region existed since before Roman times. Modern winemaking was everywhere evident in the width of the rows of vines that would allow vintners to lower automatic sprayers and implements from their tractors. At the steepest inclines, the rows narrowed, indicating vineyard workers still tended those vines by hand.

All through Burgundy, vineyards sometimes as steep as those of the Mosel amazed me. While the vines rarely rose into heady precipices as on the Mosel, the vineyards climbed to such height and steepness that despite all the modern technology used in vineyard production, the only way to access these vines was on foot. Such hillside plantings implied burgundies produced from those slopes demanded prices that justified the labor-intensive effort. Workers carried manual sprayers on their backs up those grades. They would have to drag soil that eroded downward from weather and the feet of the harvest laborers back toward the top. They would also use lighter tools, such as hoes, shovels, and shears. Workers would have to haul grapes out on their backs, heavy work that demanded strength and stamina.

I paused at one of the walls as the sky was breaking up. Rays of sun skipped across vineyards on distant hills and the agricultural fields of corn and hay on the plains below. The scene reminded me of a Thomas Hart Benton painting, the clumps of trees and winding roads distinct but beautifully surreal. A slight, warm breeze blew up over the wall, bringing the scents of soil and cut grass. I breathed deeply and took a minute, listening to the crowd chatter by behind me, glad to be free of the need to interpret or be interpreted to.

* * *

Looking off the bluff and down the rows of vines took me back to my first day in the vineyard in Trier in November 1985. That morning, I'd walked to the Avelsbach vineyard, a holding of the Trier Cathedral, from my little room. Other vineyard workers stood in the small *Hof* and along the road that wound through the vineyard. The road was a sturdy, thick, and wide concrete strip named Panzerstrasse. It was grape harvest season, and we would cut the grapes from the vines in the steepest part of the vineyard above the road. Shyly, I lined up with the other workers. I could speak very little German and decided to mimic what the other workers did. One of the full-time staff walked up the line of people and handed out shears from a bucket.

Snippers in hand, I filed with the other workers past the vineyard manager, Eduard Meyer, who smiled at me. He gently pulled me from the line and asked if I was the "new American." He could speak no English and I answered in my broken German. He took me aside and showed me how to cut the grapes from the vine and watch out for my fingers. He pulled a piece of paper from his pocket and sliced through it with one side of the shears. He held up his index finger and clamped the shears with a sudden move and drawing the shears away from his hand quickly. "*Sehen Sie? Pop. Finger weg.*"

For the next two weeks, I climbed that hill, harvesting grapes into a plastic bucket and then dumping them into the large tuns the full-timers carried on their backs and emptied into a trailer on the Panzerstrasse. We started in the dark dewy mornings when it was cold and the sun was rising. Fog filled the Avelertal above the small creek, the Avelsbach. The vines emerged from the mist below and disappeared above, making it seem as if the hill had no beginning or end. I worked up the shale slope until I reached the end of a row, and then stumbled down to start at the bottom again. At first, I struggled. My liquor warehouse job, hard as it was, hadn't prepared me for the backbreaking work of the grape harvest. Then, I'd spent a month and a half riding on trains. The backpack helped keep my back and arms in some kind of shape. But in those first days of the harvest, I often found myself sweating in the cold mornings and sopped on sunny afternoons. My legs shook and heart raced and I fought to catch my breath.

I was among the slowest workers. Clipping bunches of grapes from vines took skill and I sliced my fingertips with the shears. After the first day, I taped my fingers to protect them from my bumbling. Over time, I became better at the job. I sheared my fingers less often. I gained the heart and leg strength to work the slopes. I even sometimes donned the large tuns and shuttled grapes from the other workers to the trailers below.

That first day I was the source of fun for the other workers. Late in the morning, I heard a volley of gunfire very close to us. I dropped to the ground under the vines and covered my head. My fellow workers laughed. I looked up at their smiling faces and thought I was the butt of some joke. They helped me up from slate and leaves. "*Sie haben auf uns scheißen*," I said, which roused another round of laughter, this one heartier than the first. An English woman named Carmel, who would later become a good friend, took me aside and told me that I'd said in very bad German, "They shit on us." I was mortified, as I'd been uncertain and self-conscious to begin with. I explained to her I meant to say, "They're shooting at us." She laughed and told me the German and French armies did joint training exercises and arms testing, as well as tank maneuvers at the top of the hill. Thus, she said, "Panzerstrasse. Get it? A street for tanks—panzers, you know. Real tanks."

* * *

With memories of terror and beauty of my first days in the vineyard in my head, I breathed deeply and took in the vista at Vezelay as best I could. This was something I didn't want to forget. I stepped away from the wall and slipped back into the river of people. They walked in orderly fashion—up on one side, down on the other—but for groups whirling off now and then like eddies in a stream. I pushed past tourists of all nationalities, excusing myself randomly in English, German, French, and Italian (*entschuldigen, excusez-moi, mi scusi*). I kept my eye out for my fellow travelers but didn't spy them in the great masses moving up and down the hill.

I reached the plateau, still with no sight of Udo, Virginia, and Nick. A peaceful copse of trees stood around the back of the church and I spent a few minutes strolling around the edge for wider views of the vineyards and farmland below. Coming around to the front of the basilica, I stepped up to the tympanum and gazed for a long time at the intricate carvings around a seated figure of Jesus with his hands uplifted. I tried to interpret the biblical symbols in the reliefs but saw confusions of sinners and saints. Visitors jammed the entrance to the basilica, clambering, their collective voices loud. Once inside, the cacophony disappeared in whispers and the electronic clicks of cameras and cell phones taking pictures. The church's sheer immensity took my breath away and made me feel as if I'd entered a space bigger than the one outside. The largest of its kind in France, the basilica was just ten meters shorter than the great Notre Dame cathedral in Paris. The sun came and went. Unearthly light filtered in from the clerestory stained-glass windows above the nave. Speakers hidden behind the massive marble pillars broadcast chants and sacred music.

Nick wandered along one side of the nave between the great pillars supporting the central atrium above. I caught up to him.

"How about this, Dad?" he said. "We don't have many of these churches in Kansas City."

"We don't have any in Kansas City," I said. He stroked the pillars. They were cool to the touch.

"I'm going to stand against this for a minute," he said. "It's hot and that hill really took it out of Mom. She's over there." Virginia and Udo were sitting in the wooden chairs at the back of the nave. When Nick had enough standing still against the pillar, he and I joined them, admiring in silence the great construction around us. Udo stood and walked about the church taking pictures with his expensive camera. Virginia and I sat with Nick until Udo made his rounds. Quietly, we retreated to the entrance and entered the crowd outside.

We moved slowly down the hill, poking our heads into shops along the way. Some seemed reputable businesses, restaurants and wine shops. Invariably, cheap-trinket merchants sold everything from tiny mock-ups of Mary Magdalene's crypt to snow globes with the basilica in their centers. I stopped at what I thought was the best wine shop I'd seen on the hill—large selection, good prices—and searched among the stacked cases and stands, remembering the tastes of the burgundies, until I found a bottle suitable for Josef. We made our way back to the car.

* * *

Udo next wanted to see the famous Abbaye de Fontenay. We drove through the larger towns of Avallon and Montbard, in and out of light rain. The sky soon broke up and let the afternoon sun do its work on the shimmering landscape. The abbey lay off the beaten path in a sublime grassy valley Thomas Moran might have painted. The vale stretched out from a creek running through the center of the abbey grounds. We arrived too late, however, and the gates were locked. We poked around the clear-water creek and the adjoining, manicured grounds. The late-afternoon sun fell into the end of the valley between the forests on either side. The mist that rose after a good rain gave the valley a stately, dreamlike air. All around us lay the quiet I'm sure the abbey's pilgrims sought.

We motored off through the last of Burgundy into Champagne. At first, I expected to be surrounded by vineyards, the great crus of Champagne looming large in my mind. Instead, we entered a plain of rolling hills and farm fields that bounded to the horizon. It reminded me again of Kansas, where factory farms and large holdings cover the land. An occasional farmhouse and farm operation—machinery, tractors, and silos—poked up in the rolling hills. The scene was no less beautiful than the Great Plains on a clear summer evening. The countryside didn't possess the grandeur of mountains or the eerie depths of a hardwood forest, but it retained a nuanced, even sublime loveliness all the same. The sun, low in the sky, lengthened shadows and gave the plains another dimension appealing to the Midwesterner in me. I remembered Van Gogh paintings of wheat fields and sunflowers.

The Seine Valley opened between hills that grew up alongside the road. Now, the great vineyards came into sight and climbed up from the river into steep heights beyond. On a knuckle of a hill above the river, vines grew around the base of the Virgin of the Vineyards, a tall marble statue that watched over the vineyards and valley. The hills rose to offer the fruit of people's labor to the sun in ways that strike an American as aged and of yesteryear. I was sure a vintner in Champagne was as tech-oriented and modern as any American farmer, with a savvy eye to the quality and price of their products, as well as to markets and new opportunities. But Virginia and I had trained our eyes and brains in a lifetime of cultural and social impressions of foreignness and stereotypes. We saw things not as they were, for vineyards in Champagne were ordinary to the people who live there, but as lusciously strange and exotic.

We saw much of the last few days as different from the life we led in Kansas City. We couldn't help but see cultural practices, infrastructure, and even household items as superior to their American counterparts. I liked, for instance, the size of things in Europe. Americans want more, or, at least, this American does. I seek out such portions, amounts of products, and time that sate my wants rather than satisfy my needs—food, drink, coffee, sleep, exercise—I crave in overabundance. I get some and want more. I fear not getting enough, so I overindulge. When we bought soda pops at European groceries or shops, they didn't flow from fountains into sixty-four-ounce plastic monstrosities but were packaged in small cans. I wanted to get to a point where what I desired was practical in size and price, reasonable rather than gluttonous. This European sensibleness in many things—appliances, cars, roads, houses—I think I liked most of all.

* * *

Bar-sur-Seine, a town of about three thousand, fluttered out along the riverbank. On the opposite side of the river soared the great vineyards I'd once imagined covered the whole of Champagne. We'd decided to stay one night of our trip in a French hotel and eat at least one example of typical French cuisine. After our fare of cheeses, spaghetti, salads, and sausages, the idea of a dinner in a fine restaurant enticed our minds and stomachs. We searched the narrow streets off the throughway for a suitable hotel, something small and local. We settled on the Hotel du Commerce, which was built into a row of houses all adjoining one another in a solid façade running down one side of the street.

Every French town has a Hotel du Commerce, or so it seems. None of them, as far as I could tell, belonged to a chain or franchise operation. This Hotel du Commerce was no exception. We parked at the public parking lot in the town square. Udo, with typical shyness, let me lead the way. I walked into the homey little bar and restaurant and looked for someone who could help us. A woman, about thirty-five years old, appeared behind the bar and, I supposed, asked in French what we would like. This was the break Udo was waiting for. He talked to her a while. I asked him to ask her if we could see a room before we rented one for the night. If the Hotel du Commerce didn't fit our ideas of good, comfortable accommodations, we would move on to the next hotel. She gave us keys to two upstairs rooms and the security code to the side entrance. She said if her place wasn't to our liking, we should leave the keys on the bar when we moved on. She left to tend to other business.

Udo and I walked up into a warren of rooms along a narrow hallway on the second story above the bar. When we looked the rooms over—a suite for Virginia, Nick, and me, and a separate room for Udo—we were pleasantly surprised. At the Hotel du Commerce, there was enough. The rooms were Spartan but civilized and clean. They were not the sprawling size of the modern American motel room hanging with amenities, but human in size and shape. The windows opened to an alley, where we could hear the town. The hotel itself was quiet, which made the sounds outside all the louder and more revealing. In the room we chose for Virginia, Nick, and me, Udo and I stood still and wordless for a minute. We could hear a motorbike drive down the street in front of the hotel. The clicks and squishes of walkers' shoes came up through the alley. A couple of kids played basketball in a courtyard behind one of the houses on the block.

Back at the bar, the woman asked if things were in order and we said *oui, merci*. Well, then, she said, enjoy the evening. If we wanted dinner, she'd put it on the bill, and we could pay in the morning.

There was no taking of credit cards or signing of registers. She didn't fill in any forms or give us any receipts. She wished us a good stay. Udo and I looked at each other quizzically. Was that it? The hotel, at first blush, was one of the most agreeable places I'd ever been.

And it stayed that way. After we brought up our bags, we took time to clean up and lay down in the beds. Again, these were not giant, king-sized spreads but comfortable and cozy. I listened for a long time to the sounds of the town as they wafted through the window. Virginia took a few moments to close her eyes. Nick busied himself in the next room turning lights on and off, looking through the desk drawers.

We met Udo downstairs for dinner. The restaurant held seven tables. The wood-paneled and stucco walls made the place intimate without being imposing or overly cute. Historic maps and old photographs of Bar-sur-Seine hung on the walls. Heavy wooden beams framed the space above us. Other customers, mostly couples, sat underneath sconces set into the walls. These and a small chandelier lit the interior with warm, yellow light. Frosted windows separated the customers from the walk outside. The woman we spoke to in the bar was also the hotel chef. The waiter, a young woman, went from table to table in the small restaurant, whispering to customers, as if the atmosphere of the place depended on her silence.

"What I like about French eating is the time it takes to get through a dinner," Udo said.

"I just like the idea of French food," Virginia said. "Courses and salads. Sorbet. Entrees. But I've never eaten French food in France."

"It's wonderful," Udo said.

"Do you remember when Ivo took us to Metz to eat real French cuisine?" I asked Udo.

"Indeed," he said, turning to Virginia. "The occasion, I believe, was Patrick's coming departure from Trier. We wanted to do something special for him. We drove from Trier through Luxembourg City and down into the Lorraine to Metz."

"The five of us crammed into Ivo's Renault R4, a tin can of a car so small the gear shifter was in the dash," I said. "Evening fell as we weaved through the hills and small villages along secondary roads with hardly any traffic on them."

"How big is Metz?" Virginia asked.

"It's about the size of Trier," Udo said.

"Then, it's pretty big," she said.

"Trier's not so big as you might think," he said. "But Metz has nearly as much to offer. We entered the town and shortly found the center, a series of old islands where the Seille flows into the Mosel. We parked near the cathedral. It's magnificent, a large church with stained-glass windows rising six stories to the roof."

"I remember, we spilled out of the car," I said. "We were happy to stretch our legs after an hour and a half in that little car and bumbled over to a restaurant Ivo knew."

"Of course," she said. "Ivo knows just about everything, doesn't he?"

"Well, he doesn't know everything," Udo said with a smile. "But he knows more than me. He gets around with his work in churches, you know, and takes in as much local culture as he can when he's in someplace new. He has that kind of confidence, you know. He just takes off and does what pleases him."

While the food culture of Alsace-Lorraine has strong German influences, I explained, Ivo chose a restaurant that served strictly French cuisine. "I wanted a salad for my entrée, something big and green. Nearly a year of fruit, cheese, bread, and sausages had me hankering for a change. The chef made me a heap of fresh greens covered in walnut oil and cracked pepper. He cut new potato slices and ringed the plate with them. Each slice was topped with a perfect cube of sharp blue cheese."

"The place was atmospheric with candlelight," Udo said. "Colorful liquor bottles behind the bar had lights beneath them."

"We sat in that restaurant and ate for almost two hours and talked and talked," I said. "The food was really a centerpiece of discussion. It seemed like we ate so much. But we walked away full but not stuffed. It was a revelation."

I told them how, in 1993, when Ivo lived in Freiburg, I'd finished my grad work at the University of Wyoming and wanted to see my friends after six long years. I was on a balanced plateau after months of manic and depressive peaks and dips. I took the train from Koblenz to Freiburg over Frankfurt, Heidelberg, and Mannheim, the train stations like pictures on a wall in my mind. When I arrived at Freiburg, Ivo waited for me on the platform. It was a good meeting. I cried on seeing my old friend again.

Over the next few days, Ivo showed me around Freiburg. I'd already spent time in the town in little bits between trains years before. He wowed me with a trip to the cathedral, where he explained the odd roundish marks carved on the sides of the building as the amount of bread a mark would buy in a particular year. The priests and abbots, as trusted mediators between buyers and sellers, determined the size of the loaf. Since harvests varied in amounts and quality, so the size of a loaf would change. The money, the matter of exchange, remained constant. I had difficulty wrapping my head around it. As an American who saw prices change seemingly by whim, I thought the loaf would remain the same and the price change. But this was medieval Europe. This history impressed me although I'd lived in Trier, a city ten times older than my own country.

One afternoon, Ivo took me into France for another real French meal. The day lay on us like a blanket, warm and humid under the overcast sky. We drove across the wide Rhein Valley and up into the hills on the French side. Colmar climbed up out of the river valley to a flat plain above. The town resembled my childhood imaginings of a European town with churches and houses of medieval construction behind the remnants of a protective wall.

Ivo and I wandered the town between timber-and-plaster, three- and four-story houses. He took me to museums and showed me churches he knew. Pointing out the symbols on the altars and telling the stories the windows portrayed, he identified the patrons and craft guilds who sponsored the structures. When we weren't in churches and museums, we meandered dark alleys and open plazas. The people in the shops were friendly and accommodating without being pushy.

We ate lunch at a stand-up bistro and moved on through the old town and down toward the river Lauch to the old fishmongers' quarter called "*la Petite Venise*," Little Venice. The Lauch was hardly more than a large creek. Fat and slow, it coursed through a canal with houses and shops standing atop walls that formed the river's banks. We walked easily and slowly, talking about Ivo's studies and what had happened to me in the intervening years. I told him about my history with drinking and how my life came to a complete dead end. I was only sober for three years and still making my way but going over the past with my old friend helped bring some perspective to what I'd experienced.

When the time came, we ensconced ourselves in a little restaurant called La Petit Gourmand. The place sat eighteen or twenty people at six tables. It was dark inside, the light coming mostly through the front door and from candles on the tables. The kitchen stood behind a couple of French doors off the main room. The restaurant belonged to a married couple. He took orders and served tables; she worked the kitchen. They limited the menu to two entrées. I ordered pork tenderloin medallions in a blueberry-onion sauce. Ivo opted for the trout. The meal started with a small salad. A ball of sorbet on a grape leaf followed and then bread and cheese, and again sorbet. The entrée came. The chef made the display of food a thing of beauty—spare on the plate but toothsome and enough following the previous courses. After the entrée came another small sorbet on a grape leaf. The waiter, now known to us as Frank, set down the dessert of fresh fruit in heavy cream.

In three hours, we'd eaten a great deal but didn't feel the heaviness that often accompanies an American restaurant entrée. Everything was enough. The complexity of the flavors and the dishes served up a feast for eyes, nose, and mouth. The atmosphere of that tiny restaurant, where people talked a lot but spoke in low voices, was soothing.

* * *

The Hotel du Commerce served up food very much like that I'd had in Colmar twenty-some years before. The woman who greeted us at the bar wandered from table to table, checking to make sure her presentations made it to the guests. She chatted with familiar customers and checked with us to see how it was going. Each of us ordered a different entrée, each to their own, with Nick eating chicken nuggets and French fries. The meal came in flights, with a salad first, bread and cheese, and then the entrées. We spent almost two and a half hours over dinner, going over what we'd seen and done the previous days. Nick chattered away, seemingly forgetting his staid shyness. We walked away sated. I was starting to prefer enough to more.

Udo and Virginia wanted to walk through the town. Normally, I wouldn't pass up the opportunity to stroll any new place as night fell. It was that time of day when the magic of a small town reveals itself. People come home from work and settle into their free time. Some, like the people we saw at the restaurant, use their leisure for social pursuits. Most go home and spend time alone or with family. TVs come on and fill houses with blue flickering light. With streets empty and traffic at a lull, I can get a sense of a place. What kinds of businesses dominate the town? What do people do in their free time?

I would've invited the chance to walk along the Seine on the town's riverfront. But heaviness lay on my shoulders and I wanted time alone. The day's events, the drive, and the closeness of my companions overtaxed me. I've found in dealing with depression that a break from people at close range allowed me to get my thoughts together and my head on straight. Sending my travel companions off, I sat back at the writing table in our room at the Hotel du Commerce. The sounds of people walking down the main street filtered through the alley window. A hush fell on the town, making the sounds of a lone motorcyclist or pedestrian even more pronounced. I took up my pen and scribbled thoughts and events from the previous days. I wrote with urgency, not knowing when my travel mates would return. I worked out the myriad feelings the French countryside produced in me. I recalled our camping adventures and detailed with delight the people and atmosphere of the Hotel du Commerce.

This journal and many previous ones gave me the solace of working alone. In them, I place myself in context, gather disconnected thoughts and impressions, and work out the complex emotions of everyday living. I go through those journals now, some of which helped me write this text. Many entries are just diary accounts of the day. Others are impressions, contemplations. But the journals always remind me of who I was and what I was thinking. In the Hotel du Commerce that evening, I was sated in more than stomach. The French countryside presented enough of an alien view of the world to make the travel delicious and exciting. The landscapes and towns captured bits of stereotypes of European life I'd learned about in school, but then undid those stereotypes. Certainly, the French have a common culture, but it was as complex as my own. No longer would I think of France in terms of scenes from movies.

It turned out I had all the time I needed. My fellow travelers took in the breadth of Bar-sur-Seine. They ambled along the riverfront and down through the back alleys and streets off the main drag.

I envy them today. I missed something by staying in that night. But I am satisfied I sat with my journal. I look back and feel the atmosphere and newness of the territory. Writing in the journal, reflecting on what we'd done and seen, did more than steel me for another day in the camper van. It prepared me for more time in the cramped world of my workaday life.

CHAPTER THIRTEEN

THE WAFFLE

WE GAVE UP our atmospheric rooms at the Hotel du Commerce with reluctance and started on the road toward Koblenz and Ivo's house. As I drove, I felt a heavy kind of melancholy. We still had two days and another night of camping in front of us. But our time with Udo was growing short. School and work limited the Dobsons' stay in Europe. That was the sad thing about travel, particularly with people I love and miss and can't really do without. Journeys can never last. Of time, there's never enough.

* * *

Beyond the hills of Champagne, the landscape opened up again into rolling plains blanketed with wheat and corn to the horizon. Distance between villages grew and then they disappeared altogether. We drove many miles of farm fields and woods. Isolated farmhouses dotted the plains. Here and there a bank of grain elevators punctured the sky. After a long while, the landscape began to break as we approached Troyes. Hills and valleys of Aube became more picturesque, with little villages beneath hilltop castles and churches.

We stopped in Troyes to tour the town's cathedral and the Eglise de la Sainte-Madeleine, two twelfth- and thirteenth-century churches a few blocks from each other. Both were French national monuments, and we could see why. The structures' sheer sizes impressed us, each spreading over a city block. Stained-glass windows covered the walls and the clerestories above the naves. Sunlight through the glass threw particolored sheens over pillars and floors worn smooth by centuries of supplicants.

Despite the number of tourists, a hush fell on the interiors that reminded me of nicking solitary minutes in the churches of my past. My childhood church, Christ the King, was built in the 1950s, a modernist structure of brick and glass. The moments I stole alone in the space were liberating. Beyond the prying eyes of parents and nuns and priests, I felt free to run the aisles. I made noises that echoed up through the nave. I yelped and slammed kneelers to the floor. Later, as a Boy Scout, I frequently snuck out of our meetings in the basement to sit blissfully drunk in the middle of the empty church. The space at night took on an eerie air, frightening and spooky.

As a grown-up, I've found peace in big Catholic churches, the times I've visited them since I quit going to mass when I was nineteen. After that, I only ever went into churches—except for weddings and funerals and a few concerts—when there were few or no people in them. Their walls gave me respite from the world swirling outside. When I lived in Trier, I sometimes dodged into the cathedral after working in the cellars. Open at any time of day, the great church gave me moments to collect my thoughts and contemplate the course of my work and life. In melancholy moments, the quiet and reverence the space commanded gave me escape from the worst of depressive episodes, the solitude a balm for my tortured insides. When suffering mania, sitting in the church shaved off the ragged edges of my elevations and allowed me periods of calm before I hit the streets again for maniacal, hours-long hikes through the city and up through the vineyards. Sometimes the quiet disturbed me, and I fled the church as if I didn't want to take an inward look for fear of what I might find. But I always went back.

Here in Troyes with Virginia, Nick, and Udo, I found solace from the inner foulness that haunted me. We sat alone among the wooden chairs. Masses of tourists made rounds of the church, whispering, taking pictures. Our presence made me wonder about the parishioners who regularly attended mass here. What did they make of the tourists and the picture taking? While the spaces communicated otherworldly endeavor, the tourists' activities, like ours, seemed on some level profane and ephemeral, like stains on the dignity of the structure and its purpose. Still, I was grateful to sit in the quiet beauty.

Elaborate stained-glass windows kept Udo and his camera at work. While he wandered the church, Nick, Virginia, and I watched the tourists and clergy in the cavernous cathedral. As I sat there next to a silent Virginia and a still Nick (a state he almost never entered except when reading), I remembered a *Pilgerfahrt* (pilgrimage) I'd made with a trainload of Germans when I was an intern at the winery in Trier. It reminded me not all my adult experiences in churches had been positive.

* * *

Günther was a career employee at the winery. He was shorter than me. His brown eyes sparkled. He smiled often and gestured with baseball-mitt hands when he talked. Early in April 1986, he surprised me and my English friend, Carmel, with an invitation to accompany him on a pilgrimage to Rome. He'd worked for the company for decades as a driver and errand man. He possessed the mental capacity and bearing of a teenager, though he was well into his forties. I always liked him. He was kind to me and gentle with others, though fellow winery employees, men mostly, often made sport of him. We were standing in the bottling hall and he said something about a pilgrimage to Rome aboard a chartered train. I hardly ever understood a word he said, his voice soft and speech heavily dialectical. I always had to ask him to repeat himself and I'd bend in to listen. I asked him to slow down. He took a deep breath, lowered his head, and in a halting voice said I'd be his roommate on the trip if I wanted to go. The journey would take me places I wouldn't otherwise have had the opportunity to visit.

I demurred and told him I'd never raise the money for such an adventure. I also said that as a nonbeliever I'd be out of place. Carmel came up to us to discuss the trip, which she had spoken to Günther about earlier in the day. He told us he'd already paid the bill and was waiting for our assent. In fact, he said, he wanted us to say yes so he could avoid the difficulties of getting his money back. When I asked him why he made such a generous offer, he said he'd taken to me and Carmel. We had been kind to him, and he wanted us to accompany him.

It was early May when we boarded the train with five hundred religious tourists headed for Rome. I loved being on a train again. This time, I didn't have to worry about changing lines or sleeping in stations, as we had nightly accommodations in hotels along the way. This train traveled on its own schedule through Switzerland to Rome and back. Plus, all the people on the train seemed to know each other. I was introduced around and soon found myself at home—except for the not-being-a-believer part. But if it didn't come up, I wasn't going to make it an issue.

Our first day, we traveled the length of the Rhein to Basel and then though the Swiss Alps. The sun was out full. As the train wound higher up mountainsides, we could see peak upon snowy peak rising to the horizon. We stopped that night at Stresa on Lago Maggiore in the Italian Piedmont. Our hotel presented luxurious and extravagant accommodations to me. The commodious suite with an ornate coffee table and armchairs contrasted sharply with what I'd lived with the better part of the year in my Spartan room at the top of the winemaker apprentice school and in my friends' apartment in the Saarstrasse. Günther and I each had a king-size bed with piles of pillows and lush featherbeds. After testing the mattress and ditching my bag, I filched two bottles of Amarone (a rich wine made from partially dried grapes) from the hotel lobby and shoved them in my jacket. I walked down to the lake cove, where lights from the bars and casinos shimmered on the black water.

The foreignness of the place and the depth and quiet of the night captivated me. I could hardly believe my luck. Here I found myself, a twenty-three-year-old kid from a working-class background, living and traveling in Europe. I was sitting on the shore of a fabled lake with two bottles of wine, a pack of cigarettes, and a place to stay for the night. I watched patrons filter out of the bars and cafés as they closed one by one. Lights reflected off the lake and contrasted with the deep of night beyond the village and out on the water. When the last of the bars closed and turned off its lights, I puffed one more cigarette. Smoke hung in balloons above my head in the still night. I watched bar employees sit down to an after-work drink at the sidewalk tables in front of the last café open. When I'd drained the bottles, I tottered back off to the hotel.

The next ten days rushed by, helped in my part by a heightening mania that kept me on my toes. I hardly slept and drank a great deal, as wine flowed like water on that journey. We took in pilgrimage sites and old churches in Turin, Genoa, Pisa, Rome, and Assisi. We filed past saints' relics (though viewing pieces of bones struck me as ghoulish). We stayed in spacious hotels and bed-and-breakfasts, one above Assisi in an olive grove. The view from our balcony there took in a great swath of the rural Umbria, with its rolling hills and variegated fields and vineyards. I was, of course, enraptured by it all.

At each successive church tour, however, I became more agitated and self-conscious about my tourist status. I wondered how the locals coped with interlopers infesting their holy sites and daily lives. When we were in Rome, our loud and chatty Germans—self-righteous, demanding, complaining, full of expectations that locals would cater to them—walked into a basilica, the San Pietro in Vincoli, to see the resting place of Nikolaus of Kues, the Renaissance humanist philosopher who became the vicar general of the Papal States in 1459. The village of Kues, a part of the modern vineyard town of Bernkastel-Kues, interested my German companions. They connected Nikolaus with the Mosel, the once-powerful Diocese of Trier, the Trierer Cathedral, and then to their own lives. Not one, I think, understood Nikolaus's influence on German daily life. The polymath, whom I'd read about over a lonely weekend in Trier, influenced the German university system and its emphasis on the liberal arts. He would encourage the adoption of liberal arts university systems in Europe, which the United States emulated.

This was unimportant to my fellow pilgrims, who enjoyed being at the burial site of one of their own. The Germans streamed into the church in the middle of a wedding. The priest and the couple stood at the ancient altar. A small group of family and other well-wishers sat in pews in the dark. All around them our Germans yakked and shot pictures. A few, oblivious to the importance of the ceremony, sidled up to the priest and took pictures of him and the couple as they recited vows. I cringed with embarrassment. Anger took hold. I steamed around a while in the back of the church. Before I blew up at the insensitive pilgrims, I rushed off without telling anyone and spent the rest of the day into evening marching across the city to our hotel.

On the way back from Rome, the train stopped in a tiny Swiss town right out of Herman Hesse's novel *Peter Camenzind*. The village inhabited a tiny spit of land along Lake Lucerne that backed up to the sharp inclines of the Alps. The springs of mania were on me, and in that time, I had no control or self-awareness of manic depression and haphazardly went through familiar behavior patterns tested over much of my adolescent and adult life. In other words, I'd learned by trial-and-error behavior what caused the least amount of trouble (personal, social, and legal) without really realizing what I was doing or why. I drank and exercised more. I isolated myself and fumbled around and slept at odd hours. Instead of breaking public and private property, I took to destroying disposable things if I had something around. I tore aluminum cans into tiny bits. I broke some mechanical device I found in a trash can. I shredded plastic bottles with my pocketknife.

By the time we arrived in the Swiss town, I'd had enough of the pilgrims and was growing claustrophobic and agitated at the press of their presence. Instead of touring churches that day, I told Günther I wasn't feeling good and sent him off with the other religious tourists. I sat that morning in the hotel room and knifed a shirt I didn't like much anyway into tiny shreds. Then, feeling cooped up, I walked from one end of the town to the other and back. Finding time on my hands and my mood ebullient, I struck out on a wooded path behind the village that wound to the jagged heights above. It rained on and off, and I hiked through clouds hanging on the side of the mountain like fluttering sheets. The trail led me through miles of wet, piney woods and alpine pastures, where, when the sun came out and the sky cleared, I could see the sky-blue Lake Geneva stretched out before me, mountains lining its shores. I screamed and yawped, and screamed some more, the cries relieving the tension in my chest and neck. The path ducked back into the dark woods and made its way up into rocky inclines to the edge of a waterfall. There, a memorial stood to hikers who'd died crossing the falls. I was stunned for a moment and considered my position. The falls and the woods beyond were sublime.

I tiptoed my way across the cataract on rocks sticking above the surface of the stream. On the other side, I continued up until the trail gave out in a pasture where sheep grazed with bells around their necks. I stood and listened to the uneven clanking and wind in the pines and the water falling far behind me. I raced back to the town as night fell. When people asked where I was that day, I told them I needed some time alone and spent the day up on the mountain. Secretly, I felt good about not interfering in other people's weddings. Our compatriots already thought I was an odd bird and lifted their eyebrows and said, "Well, then." When Günther and Carmel asked if I was all right, I made up a story of sleeping a little longer and then feeling better before taking off on my hike. I then commenced drinking the banquet's generous wine offerings.

* * *

Sitting in the Troyes cathedral now, I wondered how the cathedral's congregation—which should be large, considering the size of the church and its maintenance—dealt with tourists. Did they close the church to all but congregants on Sundays? What of weddings and funerals? How do you balance the needs of parishioners with the desires of others in what is a tourist attraction, national monument, and pilgrimage site? And there I sat, part of what I dubbed the "tourist problem."

When Udo had finished and we had enough of the beautiful churches, we wandered the oldest section of Troyes. The town had escaped destruction in most of the many wars that had stormed over the European continent over the last several hundred years—particularly the First and Second World Wars. Buildings dating to the Middle Ages towered over the town square and through the residential districts on the banks of the Seine. Apartments reached five and six stories in the timber-and-plaster buildings. Shops of all kinds inhabited the street-level floors.

Though I was feeling low, rambling through the town and down by the river with Udo, Virginia, and Nick diverted me from my depression and the brooding thoughts it produced. Exotic and ordinary offerings in shop windows distracted me. Tourists and townspeople thronged the town square and crossed the Seine on ornate bridges. The sun shone full and the day was warm. We dawdled in the center of town, eating crepes at a small shop off the pedestrian plaza.

I was fortunate Udo spoke decent English. That day, depression made it difficult to keep coherent strains of thought in my head. I had a difficult time with German. All morning, my language ability came and went. Udo would often say what he wanted in English and turn to me to communicate more complex ideas and very specific information. Sometimes, I could hardly express a thought. Other times, German flowed in fluent streams. The worst came in the late afternoon when I could neither speak the language well nor translate at all. Virginia thought there was something wrong. I told her the languages tangled together in my head. My abilities, I assured her, would soon return. In the moment, though, it felt like I would never speak a lick of German again.

As we sped away from Troyes, we came closer to the area of the Western Front in both the First and Second World Wars. Isolated monuments several meters high glorifying soldiers and military leaders appeared on the side of the road. Many suffered the ailments of age, corroding edifices reminding me of Ozymandias, whose broken monument to himself looked out over the great, empty desert. French patriots maintained some of the statues and memorials in pristine condition. Metal engraved panels stuck upright on poles, some in the middle of nowhere, others standing in trimmed parks. We passed through Lorraine, a vast rural area around the towns of Metz and Nancy. Our route took us into Ardennes through Vouziers and Sedan. We crossed the Dutch frontier and drove into a region of smaller farms more diverse than those we'd passed through in France.

We found our campground as we had in previous days—by bumbling into one. As we neared Neufchateau, Belgium, early evening sun threw long shadows down from the hills and steep road cuts. We followed "camping" signs to dead ends and fields. We traveled narrow two-lane roads into the hills around the outside of town until we came upon a lone farmhouse with a restaurant in it beneath heavily wooded and trimmed cemeteries of identical crosses and stars of David. We stopped to ask about where we might find a campground and saw one spread out behind the house. What luck, Udo and I thought, and clapped each other on the back.

The evening lay soft, cool, and humid on our little campground. Full mature trees towered above and low hedges separated the camping spots from one another. After dinner, we lined the stools up against the back of the camper van and leaned against it. The activities of a campground—the voices, the sounds of cooking and cleaning—accentuated the hush that fell with the evening. Children played in the pond behind our campsite. Strings of Japanese lanterns hung on the house and down the road along a long trellis supporting a massive grapevine. Nick unfolded a red paper lantern with Chinese characters Marlies had given him. He lit the candle and hung the lantern in a bush at the end of our campsite. As night advanced, we could see the stars through the oaks and elms. Nick played in the campground playground until it was too dark to see.

Udo and I sat in our chairs long after Nick and Virginia had climbed the ladder and gone to sleep. The moon hung in the trees and the stars shined brightly above. Low voices of other campers rolled through the mist settling in over the camp as night advanced. The lantern Nick hung on the bush at the end of our campsite sputtered and went dark.

Since it was our last night camping, Udo and I took an inventory of the previous days. We'd done and seen a lot but hadn't overexerted ourselves. We'd driven almost 1,200 kilometers (about 745 miles) in five days. That's not a lot in American terms, Udo said. "We drove over 900 miles from Kansas City through Great Sand Dunes to Mesa Verde in less than two days." We agreed the French two-lane made the distance seem much longer, somehow. The curves and the way we had to slow down through the many villages we traveled through made our going leisurelier. Ancient French villages gave the road an ambience decaying American small towns cannot lend to their byways. We'd taken frequent breaks to see things and stopped each day in enough time to enjoy the early evening, make dinner, and then sit in our campsites or in the hotel without hurrying.

Udo said he wanted more time. I did, too.

"When I'd canoed the Missouri," I said, "I so wanted to get home to see Sydney. But I didn't want to go home. It meant routines and living in the city. Life on the river was too easy. I camped where I wanted and did what I wanted. There was no time clock or anyone telling me what to do. I wished the river were longer, that, somehow, it'd gain more miles before it reached Kansas City."

"I have that confused feeling now," Udo said. "I wonder if Belgium can somehow grow larger for us, put more distance between us and Ivo's house in Koblenz."

When Udo and I finally gave up the day, we both collapsed in our bunks. I listened to Virginia and Nick, their sleeping sounds close against the canvas of the tent. Underneath, Udo stirred and bumped for a few minutes, and then everything fell still. The silence outside our cocoon closed in. I slept like a worn-out hound.

* * *

To get up from beneath the depressive weight the next morning, I walked up onto the road we'd come in on before the others woke. The countryside beyond the hills spread out across farmland and fields. I spent melancholy moments in one of the roadside cemeteries where rows of crosses sat in small paddocks under tall trees.

We drove through hilly country to Bastogne. A Sherman tank sat in the center of town with its muzzle pointed toward Germany. The main street meandered with heavy traffic between two- and three-story timber-and-plaster buildings filled with shops, restaurants, and bars. We found ourselves a parking spot and wandered slowly through the people toward the tank. An armor-piercing shell had punctured an almost perfectly round hole in its side. It looked to me the men inside all died in that attack—four universes extinguished.

* * *

I'd been here in 1993 with Paul Legill, the tall and powerfully built Luxembourger with whom I'd gone to school at Geisenheim. When I came back to Europe that summer, he and his girlfriend, soon wife,

Violette, took me on a long drive up from Schengen at the German/French/Luxembourgish frontier through the length of their tiny country into Holland and back down through Belgium. We drank coffee and ate waffles at a sprawling restaurant across the street from the tank.

Paul, Violette, and I continued after our coffee and waffles and drove along the Luxembourg border to Arlon. We entered Luxembourg again at Differdange. The day grew cloudy and threatened rain. It made the car and our conversation dearer, cozier. As the day closed in around us and the countryside changed on the dimness of the evening, we slowed down. We puttered on that two-lane through the forest and hills and ravines. The occasional car took us by surprise, and we pulled into turnouts in the road to have the time together outside to talk. We arrived in Luxembourg City, where we walked for hours before settling down to dinner in a dark café where lights illuminated bottles of various-colored liquor from beneath. When we arrived back in Schengen, it was nearly midnight. We'd been underway for fourteen hours.

* * *

In Bastogne now, Virginia made it her singular mission to eat a Belgian waffle in Belgium. I was jumpy and anxious and didn't want to go traipsing around for waffles. As we walked down the block, I was keeping a lid on my irritation when I remembered my trip with Paul and Violette. I directed our little group to the restaurant across the street from the tank where Paul, Vio, and I had eaten more than twenty years earlier. We settled around a table looking out on the street through a large, open window. We were nearly alone in the sprawling establishment. When the waiter came, we all ordered variations of waffles. We had little cups of dark, thick coffee that filled the air with wonderful aromas. Along with the coffee came fresh cream in little milk jugs. I sipped the coffee and thought things couldn't be more perfect. Virginia ate with delight. "This is exactly what I dreamed of," she said. Even Nick was impressed. "I wish we had waffles like this back home, Dad," he said. "You're gonna to have to figure out how to make them."

* * *

Back on the road, we drove along byways that flashed through my memory. When I'd lived in Germany the first time, Udo owned a small motorcycle. We made short excursions into the countryside around Trier for the most part. But several times, we drove into Luxembourg at Grevenmacher, directly west from Trier, and toured around the duchy wherever our hearts fancied. Once, we spent an afternoon rolling up and down the hilly countryside to Junglinster, a picturesque village dating to the late medieval period. We walked its tiny square and had coffee in a lonely café before taking off on even narrower two-lane roads to Altlinster, a village smaller and older than Junglinster (*Jung* = young, *Alt* = old). That day, the sun shone through puffy clouds. The clean, clear air accentuated the hills and forest around us and made each vista a calendar picture. The wind felt cool but not so much we needed heavy jackets against it. Our sweaters and windbreakers did well enough.

I remember that trip and ones like it because we had no worries. My vineyard manager thought highly of my work, which guaranteed an income, no matter how meager. Udo worked his apprenticeship at the stained-glass-restoration firm and would continue until he became a journeyman and then, two years later, *meister.* Our weekends were our own. No one told us what to do. We rode the motorcycle through lovely, almost precious landscapes and into fairy-tale villages. We spoke to no one unless we wanted. Many times, we didn't even speak to each other. Our company was enough.

I'd traversed the Eifel—a region of ancient volcanic hills north and west of the Mosel River—numerous times with Ivo and Udo in 1986. When they stayed at home in Trier on the weekends, we sometimes found ourselves without much to do. So, we drove. I think, too, the spirit of adventure welled up in us. Anything new excited me. Udo was exploring. Ivo knew the area because he'd lived in Koblenz his whole life. But with an American by his side, he discovered the hills again, reminding himself of the history and people as he explained them to me.

Ivo and I stopped one day atop a hill on a remote road in the Eifel. We looked out over open fields and steep, grassy inclines. Rain had passed. In my mind today, the scene shimmers under a dark sky opening in places, dropping rays of sun to the valleys below. On a rise about half mile distant stood an abandoned church, alone in the landscape. Ivo explained the village that once surrounded the church was destroyed in World War II. On the church's slate roof, we could make out a light, almost indistinct square with a darker blocky cross in its center. Ivo said the Germans, and then the Americans, had used the church as a medical aid station. The cross and square, once red and white but now with their colors weathered away, indicated the use of the building to passing bombers and fighter planes overhead.

"Who knows," he said as he shrugged his shoulders, "if either the Americans or Germans really used the abandoned church as a hospital or as a command post. You could never tell who was telling the truth. It was war, after all. Both sides did sneaky things."

We stood on that hill a long time, contemplating the war from our own perspectives. My war came out of history books and movies praising American efforts against the Third Reich. His war came from relatives living on ground the war had shaken and from German history texts—the story of the defeated. Not having contact with many educated Germans, except for the men at the Saarstrasse, I had no idea what story of the war Germans read in their schools. I hadn't seen the German movies or read German war encyclopedias like the American ones my father kept in the living room. In my German travels when I stayed in strangers' houses, I'd seen black-and-white pictures of family veterans. What did Germans think about their veterans, the people who'd fought the war, transported the people to death and labor camps, and those who staffed the camps? In that moment, I realized the cultural distance between my friend and me.

I remember looking over at Ivo. He leaned up against his cheap car and took in the melancholy beauty of the scene before us. Our differences in upbringing, learning, and culture touched our friendship not at all. As human beings, we came together and found interesting commonalities. Ivo, Udo, Martin, and I all struggled. Each of us had small incomes, though Ivo, Martin, and Udo received some support from parents. They'd taken me in and made their home mine. I could depend on them in times of need and want. They fed me. The past, our national pasts, mattered little, if at all. We lived in our moment and would for the next thirty years.

As I drove our camper van, I told Udo about my memories of the times he and I had traveled these roads together, about Ivo and me on long drives in the Eifel, the church, and the way that travels with him and Ivo made me feel. We sat back and looked out the window up at the sky. We were quiet for a long time. My thoughts turned darker but I realized how I had come to terms with my compatriots. I'd done well so far keeping my malady from my mates or, at least, I thought so. But for a moment at Vezelay, we had gone almost six days without disagreement or struggle between each other.

* * *

I just now talked to Udo over the phone about the past and how our trip to France reminded me of the way I used to see the world. "I remember most how I saw it all with new eyes," I said. "Our trip into France showed me I have those eyes still."

"Of course, you do," he said. "Think about what we talked about on that last night in Belgium. We'd spent six days in a world new to the both of us. Don't you feel a little changed?"

"Yes, I do."

"That waffle really made the difference, didn't it?" he said.

"Yeah. It sure did."

CHAPTER FOURTEEN

ANDREA

We wheeled through the Eifel under puffy clouds and air so clear that when we crested hills, Udo and I gasped at the view over the woods and deep valleys. As we drew closer to Prüm, his face relaxed. Soon, he would no longer be in charge. Now out of France, his translating responsibilities were over. Within a day or so, he would be free of the campervan. He looked forward to seeing Ivo as much as we did. I asked him how long it had been since he'd seen his old friend.

"Months," he said. "Far too long."

We talked briefly about how we both missed Ivo's wife Andrea and that her death in June 2011 had left a vacancy in our lives. We fell into reflection and took in the scenery, dreading the end of our time together but looking forward to a new chapter of our lives.

* * *

We arrived at Ivo's house in the Niederberg section of Koblenz in the afternoon. We piled out of the campervan and stretched our legs in the sun. Nick wandered up the street a little, glad to move his body after hours in the campervan. Ivo met us at the bottom of his steps and gave everyone hugs. "I'm glad you made it," he said. "I've made coffee and put out some *Teilchen* (baked goods and pastries) for our little discussion." We sat in his kitchen and he asked us about our excursion.

During our conversation, the subject of his wife, Andrea, came up and we remembered her fondly.

"I first met her in spring 1997," I said, "when you and she had stayed a week at my tiny house in Kansas City."

"I remember that trip well," Ivo said. "You were proud. It was your first house. It was so tiny, you had to sleep on the floor while we slept in the bedroom and Sydney on the couch. I remember the neighborhood most. It was so close and the people so friendly. You marched us around to their houses, introducing us. We had good conversations."

"Andrea and I got to know each other well and found much in common."

"She always had a special affinity for you," he said. "It made me very happy. Then, well, you remember our skiing trip?"

"I'll never forget it."

I told our mates that in winter 1998, Sydney and I flew to Germany to accompany Ivo, Andrea, Martin, and our old friends Barbara Windelen, who was a young medical student in Trier in 1986, and her partner Harthmut, on a skiing trip to Savognin, Switzerland. I was working for a weekly newspaper at the time and we lived from paycheck to paycheck. But Ivo's business was doing well, and he'd offered to pay half the price of plane tickets for Sydney and me. I'd have to pay for skiing and other costs for the trip. I scraped together my end. We were able to join them due to Ivo's generosity.

Ivo picked us up at the airport in Frankfurt. I was in a manic phase and things couldn't move fast enough. I hugged Ivo enthusiastically and hurried the operation along, pushing Ivo aside to get on with it. I'm sure he thought I was just happy to be back in Germany, and I was. But we wouldn't know the extent of my frenzied demeanor until a few days later.

Sydney was seven years old. To her, this whole world—the language, the sights, the way people carried themselves—fascinated her. Andrea with her fierce red hair and deep brown eyes met us at the door of the house where she and Ivo lived at the time. She smiled and gave me a hug, telling me she was glad to see us. Giving Sydney a handmade stuffed animal, Andrea welcomed us in. Their home had a kind of soft hush my life in Kansas City didn't. The house was a narrow but roomy place smelling of flowers and baked goods. The interior glowed. Evening was falling.

After a simple, solid dinner, Andrea brought out cookies she'd baked. Sydney was happy but tired. We set her up in an extra bedroom where she and I would sleep. Andrea told her a bedtime story. Sydney fell asleep immediately.

Unexpected tension filled the next few hours. Andrea had a compelling and forceful personality. My mania drove her to the edge of her temper. We clashed on small subjects—how to cook potatoes, for instance. Heated arguments climbed out of simple everyday topics. Soon, we weren't talking to each other. Or, rather, I'd alienated her, and she wasn't talking to me. I muffed around the house and went off by myself. By the time I went to bed, I thought of the strain I was putting on Ivo, who certainly wanted us to get along. I cursed myself for being so selfish. My thoughts raced. I hardly slept.

The next day Andrea and I barely said a word to each other. The four of us rushed from one place to the next until we piled into the car for the drive to Kirchzarten in the Black Forest outside of Freiburg. I could hardly contain myself for the four-hour drive. Underway, I couldn't wait to get out of the car. At rest stops, I fidgeted around, impatient to get back on the road. When Andrea and I spoke, it was obliquely and about indifferent subjects. Rain. The weather. The sound of the car. She and Ivo, and she and Sydney, however, maintained long-running conversations that agitated the part of me that couldn't just listen but had to be the center of attention.

In Kirchzarten, we picked up Ivo's friend Dorothy (Doro) and her son Max, who was Sydney's age. It was raining lightly, and the day was cold and windy. I pushed people around, my mood expansive and overly familiar. We were fighting the wind, and I moved our things briskly from Ivo's car to Doro's station wagon, which had enough room for the six of us. I heaved backpacks and sleeping bags from one car to the other and forced bags into the small space in the back of the car, shoving people aside to do my work. When Ivo settled behind the wheel, we headed up out of the valley toward the Swiss frontier at Schaffhausen.

We had driven about forty-five minutes when I checked after my wallet. We'd need passports to enter Switzerland. I reached into my pocket. My heart stopped and my breath seized in my chest. The nylon wallet that held our passports, plane tickets, money, credit card, and (in those days) travelers' checks was missing. I panicked and yelled at Ivo, "Pull the car over! My God, pull the car over." We tumbled into the cold and wind. While our compatriots shivered in the sleet, I unloaded the car, throwing bags and suitcases to the side of the road. Ivo and I searched the car over and over and found nothing. I again chucked the bags in the car, elbowing Ivo, who was trying to be helpful. I cursed myself for my stupidity and apologized effusively to our fellow travelers all the way back to Kirchzarten.

We returned to Doro's second-story apartment and turned it upside down. Again, we found nothing. Feeling on the edge of despair and like my head was going to explode, I pushed people harder. In committee, we determined I must have left my wallet on top of Doro's car as I shifted luggage and clothes from one car to another—my rushing people around hadn't helped. We searched the street where Doro parked her car, but it was empty. We split up. Doro and I went one direction door-to-door and Ivo and Andrea went the other way to ask if anyone found the wallet. Again, after an hour and a half of knocking on doors, nothing.

Ivo decided he, Andrea, Doro, and Max should head off to Switzerland—he'd made reservations at an old friars' house in the village of Mon on the mountain above Tiefencastel. Sydney and I'd stay in Doro's apartment over the weekend. It was Friday, and Sigrid, Doro's best friend, would go to the town hall on Monday and see if the wallet had turned up in the village lost-and-found. If we found it, Syd and I'd take a train to Tiefencastel, where Ivo or Martin would pick us up. Doro left us her train commuter pass, so Sydney and I could go into Freiburg to the bank, where I could replace my travelers' checks. There, we could also spend an evening with Barbara, now a practicing physician, and Harthmut, who were not leaving for the skiing trip until Monday.

After our fellow travelers left, Sydney and I were alone in the quiet apartment. Anxiety lay on me like an enormous stone. I feared the worst—that the wallet would never be found. We spent the rest of the day watching *Powerpuff Girls* and *Johnny Bravo* cartoons, which, thankfully, were broadcast in English. I'd sit down with Syd for a while and then get up and pace. I went through these gyrations dozens of times. I berated myself mercilessly. Time poked by. I felt like I was brushing my teeth with sand.

Meanwhile, I canceled the credit card and called the American embassy in Frankfurt and American Express to determine our course of action should we not find the wallet. The American at the embassy was skeptical and dismissive. Whether she was, or this was what I perceived in my heightened state, I can't say. To me, she seemed to treat me as if I were a foreigner trying to ease my way into the American Dream. I argued and harangued before I hung up on her. After a few minutes, I called again and wound up talking to a concerned embassy representative who explained people feigned lost passports all the time. If what I said was true, then everything would be taken care of. We'd have to present ourselves at the embassy in Frankfurt, he said, apply for temporary passports, and leave the country immediately. Once back in the States, we'd have to give American officials our birth certificates and apply for new passports.

I also called Barbara and made a date for dinner with her and Hartmut at their apartment in Freiburg the next day.

Sydney understood we were in a tight spot. I tried, as well as I could, to act like I was on top of the situation. She lost a tooth that afternoon and worried the tooth fairy wouldn't know where to find her. I told her everything would be fine. After she went to bed, I felt around my empty pockets, now convinced I'd disappoint my kid. I scoured the apartment to find some change I could put under her pillow. I rifled the kitchen and utility drawers like a madman, but Doro had nothing lying around. I searched for piggy banks and in the pockets of coats hanging in the hallway. I combed dresser tops. With the persistence mania can inspire, I found two ten-pfennig pieces in dish behind some bottles of lotion and perfume in the bathroom.

I didn't sleep that night but strode around the small apartment in tight circles, excoriating myself. I remembered to put the coins beneath Sydney's pillow but then went back to my rounds of the house. When dawn arrived, I realized I'd wasted a whole night.

Thus, sleep deprived and on the edge of collapse, I took Sydney and boarded the commuter train to Freiburg with Doro's pass. We went to the bank to replace the traveler's checks. The bank representative told me there was no way to replace the checks immediately. We would have to wait until Monday, the bank employee said calmly, when they could investigate the record of our spending and see whether any of the lost checks had been spent anywhere else. I blew up and made a scene. A security guard appeared and told me I should calm down or he would remove me forcibly from the bank and call the police. I stalked outside with Sydney. We sat on a bench in front of the bank and I pulled at and twisted seat staves until my hands were raw and arms ached. The guard watched from behind the bank's glass doors.

We passed an hour at a public playground near the cathedral—Sydney playing and me pacing the perimeter at nearly a run—and then headed toward Barbara's. Dinner with her and Hartmut, I thought, would take my mind off our troubles, for a while, anyway. We easily found Barbara's apartment near the center of town. But the doorbell wasn't working and there was no way to get her attention. Near her front door on the shaded street stood a phone booth. But I had no change to call her.

I sat Sydney on a bench in front of the apartment. I dithered about, paced the sidewalk under the linden trees, and wrung my blistered hands. I looked up at the apartment building. It was several stories high and I didn't know which apartment was Barbara's. I thought of ringing a random bell and asking to be let in the building but put that notion aside. Throwing rocks at a window to get attention was out.

Then it dawned on me. I asked Sydney if she'd brought her twenty cents with her. She dug in her pocket and pulled out the coins. "You owe me," she said. I ducked in the phone booth and called Barbara.

I calmed down a little after Barbara and Harthmut let us in the apartment but was still agitated. While I talked nonstop, they demonstrated a great deal of understanding and patience. Taking advantage of a break in my soliloquy, they turned their attentions to our evening together. We ate an extravagant meal. We sat in the living room and played board games and rounds of Jenga, my trembling fingers repeatedly toppling the tower of wooden blocks. Barbara laughed and said not to worry, things would work out in the end.

"Lieber Patrick, what's the worst that can happen?" she said as she set her hands on mine. "You will have a new adventure. It will be sad not to have you at Savognin. But in the end, you're going to wind up safe at home. We'll make sure of that. Don't worry about the cost of getting to the embassy. We will get you there. And who knows, you may find your passports and wallet."

Harthmut returned us to Doro's apartment that night. "Really," he said, as we sat in the car before Doro's house, "Do try to take it easy. Things aren't as bad as you think. It's just a situation. We'll get you past it."

After I put Sydney to bed, I stayed up worrying, lack of sleep and nervousness piling up on me. I tried to calm down, repeating to myself, "It's not as bad as you think. It's not as bad as you think. It's not as bad. As you think. As you think. It's not as bad . . ." What would we do? My God, did I really lose our passports? "What a bonehead you are. How stupid. What a bonehead you are . . ."

I didn't sleep. Without the wallet, I'd have the travelers' checks I could pick up on Monday at the bank. But that money would barely cover our train fare to Frankfurt. I'd have to tap Ivo or Barbara for more cash. Once at the embassy, I'd have to reschedule our flight, which entailed another $100 I didn't have. I still had a Sunday to live through before we could hear from Sigrid about the lost-and-found or get to the bank and retrieve our replacement travelers' checks, and then figure our next move.

By mid-afternoon the next day, I was haggard and frazzled but still buzzing with manic energy. Sydney was content to watch television. I was pacing the apartment and waiting to the end of an episode of *Johnny Bravo* so we could take a long walk—the only way I knew to relieve pent-up energy and anxiety. The doorbell rang. Sigrid walked in and handed me my wallet. She smiled. She knew the *Burgermeister*, she said, and had seen him at church. She asked if they could look into the city hall's lost-and-found. There, they found the wallet on top of the bin. Nothing had been lost or stolen.

I hugged Sigrid and felt light, almost levitated. My breaths came apace, and my heart raced. I looked back over my shoulder at Syd. "It's all taken care of then, Dad, isn't it?" she said.

I called the rail company to see about trains to Tiefencastel the next day, Monday. As I put down the phone, it rang. Ivo said Sigrid had called and told him about the wallet. When he learned of our good fortune, he said he'd rung the station at Tiefencastel about the train. He told us to pack and get on the 4:30 p.m. commuter to Freiburg and then the 5:30 p.m. international that would take us to Tiefencastel. It was 4:12. I'd already lived through a great deal of stress and said I'd wait until the next day to take the train. "No, no," he said. "You must leave immediately. We will pick you up tonight." I threw our things together, hefted the bags over my shoulders, and struggled down to the Kirchzarten station, my knees buckling. We stepped on the train as it was pulling out.

Sydney and I traveled five hours to the station at Tiefencastel, where Andrea and Martin met us. We stood on the platform with our bags. Andrea stroked my face with both hands and gave me a kiss on the cheek. "I was worried you'd have to leave without me," she said.

The gulf that had seemed to separate us disappeared. She was so gentle and welcoming. I could see in her eyes genuine happiness at our arrival. I apologized for my unseemly behavior. We spent a wonderful hour with our friends in the common room before trundling off to bed among the timbered rooms in the old friars' house. I slept until four the next afternoon, mania and anxiety having worn me down to an exhausted nub. When I woke, I felt punchy, confused, and embarrassed. It took me an hour to wake up, but I was much better. My thoughts had stopped racing. I apologized to everyone calmly, rationally.

Barbara and Harthmut joined us that night and we all crowded into the common room. The friars' house had been built of timber and plaster in the seventeenth century. It served as a monastery until well into the 1900s, and then reverted to village ownership in the 1940s. A group of citizens and the local church had come to own it, and since Ivo knew people who knew people, he had rented it for a good price. Large, multipaned windows looked out over the steep valley that dropped to Tiefencastel in the long narrow gorge below. Mon lay on the shady side of the valley and drifts from a recent snow covered the village in wide swaths. The place had steam heat, but cold still crept in from all sides. We heated the common room with a wood-burning ceramic stove that added ambience to the timber-and-plaster chamber.

Andrea and Sydney hit it off again. I remember watching them walk down the narrow road in Mon, hand in hand. My father's instinct took over. Sydney's friend was my friend.

The mania had disappeared as quickly as it had come. I didn't fall into depression but rather to a plateau that held for the next week. We went to the ski slopes at Savognin in the mornings after a healthy breakfast of sausage, eggs, and fresh milk we'd bought from a farmer around the corner.

I was no good at skiing. I'd skied once in Laramie and then went directly after my descent of the first slope to a hospital for ACL and MCL reattachment surgery. Barbara was also no skier. While our mates absconded to the heights, she and I spent our days sitting in the sun on a wood patio outside the resort's main building reading and talking. The ski lifts disappeared up the mountain. Under them, Sydney attended a children's ski clinic every day and seemed to be getting the hang of the sport. Sydney and Andrea spent afternoons together in the friary's little playground.

I felt relief in the abatement of mania. It was on this emotional plateau that I was finally able to absorb the events of the next week—conversations with Barbara, late dinners in the friar house, long walks on the mountain above Mon. One afternoon, Sydney and I took a cable car to the top of the ski resort, a thirty-minute ride that took us over forested valley and rocky bluffs covered with scree and tufts of grass. Near the mountaintop, we ate at the restaurant and played in the snow. The weather drew down on us and the resort demanded everyone leave before the storm arrived. Instead of using the ski lifts or tram, we rented a sled and took off on a road snaking down the side of the mountain and to the main resort buildings several kilometers below. With Syd in my lap and my arms around her, we rode that sled for over an hour and a half, sometimes whipping along, other times rattling along at walking pace. The road took us down through densely forested alpine forest. We slid along the side of the mountain, the inclines and bluffs dropping hundreds of feet to the valley below. Andrea met us when we arrived at the resort. Somehow, though we had not spoken to her all day, she knew we were coming.

* * *

When I visited Joachim in Berlin in 2011, I stayed with him and his wife and daughter for five days. Then, I took off across country to visit with Josef and Marlies. Underway, I stopped over to see Ivo and

Andrea. We had one full day together. Shortly after I arrived that morning on the train, we packed into the car for a drive to nearby Höhr-Grenzhausen, formerly the center lower Westerwald's ceramics industry. When she was younger, Andrea had apprenticed with a master potter who taught her traditional ways of creating fine ceramics. Andrea was greatly influenced by him.

We spent the day touring little Höhr-Grenzhausen, which had become an outpost for artists and craftspeople of all stripes. The great ceramics industry had long since ceased. The factory that'd once made bowls, cups, and vases stood empty and boarded up. But the fine art of ceramics lived on in tens of shops and studios peppering the village.

The day was overcast and rainy. Andrea took my arm and we wandered under an umbrella along the quiet, abandoned streets, glad to be with one another. We visited her mentor, a sturdy man of about sixty-five who sat behind a potter's wheel in a small, residential studio. Cups and saucers, vases and bowls, all unfired and raw, stood on wooden shelves dusty with clay. His finished work lined the walls of a small showroom, yellow and warm, paneled in rich wood. He and his old apprentice embraced, and Andrea set about telling me about her work with the potter. Her old bench, certainly the workplace of many young apprentices, sat in the same spot she'd left it over twenty years before.

We walked down a narrow alley and into a warren of studios near the town center. Several artists took residence there. They kept a common showroom in a square, plain room whose only object was the artists' work. They displayed their wares on separate tables and wall shelves. Andrea and I contemplated the pieces a long time, lifting cups and bowls, scanning the prices. As I held up works of various types and styles, she explained the methods the artists used to make the goods and the diverse kinds of glazes and colors. I chose some whimsical, brightly colored pieces for Virginia, Nick, and Sydney.

Slowly and without effort, Ivo, Andrea, and I strolled up the hill toward an ancient communal kiln, a large house with an open-slatted roof that kept rain out yet vented the exhaust from the kiln inside. The kiln was big enough to walk into—forty-two cubic meters. From 1840 to the Second World War, the community of potters operated it several times a year. Potters would work for months getting their raw goods in order before stacking them carefully in the kiln. It was then fired with cords and cords of oak and pine until it reached 2,200 degrees Fahrenheit. At the right moment, workers poured pure salt into the upper reaches of the kiln. Through a reactive process, the salt bonded with the clay, creating a glaze both beautiful and durable. The village's signature glazes were gray and Prussian blue.

Andrea explained that at one time, there were three other similar kilns in the village. We climbed steps up the side of the kiln and stood under the great, darkened roof that rose many meters above up. Since the kiln was made of mortar and brick, she said, weather did it no good, particularly the Westerwald's heavy winters. The roof had to keep out the weather yet stand high enough over the superheated kiln to keep from catching on fire, which happened frequently anyway in former times. We looked down into the heart of the kiln through exhaust holes and the openings where workers poured in the salt. Around us, goods fired in the kiln were displayed on shelves. Andrea explained that the machine age replaced the old kilns. This extant communal kiln was restored after the war. Since the operation was such a huge production, entailing tons of wood, hundreds of pounds of salt, and enough ceramics to make the firing worthwhile, the owners fired the kiln once a year. Tourists, potters, and ceramic artists came from all over Germany to witness the event.

We ended our day at a dim and warm café. We drank a coffee and ate some village specialties. Ivo and Andrea sat together on one side of the table. They held hands. I remember thinking she'd never looked more beautiful. Andrea bought me a coffee mug with *"Jammern hilft nicht"* on the side. It was a lesson I took to heart. Bitching never helps.

When we returned from Höhr-Grenzhausen, Andrea and I sat in their kitchen and talked while Ivo puttered around the house. The light was perfect and we were all sleepy from our long day. Andrea had to work early the next morning and would be gone when I woke up. She gave me a hug and kissed my cheek. It was the last time I saw her.

When Ivo told me of her death later that year, I cried and didn't fully recover for days. Since our first meeting, Andrea and I had often talked over the phone and exchanged letters. When Virginia and I visited them in 2000 and again in 2002, Andrea treated Virginia as if they'd known each other their whole lives. Andrea continued her relationship with Sydney. Their fondness for one another impressed me every time I saw them together. When we heard she died, our thoughts were first with Ivo, that impressive, friendly soul who shouldn't have had to deal with such hardship. Sydney was inconsolable.

When Ivo came to visit us in May 2012, about a year after Andrea's death, he wanted to show me pictures of her he'd brought in a folder. He pulled out the first one and said he liked it the best. They'd taken a trip to Italy. The photo showed Andrea in her beret and long, flowing dark red hair. She was smiling. She pointed to a street sign built into the side of the building: "Ave. Andrea." I could look at the picture for only second before I teared up. I told him I wasn't ready. I still had farther to go in accepting her passing. He touched me on the shoulder. He was doing much better with her death than I was.

* * *

Now, as Virginia, Nick, Udo, and I sat with him, Ivo retrieved the folder from his study and showed us that picture and others. He said he still missed her. Sometimes he woke in the night, thinking she was in the house. We told stories about her. Though the time had passed, Udo said he couldn't believe she was gone. Ivo said it was still hard. But he'd met another woman, Lena. She couldn't take the place of Andrea but was good for him. She lived in Freiburg and he traveled to see her on the weekends. It was good, he said, to have her at some distance. The relationship was developing. "I have a fondness for Lena," he said. "If it is right, and I think it is, we will become closer at time goes by."

We fell silent for a while. The sounds of the street out front filtered in through the windows. No one felt the need to talk. We sat there, eating and drinking. A clock struck 4 p.m.

"Well, I have more planned for you today," Ivo said, standing and clearing the dishes. "We're meeting Martin and Christine in Köln. They've picked out a fine restaurant for us. But first, we'll visit Martin in his studio."

We piled into Ivo's car for the hour trip. The day had turned gray and rainy. The sky drew dark toward the horizon. We met Martin at his studio in a large factory building that, in the post-industrial age, had been renovated into offices and artists' studios. He settled us in for tea.

The studio covered two large rooms, both essentially bare but for his paints, brushes, and some canvases. He'd hung his most recent works, pieces he'd show in galleries, along the walls. They included camera obscura photos and pieces combining his work with the camera and his painting. Most of the pictures were small, no bigger than one by one and a half feet. But he also hung strikingly large pieces. One was particularly spectacular. A camera obscura photo of the vast tympanum of the Köln cathedral measured a full twelve feet square.

He lined up chairs around one of his working tables and poured tea into various glasses and coffee cups. He'd gone to the bakery earlier, and he set pastries before us. We talked about our trip through France and the wonders we'd seen. Ivo joined in when we talked about the cathedrals and churches we'd toured. His encyclopedic knowledge of historical periods and stained glass in each entranced me and Virginia. Nick sat quietly, drinking a cola Martin had dug out of his small refrigerator. Nick was content to listen to the various languages being bantered back and forth. Every now and then, Martin or Ivo would ask him about his experience and he answered in a soft voice. I translated for Virginia, but Martin tried in his limited English to include both Nick and Virginia in the discussion.

With a sense of growing melancholy, I ducked out of the conversation and let Ivo and Udo translate. I watched my three artist friends. The bonds they'd first formed in Trier had lasted decades. I'd been in each of their houses, and each had works from the others displayed on their walls and bookcases.

As conversation expanded, I withdrew even further, looking at the space and the work in it. I couldn't help but think that Martin's work, his painting like his photographs and their combinations, illustrated soft, endless space and calm reflection. But I also knew Martin was given to periods of ill-confidence and intense doubt. His inner, self-produced noise made the world around him unbearable sometimes. Noise, I think, includes more than sound. It includes the helter-skelter of images, actions, and movements of the everyday world. Martin used his art to find order in the chaos and imagine an inner peace he might find one day.

After tea, we walked out into the parking lot and the rain. On a corner of the lot stood the immense camera obscura Martin would move to the square before the Köln cathedral. For the first time in the church's eight-hundred-year history, its preceptors had sanctioned an art exhibition on the plaza. Martin's camera obscura, two shipping containers clad in attractive black panels, would be open to the public for a month. He'd worked for over two years and spent 100,000 hard-earned euros to design and construct the piece. Now, in the parking lot of the studio building, the camera stood complete but for the panels that would cover it in the cathedral plaza. Martin unlocked the great doors of the lower shipping container and flipped on the safety lights that lined the stairs.

He'd sprayed the interior of the containers flat-black. Visitors would enter the lower container and climb steps to the one above. There in the dark, on a translucent screen, they'd see the image the simple hole in the front of the upper container projected on the screen. Everything on the image would be a backward and upside-down version of the world outside. The hole or aperture through which light entered the space projected people in front of the containers on top of the image, moving in the opposite direction they walked.

We stood behind the translucent screen and gazed at the image of the parking lot outside. Martin apologized for the spotty light. He was sorry we could see nothing more than the parking lot and part of the building. He had nothing to apologize for. The simple image projected on the screen produced an eerie, haunting effect, as if the world outside existed on another plane, one indistinct but still important. The coming and going of the light made the image a living thing, recording time as it happened. We stood speechless for a few minutes. We all took in the scene, stepped up closer to the screen to see if we could make out various aspects of what was outside, and then stepped back again. We asked Nick to walk in front of the camera to get the effect viewers might have of people outside. From inside we saw him, a ghost gliding upside down across the top of the screen. The image turned out to be as softly out of focus and ethereal as the rest of Martin's work, a mere shade of the world outside that gave the feeling of walking into another realm.

We drove back to Martin's apartment, which was itself an artist's studio. Christine, Martin's wife, worked in textiles and paint, and they'd given over one large room of the apartment to her work. After fetching her, we walked down to a crowded Alsatian restaurant, where we ate an elaborate dinner. Conversation floated all over the place, from the origins of the food we ate to the artist's life in one of Europe's great cities.

* * *

On the drive back to Koblenz, Virginia said she loved being with Martin in his element—his studio, his house, his city—and to see Udo, Ivo, and Martin together again, to watch the old friends and artists interact as people who knew each other perhaps more than they knew themselves.

I found the evening difficult in one way though. At dinner, I sat between Nick and his reluctance to eat anything foreign or new and Virginia and her need for translation. I found myself overwhelmed. No one demanded too much, probably. But my tolerance for noise and fluster diminished greatly in the depression I was dealing with. The day had been pleasant but long. I couldn't get my mind around the translation, the competition for my interest on the part of my friends and Nick and Virginia, and their needs in a foreign land with friends who knew each other so well.

Nick and Virginia don't pick up on my deteriorating state of mind unless I tell them what's happening. At the same time, I'm not always conscious of their needs. Maybe they want attention and I'm reluctant to give it, absorbed selfishly in myself. I also don't become aware of my response to their behavior until I'm too far gone and have reacted unpleasantly to the pressure. The tension builds, one gaining as the other defends, until one side or the other breaks. Hopefully, someone gives in. But that's the point of being self-aware and coping with depression—compromise, mediation, negotiation. When it doesn't work, things break down, feelings get hurt, and people fight each other.

As I sit at my computer, it strikes me that Martin's camera obscura images are much like memory. It shifts with mood and feelings and in context with other memories. Meanwhile, many memories overlap each other in time and place so I can't know when or where particular events occurred. One minute they are so distinct and tactile and in the next so uncertain and wraithlike. The camera obscura projects images upside down and backward, and like memories, like our lives, it takes time and perspective to make sense of them.

And I remember lightning illuminating the horizon that night as we passed over the plains and through the river bottoms connecting Köln to Koblenz. I apologized for being short with my family, and Virginia assured me she noticed my behavior in moments and between lulls in conversation.

"Everything," she had said, stroking the side of my face, "isn't about you."

I take heart in that every day.

CHAPTER FIFTEEN

DAYS OF REST

THE TRAVEL THAT threaded our lives together with people and places left a buzzing in the skull. It was then, at the moment of repose in our busy schedule, I realized all travel passes too quickly, no matter how much waiting in lines and sitting in cars, trains, and buses we do. The days dawn only to end before we know what's happened.

So it is with friends. The time we spent with Josef and Marlies had zipped by. The aging couple kept our days filled and our minds moving. Then, the journey with Udo kept us moving. Each morning, we struck our tent, climbed in the campervan, and headed off through the French countryside to the next destination. Now, at Ivo's, the speed of the previous days and rollicking drive to Köln contrasted with the laziness of our day. I wrote and read, occasionally looking out at the broad sweep of orchard at the back of Ivo's lawn. The clouds broke from time to time, and the scene shifted in light and color. The quiet was astounding. The smell of cut grass and flowers filled the air. The horses the orchard owner kept grazed by, slowly, like something out of a pre-impressionist landscape. Virginia sat close by, reading. She occasionally broke off to write a postcard or letter. Udo and Ivo read and talked at the kitchen table. Nick played with the handheld video console. None of us made any demands on one another. Conversation came on its own and disappeared as quickly as it rose.

* * *

Toward the afternoon, Ivo, who'd also been resting for most of the day, suggested we make the short drive to Höhr-Grenzhausen to look around. We took to the road at our leisure for the fifteen-minute drive to the small town. Little had changed since I'd been there with Ivo and Andrea three years before. The town sits on a steep hillside, and we walked along romantic and cobbled back alleys up toward the old kiln house. Ivo pointed out the sites—artist studios, old architecture, and cobbled courtyards—to Virginia and Nick, much the way he'd done when I was with him and Andrea. He took great delight in bantering back and forth with Nick, who posed hundreds of questions.

With my family and Udo next to me, I saw everything in a new light. I walked through memory, used those memories to form new ones, and saw the town through the eyes of my travel mates. Their wonder and curiosity were infectious. Our visit to the artist shops revealed to them the processes of ceramic making on the artisanal scale. Since Ivo knew a few of the artists, he procured us private tours of studios, where we watched ceramicists throw their cups, pots, plates, and vases. The artists stacked their pieces on movable bakery shelves until they had enough to fire their kilns. One potter explained with teacherly mastery the fine art of porcelain. He held his pieces to the light to show his work's delicate nature. He demonstrated various kinds of glazes, showing first unglazed pieces, then the glazes, and then how each looked once fired in the kiln.

The day had grown rainy and changeable. The depression that had dogged me the previous week turned with the weather into reflection. The dim afternoon bled into the evening's twilight, and we headed back toward Ivo's mostly quiet and happy.

Back to Ivo's house, we puttered around the kitchen, letting things sauté and boil. We chopped vegetables and sliced bread, nibbled on apples and drank drinks we made from Ivo's homemade fruit concentrates—normal, everyday things we don't celebrate until we remember them. Conversation with Ivo was easy, and his erudite, masterful tone enlivened the evening.

After dinner, we climbed up to one of Ivo's upper-story balconies, where we watched the immense fireworks displays of the annual "*Rhein in Flammen*." The event took place in conjunction with a large festival on the riverbank around the *Deutsches Eck* (German Corner), the narrow peninsula where the Rhein and Mosel meet. The fireworks event started several decades ago as a show for tourist cruise ships that ply the river. The boats convoyed from one town to the other and from one fireworks display to the next, so it seemed the river was in flames. The fireworks bloomed over the fortress Ehrenbreitstein on the bluff across Niederberg above the river. They exploded straight across from us, giving us a feeling for how deep the Rhein Valley lay beneath us. The night was brisk and humid and the air clean and clear. For more than a half an hour, we watched bombs burst, rosettes flower, and streamers stream. We thought it was a fitting prize for the end of a lovely, calm, quiet day.

Udo set up his bed on the comfortable couch underneath the windows in the living room. Nick slipped off to his room, an extra bedroom in the attic that at one time belonged to an apartment and where Ivo now kept his offices. I bedded down that night on the floor of Ivo's extra room. Virginia fell asleep quickly in the single bed next to me. The night was inky black. The lights on the street in front of the house barely made an impression on the backyard, open to a rural landscape as it was.

* * *

I lay in bed and stared up into the dark and quiet for a long while and then stepped out onto the balcony into the chill of the night. I listened to the silence and tried to imagine what impressions the trip was making on Nick. He was likely asleep in his roost with dreams of fireworks and fired porcelain. Throughout the trip, he'd ridden trains and flown in planes for the first time. He passed through countryside where Neanderthals and the great barbarian tribes had once wandered and seen the villages and towns that descended from tribal strongholds and medieval fiefdoms. He meandered through buildings centuries older than his country. Huge, ancient statues had passed by our windows. Farmhouses and settlements dated to the medieval world. He saw castles and cathedrals. He watched cows graze under vast vineyards. He walked along streets first cobbled in the 1200s. And finally, he watched a magnificent fireworks display.

Everyone—Marlies, Josef, Ivo, Udo and Martin—had treated Nick as his own person, not some child who happened to tag along. Except for one morning when he decided to act the contrarian—playing his video game before he got out of bed, overeating candy, throwing a fit over food he'd never eaten before—Nick participated in every activity we undertook. He'd been excited and easy to get along with. He observed everything closely and realized, I think, we don't travel to Germany every week or year, and it might be a long time before we'd do this again.

I was also melancholy, as I get whenever I come to visit my friends. Perhaps, this was the source of my bubbling depression. I fear the next time I cross the ocean it will be for a funeral. I returned when Joachim was sick and dying, and when he most needed my presence. But I missed his interment. I didn't have the money or time in my school schedule to make it back for his rites. Ivo and Udo were a few years older than I was, Martin a couple younger. But Josef and Marlies are nearing the end of long, fruitful lives. Someday, I will get the call.

When Joachim died, the pain weighed so heavily on me I wished I'd never met him. Grief was one of the factors motivating my suicide. But his death revealed the processes of friendship. I get into relationships with people based on the present. We build bonds and increase our knowledge of each other in a series of moments, none of which speak to a future. It never enters my mind at the first meeting of a new friend or in the moments we share that those relationships will end someday—with a phone call from a person with a sad and quiet voice. I knew if I'd never met Joachim, never pursued the bonds of comradeship—even of those between soul mates—I wouldn't hurt the way I did. His death made me think of how often I'd have to suffer the pain of loss before I, myself, would die.

It was selfish, the wish never to have met someone because their loss caused such riveting pain. But I am a self-centered person, and in the moments of grief, I think of myself. Better, sometimes, to be the true loner, the person who knows no one closely, the person who has no reason to grieve at death. I don't know what such a life would entail. I have only ever tasted the agony of complete loneliness. More often, I have felt lonesome, sometimes for long periods, particularly when depression or anxiety overwhelmed me. Even in Trier in my loneliest moments, I knew I'd be at work again or off with Monika, Carmel, and Wolfgang on the coming weekend. But I have never come close to being truly lonely. In grief, I long for such loneliness.

I have funerals in my future, and since I'm selfish, I imagine everyone I love will die before me, and I will have to endure the pain of their losses. I can comfort myself, as I have with Joachim, that my friends live on in their influences on others and the world around them when they die. Like the sound a yawp makes in a vale, the echoes become more diffuse over time, but the valley is never the same once the human voice penetrates its surface. The voice has shifted the foundations of the ravines and streams and bluffs. The sound waves have moved the stone, the stone the rabbit. The rabbit climbed out of its hole in a little different way. The hawk ate the rabbit that before the voice entered the valley would not have come out in the open.

If the valley is different, then so am I. But none of that kind of thinking eases the immeasurable weight of loss. At every death, I am more bitter, less satisfied, more doubtful, less confident of my place in the world. In grief, I find it exceedingly difficult to remember these people have made my life better. They influenced me in ways I cannot comprehend. They have helped make me who I am, and, therefore, are part of me.

I looked up at the starry sky and thought of how different my relationships with these Germans would have been if I'd lived around the corner from them. Would I have maintained the relationships with Ivo, Udo, and Martin if I they had experienced firsthand the ugliness of my final drinking days? Continuous contact instead of isolated moments of closeness certainly would have produced different kinds of relationships. How would our friendships have been different if we could've bounced over for dinner or a hike whenever we had the time? I wondered if they could've tolerated my quirks, or if they would've fled from my neediness. What would they think of me now if they would've had to deal with my depressions and manias over the course of three decades? If I'd lived closer and kept contact, would we still feel the same connections between one another and to the past and present that we feel now?

Would we even have maintained contact over the years? I have two or three friends in the States whom I knew as friends thirty years ago. I alienated many others in my dissolution. Some have moved away, or I have lost contact with them for one reason or another. Was the nature of the friendships with these Germans different because of our respective cultures? Many people have told me over the years that Germans make intense friendships and keep a wide body of acquaintances. Americans are more likely to conflate the terms friendship and acquaintance. In America, I can count my close friends on two hands, and I believe my circle of true friends is not as broad as most. I keep a wide circle of acquaintances, people I am truly happy to see and keep up with, many of whom I've known for decades. But friends . . .

I stepped back in and closed the door. Images of Joachim, Josef, Marlies, Udo, Martin, and Ivo raced through my mind. When I went to sleep, I was thinking that whatever happened, I needed to call, e-mail, write letters, and send postcards more often.

* * *

At breakfast we planned our day. Udo would head back to Reutlingen and return the campervan to its owners. The rest of us would go to Bad Ems for a soak in the hot springs. We spent an uneasy morning, each of us avoiding the moment when we would have to tell Udo goodbye. I thought of the farewells of the past, how they all seemed final, as if the people I departed from would never enter my life again. A pang of loneliness shuddered through me. What if something happened and we were never able to visit one another again? The telephone and e-mail were insufficient substitutes for a firm hug or the whiff of someone whose smell we'd forgotten, the companionship that comes with proximity. In goodbyes, everyone always dies before I do.

* * *

Early in the afternoon, the sun shone and the street in front of Ivo's house sparkled with the recent rain. I gave Udo a long hug. We would see each other again, if death or finances didn't intervene. But in that moment, the idea of never seeing my friend again haunted me. I didn't want to let him go. We checked the campervan again for things we might have left behind. We tried to put things in order and reduce the work Udo would have to do once he returned home. Finally, he climbed into the campervan and rolled away from Ivo's place slowly. We listened to the sound of the engine as he disappeared around the corner and deeper down the Arenbergerstrasse.

We turned and entered the house again, not morose but silent. We went about gathering our things for our trip to Bad Ems with hardly a word. Ivo fixed us a last bite to eat before we headed down to his car. Once we broke free of the driveway, our moods lightened. Nick was excited at the prospect of swimming, one of his favorite activities. Virginia was happy to be along for the ride but self-conscious about being seen in a swimsuit—one of Andrea's friend's suits she left at Ivo's before Andrea's death.

Remembering the unique situation I found myself in and the friends and family who surrounded me, I pulled myself from my depressive funk and began to look forward to our visit to the old resort town.

Bad Ems lay in the Lahn Valley about thirteen miles from Koblenz-Neiderberg. It had all the earmarks of a nineteenth-century playground for the rich and famous, the socialites and the powerful. Along both banks of the Lahn stood grand buildings dating to the beginning of the German Republic, vast palace hotels, casinos, and ballrooms. Princes and their ilk had long abandoned the town, which now concerned itself with the pedestrian but lucrative tourist trade. Rhein cruise ships made regular stops here. The hot springs, which used to attract a wealthy clientele looking to take the cure and avail themselves of the healthful waters, had closed long ago. But in the past few years, the same corporate parents that operated the springs at Baden-Baden had opened a facility as posh as it was big. It took subscriptions to the gym and health facilities but also dealt with a brisk tourist trade.

We entered and stood in line at the registration desk where buff, suspiciously Aryan Germans took credit cards and doled out towels. All around us, athletic-looking representatives of the young and up-and-coming jogged in and out of the place. We more rotund and pasty people paid for entry, picked up our towels, and went into the locker rooms. The vast, ultramodern interior echoed with the voices of hundreds of lumpy tourists, including us. Nick found himself at home, swimming from the interior pool, through a plastic gate, and then into the pool outside. The day was cold, which made the warm pool steam and obscured the loungers who took to the patios to cool off and enjoy a moment in the soft rain.

Ivo and I left Nick and Virginia to use the hot tubs and pools of various temperatures. We joined the naked people outside. We doffed our swimsuits and walked luxuriantly through the steam rooms and hot pools, and then over a large, green lawn. The rain pattered down on us as we took a while to sit in the cool day on fancy lounge chairs arrayed on the green. We made our way slowly down to a riverside facility with yet another steam room that let out onto a wooden deck above the river. The chill of the day felt crisp after the heat. Sitting on the deck, I imagined young boys and teens gawking across the river with binoculars and old lechers in their apartments with telescopes. No one on the green or who sat on the patio above the river seemed to think of their nakedness. I did, as I usually don't run around in the buff with other people. This was the Europe I'd heard about as a kid, a place in which the verities of Eden reigned supreme.

When Ivo and I had enough, we pulled on our suits and found Virginia and Nick inside. In the hour we were away, Virginia had tried to participate in a water aerobics class, which turned out to be something of a disaster. The instructor demonstrated the various exercises on the pool's edge. When Virginia didn't act as he expected, he raised his voice at her. Not understanding a word, she became the focus of the class, the older women there taking her aside and showing her how to do the exercises themselves. They mocked the instructor with funny faces. She'd had a great time.

In the meantime, Nick made friends in the pool. He ran with kids his age from one pool to the next, jumping and diving. They didn't need a common language. They spoke the universal language of kids having fun.

* * *

Two days at Ivo's provided a stark contrast to the previous six days of driving through the French countryside. Away from the worry of where we would stay, Udo's handwringing over sites and routes, and the complicated tent came an odd feeling of being on vacation. I let Virginia, Nick, and Ivo put their things away and fix dinner while I sat in Ivo's quiet study. I contemplated the poster he'd received from a Buddhist monk after Andrea's death: "I have enough."

I felt a connection with the person I was in Germany many decades before. Then, I had crammed my days full of activity, whether it was walking the streets, hiking the heights above Trier, or spending time with the men in the Saarstrasse or taking time with my mates from the winery. I'd ached for and sought out new and different experiences. When I sat still, I felt the weight of time on me. Even then, I didn't know how much longer the Germany experiment would last or whether I'd take in enough of the culture and place in the short time I felt was allotted me.

As I reflected, I found the truth is, then as now, I do have enough. The trick is to figure out how to manage those things I have enough of in ways that use all of them, especially time, which so often seems in short supply. The idea is not to take on all of what I have enough of but to meet those things in meaningful ways. Time sits at the center. How do I manage so I get all my imperatives in before the time escapes me?

I sat listening to Ivo and my travel mates go about the business of dinner. The plates clattered on the wooden table and metal forks rang against one another as Virginia gathered them out of the drawer. The smells of coffee and bread and books filled the room. A scented candle on the table gave off the aroma of sandalwood. I leaned forward on the desk and began writing in my notebook.

I thought about my future. I felt the travel in this trip. But it was very different from trips I take alone. I had to share and compromise. We had to do this thing together. The times I'd taken for myself to handle steepening depression prepared me for dealing with the people I'd met and traveled with on this journey. At the same time, the road affected me. New things, new sights and sounds, new foods and smells infected each day. France presented life much different from Germany—though a thin line on a map separated the two. German influence faded by degree as we left the Alsace and approached Burgundy. The heavy food and fastidiousness of the German gave way to the delicate cuisine and unfussiness of the French. Towns of brown plaster and stone replaced German villages with their houses in neat rows and white and gray faces. The excitement of new discoveries switched places with familiar territory and old memories.

The trip little resembled travel in the United States on freeways and in chain markets. A person driving interstate meets endless familiarity along highway exits. One suburb resembles another. If you've seen one set of the great knots and ropes of chain stores, brands, and franchise restaurants, you've seen them all. Fort Collins, Colorado, looks and feels like Overland Park, Kansas, Wheeling, West Virginia, and San Jose, California. I knew my way around Germany. I could speak the language and recognize cultural differences and forms. A German in France was as easily picked out of a crowd as an American anywhere in Europe. I knew my friends, their foibles and vulnerabilities. In France, I traveled a foreign land, one I enjoyed and loved as dearly as any other place where I wonder about life in the markets and houses.

These are attributes I share with my old self, the man who first came to Germany on a whim. He had an endless fascination with the world and always sought new experiences. I couldn't help but think I've lost some of that to the years. Our meanderings around Germany and France demonstrated to me that more than a kernel of that captivation with new experience existed within me still.

Reflection replaced the frenzied and uncertain movement of travel for us all. I remember now considering Ivo's extensive library. He owned titles running the gamut of Western classics to poetry and history. I sit here now, realizing I have more historical inquiries to make. Now free of my dissertation, I can pursue some ideas, essays, books that interest me. Unlike the young man who came to Germany so many years before, I know my strengths and weaknesses.

Of time, I must convince myself, I have enough.

CHAPTER SIXTEEN

LOVE AND LOSS

When Ivo dropped us off at the Koblenz train station, he gave Virginia and Nick hugs and told them to come back soon. Traffic bustled around us, and the taxis before the station jockeyed for position at the entrance. Horns honked. A police car sped by, its siren echoing up the street. I hugged Ivo. The world fell silent. People and traffic moved but I heard no sound. How hard it is to leave this man, my friend, I thought. He kissed me on the cheek and wished me well. "It won't be long," he said. "It'll be like no time at all."

The environment around me came back into hearing. As he climbed back in the car and pulled into traffic, we picked up our things and jumped on the train to Trier. We passed through familiar landscapes I'd never get enough of except through memory. Virginia held my hand. Before, Nick's electronic game had preoccupied him along this stretch. He now stared out the window at the wonders flashing before us. "They look so little," he said, finger against the window, of the men and boys high up in their vineyard perches. "I bet they have strong legs."

We changed trains at Trier. A small vineyard I used to tend on the grounds of the Benedictine convent stood high up on the Petrisberg alone in the woods. I regretted I couldn't take Virginia and Nick into the vineyards up and around Trier, Olewig, and then down toward Konz. I ached to walk with them through the city and tour the Roman and medieval ruins. I wanted to show them what I had seen, tell the stories. They'd see these things with their own eyes. Only I'd be able to gaze through the years. Our grand tour of Trier would have to wait for another time, perhaps even another lifetime.

I thought of the relationships I have with my family members and understood they were deepening. They would continue to do so in the last days of our European journey with Josef and Marlies.

* * *

Josef was waiting for us at Kanzem when the train arrived. I looked down at him standing next to the family car, and sadness washed through me. Seeing him again meant the journey was coming to an end and a phase of life was passing. We'd be back to visit again, but things would be different. Lives were ending. Whether tomorrow or in five or fifteen years, these people who were my parent figures would be gone. Their passing would transform my life. I again asked myself, "What about me?"

So, I tried to savor every minute. Depression made me reflective, and our time at the Fricks' eased the course of the episode. We spent our days much like we did those of our previous visit. We sat at the table on the veranda mornings, afternoons, and evenings. The days were sunny with puffy clouds. The warmth of the afternoons lulled us to sleep. We took long walks and drove up through the vineyards to take in the scenery around Wawern. We ate Marlies's food and baked goods and crunched through Brötchen fresh off the bakery truck. Nick and I helped Josef mow the grass and tend the garden. Virginia and Marlies spent time in the kitchen and sitting on the veranda. After sunset, we sat at the coffee table in the living room passing the time with conversation and tea.

Bernd, Joachim's brother and the Frick's oldest son, came by for a visit. He was a lively and energetic man in his mid-fifties. Forty or more years of long-distance running kept him athletic and young looking. He was glad to see me after thirty years. We'd kept up with each other through Joachim and Marlies and with the occasional e-mail. I tracked his career as an academic economist as he moved from one university to the next, until, at last, he landed at the university in Paderborn, where he was an esteemed member of the faculty and vice president of the university.

Bernd sat down with us to dinner. He had much to tell. His marriage was on the ropes. We listened to his side of the story, and the circumstances seemed to justify his present position. The marriage started out well and continued for decades. But in the last few years, things at home had deteriorated. Tensions arose. After almost three decades of marriage, he was pursuing life as a single man.

Marlies felt the weight of the breakup. It was difficult for her, as Bernd's wife had become as much a part of the family as one of her own offspring. She felt torn, but her loyalties lay with her son. I watched Bernd and her talk about the latest developments in the sad drama and tried to imagine myself in his place, Virginia and I separated and living apart. I couldn't foresee a life without her. If she left me or died, that would be it. I wouldn't marry again. I'd take up in a Spartan midtown Kansas City apartment. I'd walk. I wondered for a moment if I'd start a new relationship and thought of Ivo, and how he'd pulled himself together after Andrea's death. I'm not that strong, I thought.

As the shadows grew long, Marlies wanted to visit the cemetery with Bernd while he was in town. The evening was cool and the sky clear. Virginia, Nick, Marlies, and Josef chattered in a group well in front of Bernd and I as we walked together to catch up with each other. He told me of the intricacies of his career and his relationships with his colleagues and students. We talked about his work and his prospects at the university, which direction he wanted to take his career. He asked questions about what had happened with this or that event he'd heard of from my life as related by Marlies, Josef, and Joachim. We soon conversed as if the years hadn't passed between us.

He was a well-known economist and becoming more renowned for his specialty in sports economics. He, like Joachim, was often a guest on television news shows regarding one aspect of his work or another. Marlies had shown us some recordings of Bernd on national TV. As an expert, he spoke well and confidently, answering interviewers' questions without hesitation. I don't know if it's my place to be proud of anyone. But when Marlies showed Joachim and Bernd on TV, I couldn't help but be proud of my friends. They'd achieved so much over the decades. When I compared my path to theirs, they always came out on top. They excelled in their fields. Each held important academic positions. Both published widely. They had curriculum vitae spanning tens of pages each. Their careers shined brightly before them.

As we strolled to the cemetery, our conversation shifted to Joachim. It was still hard for Bernd, though Joachim had been gone almost three years. What would he make of us now? we wondered.

We walked on to the cemetery and stood for a long moment in silence at Markus's grave. The wind rustled in the vineyard above the cemetery. A few birds erupted into song and quieted again. I thought of Joachim and found I was still angry about his death. My heart ached. But these feelings soon passed. I remembered times when he and I had traveled together and the talks and walks we'd had over the years. Acceptance came with difficulty. I knew I still had work to do.

Marlies trimmed some flowers she'd planted on the grave. When she stood, Virginia put her arm around Marlies's shoulders. Nick was close by, quiet and still. Josef lit candles among evergreen branches. Bernd stood looking down at the stone. Reverence for sons and brothers was in the air. Once again, I felt selfish.

Bernd was standing near Marlies and Virginia. He seemed sad and lost in his thoughts. I first met him at the Weingut in 1986 when he was a young graduate student at the university in Trier. He and his future wife were dating at the time. One evening that summer, we had dinner at the Weingut—Josef, Marlies, Bernd, his fiancée, and I. Bernd and I talked into the evening and our conversation ranging over a broad variety of topics. He'd gone to school in the States and was familiar with American politics. We discussed Americans' characteristics and society and compared them to Germans'. By the time we looked up, everyone had gone to bed.

Our talk that night reminded me of the discussions Joachim and I'd often shared. The resemblance between their personalities was remarkable. Bernd was lively, excited, his eyes shining behind his glasses. (All the Frick boys wore glasses. Bernd and I sat in a corner of the formal living room. Above us hung a picture of Markus in his thick spectacles.) He laughed easily and made good jokes.

Later that fall, I was at the Weingut when Bernd and his fiancée visited. We ate dinner, and they drove me in their tiny car back to Trier on their way home. They lived up by the university in Trier at the time. I was slated to return to the States within the next week or so. They knew I was unsure of myself and fretting over whether I'd made the right decision. As I climbed out of the car in front of the boys' house in the Saarstrasse, they gave me a going-away present, a German-language copy of Antoine de Saint-Exupéry's *The Little Prince*—a children's book written for adults. Struck as I was with the weight of the uncertainty before me, the book moved me when I read it that night. The Prince's travels and encounters with the adult world of worry and misplaced priorities gave me strength to face what lay before me. I cried at the end of the tale, when the Prince allows himself to be bitten by the poisonous snake so he can return to his planet and his flower without his "shell."

* * *

When Bernd and his fiancée gave me the book, I was head over heels for an American opera singer. I'd met her in Kansas City a couple of days before I left for Germany the first time. She lived around the corner from my apartment. When I decided to sell my things before I left, I'd held a garage sale. Toward the end of the day, she came and gave my things a good look. I was struck by her beauty. I bumbled around, hoping she'd find something and I'd make more money for my trip. Nothing of interest struck her, but we engaged in good conversation. I told her my plans. It turned out she was toying with the idea of taking a summer course in new music at Darmstadt, a center for international music culture.

She gave her address and asked me to write once I settled down in Germany. When I set up my little room in the winemakers' apprentice school and started work at the winery, I had plenty of time by myself. After I secured a typewriter, I spent nights banging away at long letters to friends and family at home. Poems and short stories, mostly drivel, poured from the keys. Writing filled in the lonely weekends. I wrote to the opera singer, detailing my new life and work. She wrote back, and so began a correspondence that continued until she arrived in Germany in the summer of 1986.

At the time she came to Trier, I was dating Monika. I'd spent months lovesick for her but was too chicken to ask her out. Monika had wonderful grass-green eyes that stood over a strong and prominent nose and full, shining lips. She was diminutive and quiet, but these characteristics gained my attention as we spent evenings in the city with Wolfgang and Carmel. We'd spent a great deal of time together in a circle of her friends. Still, it took me months to gain the courage to ask her for a date. When I did, I fell and fell and fell.

Monika lived near the vineyard where I worked on the other side of Trier from my room. Since the city was so compact, she met me on the pedestrian plaza without much effort—a short bus ride. I don't remember how often we went out, but the time was dreamy.

One night early in our budding relationship, Monika met me for dinner at the brewery on the next block over from my room. When I walked her to the bus stop, it was raining and night had fallen. We stood under a few linden trees. A lone streetlight illuminated the shimmering trees. The rain was warm and we had no umbrellas, and our clothes were soon wet and heavy. I put my arm around her and we kissed. My heart raced and knees wobbled. Rain ran down across her face. I put my hand to her cheek and the water disappeared down my arm. It is a picture irradiating my memory, and considering what was to follow, it is a reminiscence I savor from with fondness and regret.

Not long after, the opera singer arrived, and I made arrangements to put her up with Martin, Ivo, and Udo in their house in the Saarstrasse. Mania had me flying. I showed her around Trier, which I knew intimately by that time. We went to wineries and dim, out-of-the-way cafés, where we drank delicious coffee and good wines.

Meanwhile, I continued to court Monika. One evening, Ivo, Udo, Martin, the singer, Monika, and I went to my friend Wolfgang's winery in nearby Kasel, where his mother served a magnificent dinner. Wolfgang took us into his cellar and let us sample his wines, recent and vintage, by candlelight. When it came time for us to leave,

Monika was sitting at a picnic table in front of Wolfgang's house. I gave her a long kiss. Then, all of us, except Monika, who'd met us at Wolfgang's, piled into the car and drove back to the Saarstrasse.

The night grew late and the boys went off to bed. I was buzzing, and my energy was off the charts. The opera singer and I stayed in the kitchen, where I talked a while longer before I took off for my room. She stood at the sink and, when she could get a few words in, told me she'd been hurt, watching me kiss Monika. I knew already I felt something for the opera singer, and it confused me. I was very much in love with Monika, but the opera singer was deeply attractive and overtly sexual. As I tried to explain the situation with Monika, the opera singer gave me a kiss, long and deep.

I again turned into jelly and we began an affair that lasted the summer. I quit calling Monika. I felt bad at first, but I was twenty-three and taken with the singer bodily and mentally. Mania had me whirling in circles. She was creative and sexually voracious, and she showed me things I'd never imagined. I'm not sure anymore if it was the love I once thought it was. Regardless, I was deeply, overwhelmingly infatuated, mesmerized by passion, and unwilling or unable to look any further than the fire of that desire. I mistook these pains to be real love and left Monika to pursue a relationship for which I returned to the States.

The opera singer traveled from Darmstadt to Trier every weekend. When the boys were away from the Saarstrasse, we spent our time there. We made love in every room, in every bed, in the spacious bathtub, and on the kitchen counters and washing machine. I'd never experienced anything so consciously erotic before and was taken away. She decided to remain in Germany after the new-music seminar ended. She stayed with friends she'd made in Darmstadt and with me on the weekends in the Saarstrasse. Her sister came to visit one week in Trier. It was a lonely week for her; the opera singer and I took her everywhere we went but were absorbed in each other.

When the singer returned to the States at the end of the summer, we continued to correspond via post. Her letters were expressive and, given my circumstances, haunted my dreams. In my mind, the relationship was growing. Warm, deeply seated feelings affected me whenever I thought of her, which was nearly all the time. In the last month of my internship, mania took me to greater heights. I undertook my vineyard tasks with unending energy. I drank harder, walked more. The whole time, I contemplated a dreamy life with my new girlfriend.

Finally, I ditched plans to go to Geisenheim and decided to return to Kansas City to pursue the opera singer. I had everything going for me for a lifetime in Germany. I was nearing the end of my internship, and my future in oenology and viticulture was all but assured. Marlies had even secured a scholarship for me from the local Rotary Club, a mission she'd put herself on the line for. I turned it all away. After what seemed the perfect summer and fall—work outside in an idyllic landscape, a waxing fiery relationship, and plenty of wine and friendship—I wrote to tell the opera singer of my arrival time and date.

Mania abated, and I plunged into depression. My last days in the vineyard were difficult. But I mustered the strength to pack my backpack and make it to the airport in Frankfurt. My knees shook under the anxiety of my uncertain future.

It was raining the late November night I arrived in Kansas City. The opera singer didn't greet me at the airport. I took a taxi to her house. I should've known something was amiss when she wasn't home. Streetlights illuminated the night and transformed everything into shades of dull silver and black. I sat on the porch swing in front of the empty house for several hours in the cold, waiting. My heart sank deeper. My breaths hung in the air like balloons. I started to count them before they floated into the rain and away. I counted drops falling from the eave. I didn't know where else to go.

When she came home, she stood on the top step of the porch out of the rain. She seemed not to recognize me. Then, she was stunned, taken aback. When I told her I'd written to say I was returning, she didn't recall the letter. She'd never expected I'd give up my life in Germany. Standing in her living room that night, I didn't know what to do and neither did she. She set me up on the couch in her living room. I was confused and hurt. I expected a joyful reception that would pick the relationship up right where we'd left off. But it turned out she'd taken up with a friend of mine from the university shortly after her return from Germany. She was self-conscious and distant the few days I stayed with her. I didn't feel jilted, as my senses were so dull. Instead, I despaired. I arranged a place at some friends' house, a peculiar situation where my room was literally a closet I rented for $25 a month.

Crushed in depression and deeply disappointed, I craved attention and approval. As the weeks progressed, I felt more and more the necessity to prove myself to the singer. I felt inferior to her creative friends, who were artists and musicians. In Germany, my drinking had moderated. But now I began to drink more than ever. What relationship we developed lasted a rocky month until I couldn't stand the humiliation. With my dreams demolished, I spent the next months on a long drunk. I partied as if nothing else mattered. The job I found waiting tables accommodated my drunken behavior. A succession of women found me exotic and my closet interesting. I attempted to establish relationships but nothing seemed worth my time. I contemplated suicide but drank the feelings away.

* * *

In August 1987, a letter from the winery arrived. The administration had paid my matriculation fee at the wine school in Geisenheim. I had a month before school started. This time, I had nothing to sell and little money saved. Within two weeks, I packed my backpack and flew to Germany, where I stayed with the Fricks for a few nights and a few nights in the Saarstrasse. Housing near Geisenheim was limited and expensive. Ivo and his mother—a dear woman named Else—drove me from Koblenz to Geisenheim, where we fished around for apartments. Anxiety and uncertainty weighed on me and it seemed I'd never get things right. I wound up in Aulhausen, a village about five miles from school, where I found work with several vintners in the village and subsequently ran myself ragged between work, school, and drinking.

I did well in school but hardly had the time for homework. Paul Legill became one of my great pillars of support. I made friends with many of my classmates, who looked after me and took me out to eat when I had no money to buy more than a jar of off-brand Nutella and cheap toast bread. They never suspected how much I drank when I wasn't around them. I was able to keep my charade going, as I could have a couple of drinks with them before I went to my little room and drank to pass out. Every morning, I woke with the church bells and rode my bike up the steep village street and then down through the vineyards to school. Only Paul suspected my deteriorating condition, as I lost weight and became pastier and more haggard.

Finally, it was too much and I returned to Kansas City, disgraced, after three months.

I used to look at this phase of my life as a humiliating failure. Memories of the opera singer, my stay in the closet, and failure to make it at school made me cringe. Over time, the hurt transformed into a dull pain. For many years, the opera singer occupied my dreams and I often felt as if she was looking over my shoulder, disapproving of my efforts to express myself in writing and life. I cursed myself for ditching what could have been a rewarding life in Germany.

My obsession with these times affected personal and romantic relationships for a decade. Fortunately, as I matured in sobriety, I began to reassess that period. I realized I couldn't have continued to drink and have the life in Germany I imagined. More and more, I found myself an immature alcoholic and now see myself as an undiagnosed manic-depressive who suffered under the weight of his own unreasonable expectations for himself. After I attempted suicide and discovered the depths of my mental illness, I see the decisions I made were associated with my states of mind when I made them. Depression had taken me to Germany the first time. Mania had brought me back to Kansas City. Mania returned me to Germany the second time, and depression took me back home.

Sobering up and healing slowly from my mistakes—my changes in direction—I began to grow and face my decisions head-on. I made it a point to meet Monika again when I went to Germany in 1993 and make amends for the way I'd treated her. We'd corresponded on and off in the five years since I'd left Geisenheim. We spent a wonderful afternoon sitting in the sun in the Marktplatz in Trier, eating ice cream, talking, and laughing as old friends will. She was smaller than I remembered and prettier, and we'd been close when I'd known her before. Our conversation fell quiet. I asked her to forgive me. I told her I'd been in love and still had strong feelings for her. I was sorry I'd been so shortsighted. She said she hadn't realized the depth of my affections. She'd been deeply hurt but had seen our time together as a relationship that probably wasn't meant to be, regardless how strongly she felt for me.

* * *

My memories of the relationships with Monika and the opera singer have set me to thinking about how past and future exist in my head. Life is fluid and can't be contained in a moment, a time recognizable by the abstractions of history, what might have been, and what might be. I don't live each day as if I'm going to die or be miserable in or out of love. Rather, I live, usually, without the consciousness of being alive or in love. Fortunately, I also know many moments, many days, when life and love are not conditions to be endured but tasty, corporeal things. I take them into my lungs, feel them in my chest, and know them in my heart. It's then past and future cease to be; and so the moment ceases as well. Flow. Convection in a lake. The ceaseless processes of evaporation and condensation.

It wasn't until I met Virginia for the second time in 1998 that the pain of the opera singer and Monika abated. Virginia and I knew each other briefly in 1987, shortly before I left for Germany to attend school in Geisenheim. She's the sister of a friend of mine who I'd met through my friend Bruce. Bruce and Jo Anne lived in an older neighborhood in Kansas City. I'd gone to dinner at their house, a sort of goodbye before I left for school in Geisenheim. Virginia had moved from Houston and was staying with them while she looked for a job and an apartment. We had a bountiful dinner, and I'd gotten good and sotted that night. When it came time for Bruce and Jo Anne to end the day, Virginia and I walked to a neighbor's house to have more drinks and talk. We hit it off, and I promised to write once I settled down at school.

I didn't write. Instead, I asked Jo Anne in a letter to say hello to Virginia. That was the extent of our relationship then. But there was something about Virginia that impressed me. For eleven years, we kept in touch through Bruce and Jo Anne. I'd see Virginia now and then when she'd come to their house with her boyfriends. In Missouri at that time, liquor and beer sales at grocery and convenience stores ended at midnight on Saturday. You could only buy alcohol on Sunday from bars that sold beer to-go. Sometimes, I'd forget to stock up on Saturday for my Sunday drunk and dropped by the bar where Virginia worked for a couple of take-out six-packs. We were cordial to each another. She always seemed happy to see me. When she stopped working at the bar, I kept up with her when Bruce and I went on our weekly bike ride.

After I sobered up in 1990, I kept contact with Bruce and Jo Anne, and through them, Virginia. I always asked Bruce during our bike rides about Virginia. He told me what she was up to and how her life was changing. She'd gone through some troubles but was getting her act together. The years passed. In the summer of 1998, Bruce and Jo Anne made ready for a move to St. Paul, and I suffered a kind of panic. I feared my tie to Virginia, no matter how tenuous, would be broken.

I picked up Sydney from her mother's every other weekend. I knew Virginia worked at a restaurant and was going to nursing school. One Saturday, the Fourth of July, I was thinking of Virginia when I went to get Sydney. I asked my seven-year-old if she wanted to have pancakes that morning. I was nervous and shaky, feeling like a schoolboy afraid to talk to a girl he liked. We went into the restaurant where Virginia worked on the outside chance she was waiting tables that morning.

We walked in, and Virginia was on duty. I saw her and felt struck by lightning. The place was crowded, but Virginia spotted me right off and came over to say hello. She arranged for us to be seated in her section of the restaurant. We chatted cordially when she came to take our order. As Sydney and I ate our breakfast, I was distracted, watching Virginia work. Every now and then, she would look my way and smile. When it came time for the check, I asked her if she was busy that night. Maybe we could take in some fireworks somewhere? She said she had a date who was taking her to the baseball game. (Virginia is an ardent fan of the Kansas City Royals.) I scuffled around in my head for another reason to go out with her. The local Shakespeare society was performing *A Midsummer's Night's Dream* in a midtown park that week. I asked her if she'd like to go with me.

We had our first date three days later. The evening was warm and humid. The park where the play was staged was green and lush. I'd brought cheese, crackers, and sweet cherries to eat on the lawn. We sat on a blanket under the canopy of oaks and chattered through the entire performance. Night fell and we walked back to the car, which was at some distance from the park. While we were underway, Virginia grasped my hand and we took our time. I was again nervous and unsettled when I dropped her off at her apartment. The unspoken tension between us rose. We kissed for the first time. Eleven years had passed since the night I first met her at Bruce and Jo Anne's. Our date felt like the fulfillment of a dream.

Within ten days or so, we were talking about getting married. I'd never committed myself like that before. But with Virginia, marriage seemed right, almost second nature. On October 1, 1998, I asked her to move into my little two-room house. We're both Internet reverends, so we married each other in my living room. We made my Internet an internet reverend a few weeks later so he could sign our marriage certificate.

We didn't have the money for a wedding or reception. We saved our dollars—I was working at a newspaper and she was in nursing school, working part-time at the restaurant. We planned a formal ceremony and reception for our first anniversary. We sent out handmade invitations to family and friends. Udo, Ivo, and Andrea came from Germany. We wanted to show off our close-knit neighborhood to our friends. We held the event in the basement of the Catholic church one hundred feet from our doorstep.

For our honeymoon, we took Ivo, Udo, and Andrea to a state park in south-central Missouri and stayed a weekend in a comfortable cabin that was really a new house on the property. A deep clear-water stream flowed down from an immense spring. The state stocked the river with trout. We spent the weekend hiking and fishing. It was the first time Ivo and Andrea ever held fishing rods. Andrea was thrilled to land her first fish. Ivo enjoyed hooking a trout or two, then retired to a park bench to read. The activity intrigued Udo, and he busied himself catching and releasing numerous trout. We didn't hold on to any of the fish. Cleaning them would have been an ugly business for Andrea, who felt for the creatures when she caught them. She thought, after a while, how painful it must be to get hooked in the lip and dragged to shore against your will. She'd had fun fishing, but she gave it up after a while and joined Ivo on his park bench.

This was the night Udo and I walked the length of the park in the dark. We talked about what marriage meant, and how he'd sought the right woman all his life but never found her. The frogs sang around us. Crickets chirped in the grass at the side of the road. From the deep forest echoed the call of a whip-poor-will, the loveliest sound I know.

* * *

Now in Wawern, we'd returned from the cemetery and Bernd had left. Virginia, Josef, Marlies, and I settled into another long chat at the coffee table while Nick fiddled with his handheld game. When it was time for bed, I stayed in the living room to read but couldn't focus on the page. Clocks all around the room ticked. I turned off the light and looked out the window at the village. I thought about the changes that had occurred in my life over the past thirty years. When I was in Germany the first time, I couldn't have imagined how things would have turned out. I was caught up in my delusions. I couldn't stop drinking. The opera singer distracted me from the course I'd determined for my life and changed things irrevocably. I gazed into the distance to the great vineyards now black against a starry sky. For the first time, I felt grateful for that unendingly painful break with the opera singer. It opened my mind to poetry and art, and to a life of writing. If not for her, I thought, I never would've met Virginia.

The rest of our stay with the Fricks, I had time to myself. The depression that dogged me left me contemplative. I thought about love, relationships, and, ultimately, loss. Bernd showed me even the surest bet wasn't something you could count on. The Fricks were aging and would soon, in ten days or ten years, change my life again.

In the end, I realize I was very lucky. Sobriety and control of the worst of mania and depression have bestowed great blessings on me. I have parent figures that enriched my existence. I ache to travel again. I miss the days before Virginia and I became weighed down with homeownership and the trappings of middle-class life. While I don't yearn to be young again, I want the freedom I'd enjoyed when I was twenty-two and had my whole life in front of me. But I no longer hanker to rethink my decision to leave Germany and follow the opera singer. Everything was just right. I have the world in my hands. If I pay attention, the bonds between me and my family can only grow.

I think of losing Virginia, Nick, the Fricks, Bernd, and Nick. Where will I be without them? What would I do?

Then I understand if our visits to our German friends taught me anything, it's that I don't feel loss if I have nothing to lose.

CHAPTER SEVENTEEN
LEAVING HOME

I TREMBLED BEFORE the enormity of my task. Our time at home with Josef and Marlies had come to an end. We were headed back into the routine moments of our real lives, the ones in which we must work, pay bills, mow the grass, and tend grapevines. Idyllic moments are what they are because they don't last. Their fragility makes them ephemeral; their beauty solidifies them in memory. We were leaving these people for probably the last time. Phone calls and letters would buoy us. (The Fricks don't have computers.) Our connections would remain strong. But our departure would sever physical contact, the tactile realization of other human beings, perhaps forever.

We packed our things reluctantly. The train was to leave Kanzem's tiny platform at midday. We dawdled after breakfast. Virginia enjoyed a last cup of coffee with Marlies before she joined Nick and me downstairs. We didn't speak in that quiet room but went about packing with gestures and pointed fingers. Every now and then, I looked in on Nick, who folded his clothes around his souvenirs and packed them into his bag with deliberation.

They went upstairs. I walked around the apartment again. I took a certain comfort in the books and odds and ends that stood on the shelves where I had seen them years before. The place smelled of new fabric and old wood. I fixed that in my mind and picked up and read the labels of wines in Josef's cellar. I took special wines from the rack, ones I knew

Josef saved for events and for sentimental reasons and held them up to the light. There was a '59 Wawerner Herrenberg, a dust-covered bottle that had been with Josef as long as I had known him. The vintage was probably the twentieth century's best, and the wine would likely live another generation. Webs and mildew covered a bottle of '73 Trittenheimer Altärchen, whose label was hardly readable after four decades. I noticed Josef had shelved the new burgundy I bought him with several bottles I'd sent him for gifts over time specially separated from the rest on the top shelf. I breathed in the smell of the apartment and walked around the large dining room the Fricks used for birthdays and anniversaries, looking at photographs on the wall. I stopped before a picture of the family, Joachim on one side wearing his signature smile.

Upstairs, while Virginia and Nick stepped out front, I walked out to the patio, soaking up the surroundings as if I could take them with me. The air was so clear the vineyards stood out in detail under a blue sky. The air smelled green and fresh. Fat bees buzzed in Marlies's geraniums.

Josef helped put our things in the back of his car. Marlies joined us for the ride to Kanzem. Driving the two-lane to the village, I took in the scenery as if it was the last time I would see it. Thirty years of memories floated through my mind.

Josef and Marlies joined us on the platform as we waited for the train. We hugged and said goodbyes, and then hugged again. We posed for last pictures. A woman sitting on the bench volunteered to take the camera and get us all in the photo. When the train pulled in, we looked at each other with sorrow. I felt we had to leave too soon. The couple stood next to the train arm in arm, waving as we pulled away. I looked away, freezing them in my mind.

At Trier, we boarded a bus to Frankfurt. The choice of a bus seemed right at the time I'd made the reservations the day before. Because our flight left in the morning, the train couldn't deliver us to the airport in time if we'd started out at Kanzem. We planned to bus it to Frankfurt and stay the night in a motel near the airport. But as soon as we climbed aboard the bus, I knew I'd made a mistake. It was crowded and close. Nick and Virginia had bought pop at the train station in Trier. He had the habit of drinking it all right away. I didn't worry about it, as I believed the bus had a restroom, which we soon found it didn't.

Almost as soon as we stepped aboard, Nick had to use the bathroom. Poor kid had about an hour and a half in front of him before we'd reach the airport at Frankfurt/Hahn, a satellite airport that was once a US Air Force base, where we'd board another bus for the larger international airport at Frankfurt proper. We drove up out of the Mosel Valley through industrial districts and up into the Hunsrück, where the bus scuttled around curves and up between forested hills. I felt every swerve and bump, thinking how rough it was on Nick. He squirmed but kept a good face. He began bopping up and down in his seat. When the bus stopped to take on more passengers, I dashed to the driver to see if we had time for a break. No, he said. The bus departs as soon as the passengers are on board.

By the time we arrived at the airport, which serves as a hub for European discount airlines, Nick was green, squinting, twitching, and jumping. The airport sits in a remote area, distant from towns and villages. The glass and metal façade stretched for blocks high up on the Hunsrück between the Mosel and Rhein valleys. I was relieved for Nick when we arrived. Since we had to take a different bus from Frankfurt/Hahn to the main airport, still an hour and a half distant, I gathered the bags in a pile and waited while Nick and Virginia ran inside to find a bathroom.

I'd asked the driver when the next bus departed. He gave me the time, and before Nick and Virginia left, I insisted we had to be on the next bus in a half hour. I waited out front of the terminal with the pile of our goods. And then waited some more. I had to use the bathroom and was soon fidgeting. I watched as our bus began to take on passengers. I grew anxious as I watched the crowd at the bus stop grow. The bus soon filled, and the driver secured bags in the compartments at the side. When Virginia and Nick finally emerged from the airport atrium, they looked refreshed. They had plastic shopping bags with them. I huffed and scolded. Virginia scolded back. The bus was full and we missed it.

But I remembered my mental state and took a deep breath. The next bus left in an hour. We had time to take in a snack and cup of coffee while we waited. The day was sunny and bright, hardly a cloud in the sky. My temper cooled. The coffee calmed me down. We'd get to the motel we had reserved a couple of hours later than planned. We'd have dinner and get to bed at a decent hour. A full night's sleep lay before us, with plenty of time to get to the airport for our flight the next day. Despite my worry, everything would be all right. When it came time for the next bus to leave, we were aboard.

We arrived at the hotel as dark fell. The room was comically small compared to its American counterparts. The bed filled the room. All around were tiny compartments for clothing and other necessities, not that we needed them. Nick spent a good deal of time getting to know the room, opening all the closets and glove box-sized storage areas. I was hoping to find a German Gideon's Bible I could slip into my pack, for the sake of having it. But the Gideons had not been here. We tried the television, which showed German programs and did nothing for Nick and Virginia. When we were back in the room from dinner, Nick said, "It's was a great trip, dontcha think?"

"Yeah, it's pretty good," I replied.

They went to sleep and I thought what a good idea it was to take two days to leave Germany, one on the road and in a motel and another to the airport. Somehow, the lag between our goodbyes in Kanzem and getting on an airplane the next day made everything easier. The day on the bus and my worry underway distracted me from the emotion I felt at leaving my friends. I wouldn't spend the whole of the plane ride in sadness, likely crying from time to time. The night in a motel gave me time to think through our departure and allowed me to set the scene of our last view of the Fricks firmly in memory.

Once on the plane, my ticket put me in a seat widely separated from Virginia and Nick. Again, I had a row of seats to myself and got up every now and then to check on my compatriots. They were happy and resting, even sleeping when I looked in on them.

I stared into the empty Atlantic beneath us. The electronic map on the screen in front of me tracked the journey of the plane through space. Thirty years. Ivo, Udo, Martin, Andrea, Joachim, Bernd, Josef and Marlies. The decisions I'd made in the grips of unmedicated manic depression and alcoholic grandiosity and dissipation. The great joys and despair. They all floated in my thoughts as I closed my eyes. The whoosh of the plane settled into my half-dreaming. I would be back. Things would be different. People would age and eventually die.

When we arrived at home, our trip complete, I took up my journal again. The lessons of the trip flowed out of my pen but always led back to the same thought: I vowed not to take things for granted. As soon as I wrote that, I knew I'd have to work to achieve it. Busy with day-to-day routines and responsibilities, I'd have to make a point of noticing the passage of Nick's teen years or would awaken one morning and realize he was a grown human, much in the same way I experienced Sydney's childhood. Despite the medication, I knew I'd have breakthrough depressions and manias. I'd keep going to meetings and doing what I needed to stay sober. I'd do whatever necessary to keep my head out of a loop of rope. I'd try to pay attention, wake in the morning understanding that this day was the only one like it. Good or bad—or worse, plain boring—it was something I'd appreciate in its uniqueness. I'd attempt to take life as it came and keep myself from the eternal anxiety that accompanied the turning of dawn and sunset.

I now understood, better than any other time in my life, that drunkenness, despair, suicide, as well as unmitigated mania and depression, made me who I am. I'd never have gone to Germany had I not been desperate to avoid admitting my addiction. Had it not been for the depression I suffered when Larry made the call that changed my life, I probably would have stayed in my routines, unhappy and unfulfilled. People like Joachim, Josef, and Marlies would not have influenced me or enlivened my existence. I was grateful mania drove me home after the opera singer. Without her and my disjointed thinking, I might never had met Virginia.

When dealing with counterfactuals, that is, what could have been, I must go back and understand I'd have lived a very different life had I stayed in Germany. My drinking and mental illness might have driven me sober sometime or broke and homeless or to suicide. Mental health care in Germany's much better than in the States, so some doctor may have figured out my manic-depressive illness years before I tried to hang myself. Who knows but that I may have been a vineyard worker who'd sobered up and didn't drink—drinking wasn't a necessity in viticulture. But in the end, I can't imagine what life in Germany would have been.

What I did know was that life turned out well despite me, despite mental illness, despite alcoholism.

* * *

I don't want to go back and redo my twenties with the hindsight of thirty years. The perspective of age gives me a certain bias I don't think I can ever breach. Looking back on our family trip, I realized I'd spent time with the twenty-two-year-old who took off for foreign lands on what seemed to be a whim. I'd seen what he was like firsthand. I'd wanted to meet him where he was—on trains or in the vineyard and cellar or on the plane back to the States—and had. I'd seen what others saw when he was drunk, depressed, and on manic jags. I knew what he had to say about where his life was going, what he thought he needed, and how he thought he was doing.

I'd also wanted to see what became of the years between my first trip to Germany and now. Looking at the memories of my Germany sojourns—and my German friends' trips to see me—I'd witnessed a person maturing and understood that the process continues. My drinking life and mental illness has meaning and purpose in the context of who I've become. All my drunken forays, manias, depressions, mistakes, heartbreaks, and embarrassments have a place in my past and present.

I take note of the great lesson of our family trip to Germany and France: Everything that's occurred in the last thirty years brings me to you, to this essential moment, to the end of this pencil scratching across paper.

EPILOGUE

THE MOST DIABOLICAL trick biology has played on us: When we are young, time passes so slowly. When we gain a little wisdom and experience, time flies by. As soon as I blink, the week is over. It seems like it's always Sunday and I'm getting ready for the workweek. The thirty-four years since I first landed in Germany will pale next to the coming twenty, the good years I figure I have left if I don't eat myself to death, if I can steer wide of the bottle and live a sober life, if I stay on my medication and avoid hanging myself.

It's been easy lately. My doctor and I have landed on a medicine regimen that has ended the "breakthrough" episodes of depression and mania. I haven't had a serious break for at least four years. Being on the beam is nice. Big events, changes, and difficulties don't spin me out of control anymore. I have never been more productive. One can never tell, however, when the chemistry of the brain will change and I'll be thrown into the tortures of the disease. Drug adjustments and readjustments, new coping skills will be necessary. But for now, I can say I've never in my life lived a steadier emotional and mental time.

I went back to little Wawern in May 2019 on the expressed purpose of staying with Josef and Marlies. I had not seen them in almost five years. Time has been good to them. They remain remarkably healthy for their eighty-nine and eighty-five years but note that they don't do what they used to. Josef greatly reduced the size of his garden and sold his orchard because it was too much for him. We spent a good deal of time in the garden, and he was glad to have a helper. When Marlies and I took her daily walks of several kilometers, we strolled at her best pace, which, unlike in years previous, I was able to keep up with.

Marlies had generously invited me to have friends come by to overnight. Udo came in his work van from Reutlingen. The American writer Eddy Harris came via bus and train from his home in the west of France. I was afraid three strapping men in their fifties and early sixties would be too much for Josef and Marlies. But they enjoyed their three days with Udo, Eddy, and me. Josef and Marlies told the stories of their youth, of their meeting and marriage over sixty-five years before, of their children and life in the old Weingut.

Between our long conversations with the Fricks, Eddy, Udo, and I had busy days. We walked up into the vineyard above the town, as I had done many times with Joachim and Josef and Marlies. I had to show my friends vistas that influenced my way of looking at the world. We talked of my time in Germany, life in the Saarstrasse, and of the opera singer.

One afternoon, we drove Udo's van to Schengen, Luxembourg, to visit my winemaker friend Paul Legill and tour his small winery. Standing in his cozy tasting room, atmospheric with soft lighting and bottles illuminated in small arched openings in the walls, he shared some vintages with Eddy and Udo. Conversation flowed without hindrance as Paul and I caught up and Eddy and Udo got to know Paul a little. Languages flew about the space. Paul speaks French, German, and a little English; Eddy French; and Udo German, English, and some French. I had only written to Paul twice in the five years since I'd seen him last.

"The great thing about you, Patrick," Paul said. "Every time we get together, even when it's been years, we pick up exactly where we left off, like you were never gone."

After Paul took us out to dinner, we drove back to Wawern, winding through lonely villages that had gone inside for the night, windows glowing, lone streetlights illuminating the darkness.

Udo, Eddy, and I went into Trier the next day. I'd thought I'd want some time to see corners and niches I had not seen in thirty-plus years. But walking through the Palastgarten and into the center of town with my two friends, I somehow lost that necessity. Everything was much smaller and more compact that I remembered. We met our old friend from the Saarstrasse, Stephan Weinert, who worked near the cathedral for the church's radio station. Udo and Stephan had not seen each other in almost thirty years. We sat around a table at an old restaurant near the center of Trier for a lively chat—catching up and exploring new avenues of friendship. Udo and Stephan didn't leave Eddy out of the conversation. After two and a half hours, Stephan had to get back to work. On our way back to the car, Udo, Eddy, and I stopped in at the stained glass–restoration firm where Udo had done his apprenticeship and earned his Meister. He still knew people who worked there, including the director. One of Udo's old workmates took us on a tour of the firm—the offices, workshop, and an attic that contained the rolled-up plans of every window the firm had restored in over a century of existence.

The day Udo and Eddy had to leave, we moved slowly, dreading goodbyes. Udo was reflective and quiet. As time neared for him to leave that afternoon, he had tears in his eyes, his voice cracking and halting. We stood in the street waving after him until he turned the corner. Marlies gave me a hug and told me how great my friends were. Later that evening, Josef drove Eddy to the Kanzem train stop. As I put him on the train, he, too, teared up. Whether from having to depart the Fricks' unending hospitality or not knowing when we would see each other again, I sent Udo and Eddy off to their own lives, where we would be connected with e-mails and telephone calls. Who knows but when we meet again in person, we will be old men.

I spent the rest of the week, another five days, being domestic with Josef and Marlies—doing laundry, mowing grass, taking walks, going into town for shopping and for Josef's visit to a doctor. We reveled in each other's company and spent long evenings at the coffee table where Marlies had shown Eddy and Udo photos and told stories of the long past. This is what I had come for, to spend time, quiet moments in their company. When it came time for me to take the train to Koblenz to visit Ivo, Josef, in a moment uncharacteristic of him, turned to me in the living room and hugged me.

"This is probably the last time we'll see each other," he said. "Be good to your family. Be happy in your home." I didn't want to leave. I never want to leave.

On the train to Koblenz, I again looked through the years and thought of my friends. I was melancholy but not morose or sad. I had made good friends, drawn fantastic people into my orbit. They made me and, in some small way, I had helped them to make themselves.

Two days with Ivo was not enough. I met Lena, Ivo's mate (who he married recently) and her daughter Mascha. They are both lively and personable people with whom conversations were intense and personal. It was as if I had always known them.

Ivo took me out on the Rhein in his little boat. The great stream washed up against the hull and Ivo looked as if he was in his element. Giant freight haulers and hotel ships passed by us as if we were standing still. He pulled the boat around the Deutsches Eck and into the mouth of Mosel, where we tied up to a pier and spent the afternoon talking.

"I have found a life's mate in Lena," he said. The water was calm, and we could see the tourists walking the riverfront up to the

Deutsches Eck. The air smelled of vaguely of fish and wetland. "I often remember Andrea. I loved her more than anything and though I feel sad at her passing, I do not want to lose that connection with her. I remember the good days we had and also the difficult ones at the end of her life. They are all a part of the experience of Andrea."

Ivo drove us one afternoon to Cologne to see Martin. Ivo and I first walked through the pedestrian zone at the center of town, taking in sights, touring a small church, and stuffing ourselves with currywurst and fries. We met Martin in a gallery space not far off the pedestrian zone, where he had just hung some of his pieces, those ethereal expressions of his inner turmoil and peace. He had us back to his apartment in a busy street near the center of town. We spent the afternoon catching up and talking of new things, the projects he had before him and the things I wanted to do. It was as if we had never been absent from one another.

Ivo and I spent evenings sitting out on the patio looking out into the growing darkness and watching a bat that visits the air between his hedges every night. Conversation came without effort. I felt at home again. His cigars were excellent.

I miss my friends now that I've returned, and already five months have flown by. Soon enough, it will be five years and then a whole lifetime. I call Josef and Marlies every week. Udo calls for long, deep conversations. Ivo rings sometimes, he says, just to hear my voice. Martin and I e-mail, and Paul composes dreamy, impressive letters that must come at a cost, as he must write them evenings after long days in the vineyard.

I dream sometimes about Joachim. I'm always aware he is gone but relish seeing him again. I tell him so. We walk through the woods, drive down lonely roads. When I wake, I go through a book of photos I have of him. Random events of the last three and a half decades come to me. They rush through the brooks of my mind. They merge and become a sea of memory into and from which everything flows. I am twenty-two again, eyes fresh, everything new. Ivo, Martin, and Udo are apprentices at the stained glass–restoration firm, and we are spending the weekend together in the Saarstrasse. I relive the first time I introduced Virginia to Marlies. I remember when Sydney and Nick entered my world, the run of our lives together, and the things they have accomplished and the growth they still have to do.

In the quiet moments, I find myself lucky to have been afflicted. Without my ups and downs and the impulsivity that comes with alcoholism and mental illness, I would not have known any of the people in this tale, my story. I'm glad it's mine.